The Tallaght Two

The Tallaght Two

Justice Delayed

Michael Heney

GILL & MACMILLAN

Gill & Macmillan Ltd
Goldenbridge
Dublin 8
with associated companies throughout the world

© Michael Heney 1995
0 7171 2322 7

Design and print origination by Typeform Repro, Dublin
Printed by ColourBooks Ltd, Dublin

1   3   5   4   2

Contents

Acknowledgments

No-one has contributed more to the gradual unravelling of this extraordinary story than Paddy Meleady, whose encyclopaedic knowledge of its detail and elephantine powers of recall have been allied to a ferocious will power and determination. With his wife, Kathleen, firmly at his side, Paddy Meleady has been the cornerstone of the search for justice of the Tallaght Two and an inspiration to all who have encountered him. Similarly Joan Grogan, mother of Joseph Grogan, has never wavered in the search for due process for her own son. An unsung hero throughout has been Brendan Walsh senior, who didn't have to get involved but simply believed it his duty to help correct a perceived wrong.

All these have given invaluable assistance to the author over the years, before, during and since the first television programme in 1986, and I thank them. It has been a pleasure in that time to see the two youths at the centre of the drama grow into two fine young men, despite all that has happened to them.

Another to whom a particular indebtedness arises is Greg O'Neill, for his exceptional commitment to this and similar cases—in my opinion, truly a prince among lawyers. By the same token, to Barry White, who stuck his neck out and was proved right in the end. On a different level, I have to acknowledge the sterling advice and assistance offered to me over many years by RTE's Director of Legal Affairs, Gerry McLoughlin: we have soldiered together through many battles, including the Tallaght Two, in the cause of letting in the light.

A particular acknowledgment goes to the researcher Brendan Leeson, who was one of the first into the territory of the Tallaght Two and pointed the route ahead at a time when few could see any need for a journey. Also to Eugene Murray, who first assigned me to the story, and latterly to Mary Raftery and Peter Feeney, who supported and encouraged the 'Wednesday Report' programme in 1990. To my good friend Denis Coghlan, who read the manuscript and offered invaluable advice, to Brendan O'Brien and other colleagues who offered moral support, and to the many friends and acquaintances who gave me the benefit of their support and advice over the years. To Fergal Tobin my gratitude for believing in the story, and to all his colleagues in Gill & Macmillan for assisting in a project that for me, as for so many others, has become a grand obsession. Finally to my wife Mary, who believed in Joseph Meleady and Joseph Grogan and who has left her own mark on their developing search for justice and fair treatment before the law.

Sequence of Events

26 February 1984: Assault on Eamon Gavin.

5 March 1984: Identification by Eamon Gavin of Joseph Meleady and Joseph Grogan at Rathfarnham courthouse.

8 May 1985: First trial of Meleady and Grogan, Circuit Criminal Court, Dublin. Verdict: guilty.

11 November 1985: Retrial ordered by Court of Criminal Appeal.

26–27 November 1985: Retrial of Meleady and Grogan. Verdict: guilty.

28 April 1986: Court of Criminal Appeal refuses appeal.

3 December 1986: 'Today Tonight' television programme argues that Meleady and Grogan were innocent; includes interview with man claiming to be driver of Eamon Gavin's car.

12 December 1986: Paul McDonnell charged with perjury.

Spring 1987: Completion of Garda report by Det.-Insp. Paschal Anders.

21 July 1987: First perjury trial of Paul McDonnell. Jury fails to agree.

7 December 1987: Second McDonnell perjury trial. Verdict: guilty.

10 October 1990: Broadcast of 'Wednesday Report' television programme, 'The Scandalous Case of the Tallaght Two'.

24 November 1990: Early release of Joseph Meleady from Mountjoy prison.

Spring 1991: Completion of Garda report by Det.-Supt Gerard McCarrick.

May 1993: Government announces legislation to allow Tallaght Two case to be reopened; pardon refused.

January 1995: Court of Criminal Appeal hears case under Criminal Procedure Act, 1993.

March 1995: Convictions of Meleady and Grogan quashed.

Characters of the Drama

1. The Principals

Joseph Meleady: Seventeen-year-old Tallaght youth, living at home with his parents and seven brothers and sisters; an apprentice plumber in February 1984, with a brief record of adolescent crime and charges pending for stealing a car and dangerous driving.

Joseph Grogan: Seventeen-year-old Tallaght youth, unemployed, living at home with his mother in February 1984; in trouble with Gardaí at the time, and charges pending for a car theft and dangerous driving.

Eamon Gavin: Computer sales and marketing manager, living in Templeogue, Co. Dublin, in February 1984 with his wife and two young children.

Brendan Walsh: Seventeen-year-old Tallaght youth, unemployed, living in Drimnagh in February 1984; son of a photographer; parents separated.

Paul McDonnell: Seventeen-year-old Tallaght youth, apprentice electrician in February 1984; charges pending for malicious damage to a car.

Gordon (Gus) Dunne: Tallaght youth, aged seventeen, a well-known joyrider in February 1984.

2. The Parents

Paddy and Kathleen Meleady: Parents of Joseph Meleady; in February 1984 Paddy Meleady was a self-employed heating contractor; eight children.

Joan Grogan: Mother of Joseph Grogan; a separated parent in February 1984.

John McDonnell: Father of Paul McDonnell; electrician, active member of Labour Party in Tallaght.

Brendan Walsh: Father of Brendan Walsh junior; photographer, separated parent in February 1984.

3. The Gardaí

Garda Patrick Thornton: Based in Rathfarnham in February 1984, with ten years' service; investigating officer in case against Meleady and Grogan.

Garda James Broe: Based in Rathfarnham in February 1984, with almost two years' service; motorcyclist involved in search for Eamon Gavin's car and in identification of Meleady and Grogan.

Det.-Garda Felix McKenna: Experienced detective based in Tallaght in February 1984; investigating officer in prosecution of Brendan Walsh.

Det.-Insp. Paschal Anders: Experienced detective assigned by Garda Commissioner to investigate allegations made in 'Today Tonight' television programme in December 1986.

Det.-Supt Gerard McCarrick, Supt Seán Camon: Authors of extensive report on issues raised by 1990 'Wednesday Report' television programme.

4. The Lawyers and Judges

Eamon Leahy: Barrister, counsel for Director of Public Prosecutions in case against Meleady and Grogan, state witness in prosecution for perjury of Paul McDonnell.

Erwan Mill-Arden: Barrister, counsel for Director of Public Prosecutions in prosecution of Paul McDonnell.

Michael Feehan SC: Barrister, counsel for Meleady and Grogan in retrial, November 1985.

Barry White SC: Criminal barrister, author of opinion for RTE in 1990 that Tallaght Two convictions were unsafe, counsel for Meleady and Grogan in Court of Criminal Appeal, 1995.

Greg O'Neill: Meleady and Grogan's solicitor, drafter of petition for presidential pardon, 1991.

Patrick MacEntee SC: Counsel for Meleady and Grogan in Court of Criminal Appeal hearing, 1995.

Anthony Sammon BL: Junior counsel for Meleady and Grogan in Court of Criminal Appeal hearing, 1995.

Gareth Peirce: London solicitor, known for work in Birmingham Six case; represented Joseph Meleady in extradition proceedings in London in 1987; author of letter to Minister for Justice urging review of Tallaght Two case.

Richard Walker: Solicitor in Chief State Solicitor's office in February 1984, author of controversial memorandum discovered in February 1991.

John Rohan: Solicitor in Chief State Solicitor's Office in February 1984, author of controversial file note regarding location of Walsh fingerprint.

Oliver O'Sullivan: Solicitor in Castlepollard, Co. Westmeath, representing Paul McDonnell in perjury trials; first to notice state error in fingerprint evidence.

Séamus Sorahan SC: Barrister representing Paul McDonnell in perjury action.

Bernard Madden: Barrister representing Meleady and Grogan in first trial, May 1985.

Eamon Barnes: Director of Public Prosecutions, requested by Attorney-General to inquire into contents of 1990 television programme.

Judge John Gleeson: Judge of Circuit Criminal Court in retrial of Meleady and Grogan, November 1985.

Judge Michael Moriarty: Judge of Circuit Criminal Court in second trial of Paul McDonnell for perjury, December 1987.

Judge Ronan Keane, Judge Séamus Egan, Judge Richard Johnson: Judges comprising the Court of Criminal Appeal, January 1995.

1

Ten Years of Drama

Rrrmmm! Rrrmmm!

Eamon Gavin looked up from the television. The noise was puzzling: it sounded like a car being started, but it seemed very close—too close, perhaps, to be one of the neighbours' cars. He looked over at his young son, Paul. Have a look, he indicated.

Paul went to the window. Peering through the curtains, he could see in the February darkness that the lights were on in his father's car and the driver's door open. Some youths were at the door. The engine was revving.

'It's our car!' he cried, looking back at his father.

There was a moment's hesitation as Eamon Gavin took in the meaning of the words. His car? Being stolen?

There was a scramble to the hall door, Paul leading, ahead of his father, his young sister, and his mother. The others stepped aside to let Eamon Gavin through. He could see immediately that his son had made no mistake: three lads were in the process of stealing his car and had already got the engine running. They were just settling in to their seats as the front door of the house opened and the outraged owner descended on them.

Eamon Gavin covered the twenty-five feet from the hall door to the car in no more than a second, leaping the small boundary wall as he went. He grabbed the driver's door handle. It was locked. He grabbed the handle on the back right-hand door—also locked. The car was moving now, reversing out from the cul-de-sac in the Cremorne estate in Templeogue, County Dublin, where Eamon Gavin and his family lived. Watching his car now being driven away, Eamon Gavin was about to do something that would change the course of his life.

He needed the car: his job depended on it. These youths weren't going to get away with stealing it! In one swift action he flung himself right across the front windscreen of the retreating car. If they couldn't see out, he was thinking, they couldn't drive. So, in front of his astonished family, he clung on, as the equally bemused raiders tried to swing the car towards the estate entrance.

If he hoped for a quick end to the attempted theft, Gavin was to be disappointed. And if the raiders hoped this crazy man would see the stupidity of his ways and get off smartly when they continued on their way, they too would be disappointed. A duel had begun, one that would continue, in different ways, for the next ten years.

The car was now driving forward towards the exit from the estate. The driver started slewing the car from side to side, trying to shake Gavin free. Seeing the danger, Gavin slipped back from the windscreen, down and across the bonnet, legs in the air, face down, but clinging on like grim death to the lip between the bonnet and the glass.

This crazy spectacle moved, now at speed, the 250 yards towards the open road at the point where the Cremorne estate meets the roads of south-west County Dublin. Gavin's twelve-year-old son gave chase on foot, haring after them across the grass, shouting at neighbours' houses in desperation. The calm of the family's Sunday night had now degenerated into a life-threatening horror.

Peter Lucey saw them coming as he drove along the Firhouse Road, the speeding car with the man on the bonnet. My God, he thought, they're not going to stop! He braked; but the other car also braked, and the man on the bonnet slipped onto the ground and now stood in front of the car. It seemed to Lucey to be a confrontation between the man on the bonnet and those inside driving the car.

'If you're going to take my car you'll have to run over me!' Gavin shouted.

The youths in the car stared at him.

'Get out and run away. I won't follow you. All I want is my car back.'

He was inches in front of the car, still standing, hands on the bonnet. The car revved forward. Gavin started to fall under it as the front bumper caught his shins; but it stopped again. Gavin, relieved, staggered upright, still maintaining his position, blocking its progress.

But now the youths put the car into reverse and it started to move back. Desperate, Gavin again flung himself forward onto the bonnet. Peter Lucey, sitting watching this scene, decided to intervene. He reversed also, blocking the exit of the car. But, quick as a flash, those in the stolen car reversed further, then came forward at speed, making what appeared to be a hand-brake turn in front of Lucey's car as they mounted the pavement, slewed past him, and headed off down the Firhouse Road in the darkness, once again with their human cargo on the bonnet. Lucey swung his car around and gave chase.

It was a quarter of a mile to the Knocklyon Road junction, and the stolen car was now speeding. A lot of shouting and yelling was going on between the raiders and their unwelcome passenger on the bonnet. In front of them the lights were red at the junction, but the driver accelerated through them, swinging right up the Knocklyon Road. Gavin despairingly waved and gesticulated at the cars stopped at the junction, their occupants' eyes out on sticks watching this apparition going past.

Up the Knocklyon Road the car was now travelling at 60 miles an hour. In the position he'd adopted, Gavin was staring in through the windscreen, watching the three youths. Two of them were now searching in the car for something to help force him off the bonnet. The front-seat passenger flung a container of windscreen washing liquid at him; it just glanced off his body. The front passenger had now fully reclined his seat; this allowed him to lean back, apparently in search of some implement to use against their unwanted passenger.

He saw them lower the back-seat cushions and rummage in the boot, unearthing a large golf umbrella.

Once again the front-seat passenger leaned out his window. This time he sat right out on the window edge, hanging on to an overhead support with his right hand and threatening him with the heavy wooden handle of the umbrella, wielded with his left hand.

Smack! The blows rained down on Gavin. Hanging on now with his left hand alone to the lip of the bonnet, he attempted to ward off the blows with his right. The car came to a halt once more, half a mile up the Knocklyon Road, but the umbrella assault continued. It was easier to get a blow at Gavin while the car was stationary. His gold watch took a crack.

But the violence was not working: the man on the bonnet wouldn't loosen his grip and was clearly determined to hang on. Bleeding from his forehead, his wrists, and his hands, and heavily bruised on his shoulder, Gavin was not giving up now.

Peter Lucey, having got through the lights at the Firhouse Road junction, now caught up with the bizarre scene. He could see the umbrella being wielded against Gavin by the front passenger. Since the car was stopped, if only temporarily, Lucey decided to take his opportunity and go and call the Gardaí. He drove on up the road to a private house and dialled 999.

Meanwhile Eamon Gavin had ended the umbrella episode by finally grabbing it from his attacker with his right hand. It was already broken from the force of the blows; Gavin flung it into the ditch. But his temporary respite did not last long. The car started off again.

In desperation, Gavin yelled at his attackers that he needed the car to visit his father, who was seriously ill in England. Far from touching the heart-strings, this caused hilarity inside the car.

Now, ominously, he saw them produce his heavy spare can of petrol from the boot. The third youth, in the back, placed this on the roof of the car and started to threaten Gavin with it.

'It'll kill me!' Gavin screamed, against the wind and the darkness.

'That's right, we'll kill you,' came the reply. 'We'll kill you, you fuckin' bastard.'

The windscreen was by now smeared with Gavin's blood. For a moment the back-seat passenger got back inside the car with the can, but then he re-emerged outside the window. He told Gavin he had one last chance to get off, otherwise they'd burn him and kill him. By now frightened and weary, Gavin agreed; if they would slow down he would get off.

He had travelled now just over one mile; in time it was just over five minutes since he had heard the car engine revving; but Eamon Gavin had travelled almost a lifetime away from the comfort and safety of his home that Sunday evening.

The three youths slowed down enough for him to roll off on the passenger side. The front window was wound down. 'We won't wreck your car,' the front passenger consoled him before it sped off.

Bloodied but unbowed, Gavin staggered back down the road in the darkness towards his distant home, breaking into a run as he did so.

Drama in the appeal court, 1995

The scene was electric. Eleven years had passed—eleven years of passion and distress, now packed, standing-room only, into court no. 8. Parents, lawyers, gardaí, the convicted young men, the victim and his family, the three distinguished judges on their elevated bench —all were rapt in attention as the Assistant Chief State Solicitor, John Corcoran, was being elegantly badgered and baited by Patrick MacEntee SC.

It was January 1995. The Tallaght Two saga was in its closing stages.

So then, Mr MacEntee intoned mischievously to his distinguished witness, it seems that the State Solicitor's office was on 'autopilot' when the Joseph Meleady and Joseph Grogan file reached the Circuit Court. Ripples of laughter spread through the court. Mr Corcoran protested at the jibe; his office was not on autopilot, he assured counsel for Meleady and Grogan.

But Mr Corcoran's efforts to counter the gentle ridicule were to little avail. There had been an obvious system failure in the State Solicitor's office. Above him, Judge Egan's brow was already furrowed with the concern that would receive sharp expression two months later in the court's reserved judgment. The Chief State Solicitor's office might not have been exactly on 'autopilot' but it was already clear that no solicitor had seen what the civil service called form no. 8; no-one had discovered the time bomb ticking within it. Had they done so, they would have found the 'Walker memo', a handwritten note signed *R.W. 16/5/84* on form no. 8. For six-and-a-half years form no. 8, with Richard Walker's crucial message inscribed on it, had managed to escape all attention—this within an office dedicated to precise and meticulous documentation. It was not surprising that Mr Corcoran was not finding the answers easy.

Watching him and MacEntee in their unequal struggle from the back of the court were three Garda officers, all standing. One of these, arms folded, his face impassive, was Sgt Patrick Thornton, the original investigating Garda. In his mid-forties, with black hair and wearing a short-sleeved shirt, Thornton was preparing himself for what was already clear would be another bruising ordeal shortly to take place in the Court of Criminal Appeal—his own cross-examination.

Alongside him was Det.-Supt Gerard McCarrick, his six-foot-plus frame and head of white hair towering above those around him. Another principal player in the state's handling of the Tallaght Two case, Det.-Supt McCarrick would be giving evidence relating to his 180-page report on the case. The detective-superintendent knew that in that report he had failed to identify any problem with the 1985 convictions of Meleady and Grogan, and that the safety of these convictions was now coming under serious assault. He could see that things had gone badly wrong since the appeal hearing began.

Beside Det.-Supt McCarrick that day was Det.-Insp. Felix McKenna, a veteran of many criminal investigations. McKenna too was deeply enmeshed in the story unfolding in court no. 8.

In close proximity to these Garda officers, also standing at the back of the court, was Eamon Gavin himself. Bespectacled, dark-suited, wearing a crisp white shirt, the original victim of the crime was a picture of middle-class, middle-aged respectability. He appeared outwardly urbane and calm, but the court had already seen evidence of how he was deeply distressed by the way the appeal was progressing. Years of continuing controversy over the case had left him feeling damaged and tormented. Sitting down nearby was Gavin's wife, Ann, with their young daughter alongside her.

In front of Eamon Gavin, seated in the last three rows of benches in the court, behind MacEntee and his colleague Barry White SC, were Joseph Meleady and his parents. Ten years after his conviction for the crime against Mr Gavin, Joseph Meleady, now dressed in a sober grey suit, was no longer the callow youth who had faced Mr Gavin's fiercely determined certainty that he was a guilty party in 1984. He was now employed in a regular job with a good company and was settled down in the Palmerstown area of County Dublin, the father of a one-month-old baby. Beside him sat his father, Paddy, and his mother, Kathleen, each of them straining, like everyone else in the courtroom, to catch the nuances of the cross-examination going on in front of them.

Near the window to the left, standing, as he had done all week, was Joseph Grogan, the other inadvertent victim of Eamon Gavin's 1985 evidence. Now twenty-eight, with a five-year Mountjoy prison sentence long behind him, Joseph Grogan, like Joseph Meleady, was smartly dressed, not unlike a well-turned-out civil servant, but his expression was more pinched and earnest than Meleady's. In 1995 he was a member of Jehovah's Witnesses: he had turned to the sect when he emerged from prison in 1989, alienated and depressed by his incarceration for a crime he had always denied committing. Not far from him, seated on the court benches, was his mother, Joan, who, through thick and thin, never doubted her son's innocence.

Towards the front of the court, head down in concentration, wigged and gowned, sat Eamon Leahy BL, junior counsel for the Director of Public Prosecutions. Leahy was subdued. Although he was present to represent the DPP in the appeal, he was himself an important participant in the events being discussed. It was a case in which he had been involved in a number of significant errors. Although these were clearly inadvertent, at least one of them had not been remedied in the years since and had led directly to the current proceedings in the Court of Criminal Appeal.

Another parent of one of those implicated in the crime against Eamon Gavin stood, tall and alert, at the back: this was the bearded Brendan Walsh senior, father of a young man whose fingerprint, found in Mr Gavin's car, had eventually come to symbolise the state's mishandling of the whole case.

In the front row, facing the judges, were the senior barristers: Kevin Haugh SC for the DPP, Barry White SC, Paddy MacEntee SC and Anthony Sammon BL for the appellants. Facing MacEntee and White was Greg O'Neill, Meleady and Grogan's instructing solicitor, quietly observing events.

The room at that moment contained eleven years of intense history. It was a history still being acted out, but its effects were already written on the strained faces of those present. It was, for some, a nightmare; for others it was a nerve-racking opportunity to realise a dream. All could at least rejoice that they were now approaching the final act in a drama that had gone on, by common consent, too long. The drama had changed many lives in that courtroom and had deeply marked its central players.

After nine days of hearings, the Court of Criminal Appeal concluded. Four weeks later the three judges—Séamus Egan, Ronan Keane, and Richard Johnson—delivered their judgment, the first under a new appeal procedure that allowed cases of alleged miscarriage of justice to be reopened if new facts emerged. They ruled that the conviction of Meleady and Grogan in November 1985 for stealing Mr Gavin's car and for assault occasioning actual bodily harm on him should be quashed. The court found the convictions were unsafe and unsatisfactory. A presumption of innocence, the judges ruled, now applied to the two, just as if they had been acquitted by the jury back in 1985. Each had since served a five-year sentence on the basis of proceedings now seen to be inherently and fatally flawed.

However, the Court of Criminal Appeal introduced confusion into what appeared a complete legal vindication by refusing to certify, under specific terms of the Criminal Procedure Act, 1993, that a miscarriage of justice had taken place. This meant a denial to the two young men of an automatic right to compensation through the normal civil courts. This part of the judgment seemed a contradiction in terms: on the one hand a miscarriage of justice had occurred; on the other hand, in the specific terms of the new Act, it had not.

The court's findings marked the climax of a tale littered with errors by the state: errors of judgment, errors of technique, errors of memory, errors of procedure, sins of commission and sins of omission, over many years. It had arisen from a very special kind of 'whodunnit', a dramatic thriller with many twists in the narrative, for long leaving its audience unclear who were the guilty parties.

The Court of Criminal Appeal, of its nature, did little more than hint at the full saga of the Tallaght Two, at the dimensions of its intriguing 'secret history'. What the state papers on the case— examined for the first time in this book—showed was that the real turning point should have come eight years earlier, in 1987. In the spring of that year the Garda report of Det.-Insp. Paschal Anders went to the authorities. Anders sought to sound an alarm and to alert his superiors to aspects of the Tallaght Two case that troubled him. The warning was not heeded; the report was pigeonholed and forgotten. In the eight years it took for the case to reach the Court of Criminal Appeal in 1995, Joseph Meleady served the bulk of his five-year sentence; Joseph Grogan completed his. The Director of Public Prosecutions, the Department of Justice and the Gardaí all remained wedded to a status quo that was cracking open before their eyes.

In the human arena there had been a different kind of conflict. A struggle of wills and commitment was played out, from 1985 to 1995, between Eamon Gavin, the victim, and Paddy Meleady, the father of one of those convicted. The passion and determination of these two middle-aged men overshadowed all else, though one had to be close to see just how fully they influenced each and every twist of the drama.

The two men had never spoken a word to each other in the ten years. Each of them that day in court no. 8 was busy, furiously scribbling notes to their respective counsel, coaxing and prodding to have their will imposed on the proceedings. Both were obsessed and personally enslaved by the circumstances of the case; both, with their families and the family of Joseph Grogan and of the others involved in the case, had borne a decade of suffering as the price of their respective beliefs and passions. The suffering was emotional, physical, financial, and social; whole families' lives had been subordinated to the legal tussle.

Many new and intriguing dimensions of this saga are recorded here for the first time. Some aspects will cause the reader to gasp, as they have done the author many times, either with rage, with surprise, or with disbelief. But from the first violent moments outside Mr Gavin's house in February 1984 to the climactic moments in court no. 8 in March 1995, it was always that kind of story.

The Garda investigation begins

It was a quarter past eight on the evening of 26 February 1984, and the 999 phone call had had the desired effect. Garda Patrick Thornton was in Rathfarnham station's patrol car when the message came over the radio that a gold Datsun Stanza, registration number 547-TZO, had been stolen and the owner assaulted in the nearby Cremorne estate.

Shortly afterwards Thornton picked up the trail. On the Knocklyon Road, an area where the south Dublin suburbs meet the mountains, he came upon a car badly damaged along its right-hand side, apparently by collision with another vehicle. This, it turned out, was the property of Joseph Gleeson; he had had the misfortune to be driving along Knocklyon Road moments after the three youths who had stolen Eamon Gavin's car and assaulted him finally forced him off his precarious perch on the bonnet.

Joseph Gleeson was minding his own business, driving at a leisurely 20 miles an hour, when he saw the car coming towards him. Sensing danger, he pulled in to the side. But he thought his days were numbered when the car continued to come straight for him. There was a collision, it bounced off his car, and the left-hand side of his vehicle was jammed brutally against the wall. The stolen car ricocheted off the far ditch as the driver lost control, but then recovered its balance, straightened up, and disappeared towards Tallaght.

Gleeson breathed again; and he was relieved when the Garda car driven by Patrick Thornton arrived shortly afterwards and he was able to point him in the direction of the culprits.

Thornton established the facts briefly, then continued his search. He found the car abandoned in the middle of the road at Tymon Heights (later renamed Killakee Way), Rathfarnham. It was wrecked. The two right-hand doors were damaged, the ignition wiring was pulled out, and the steering lock was broken. One significant item of damage, though it was not noted as such at the time, was the breakage to the small quarter-window on the back left of the car. This was clearly the point of entry to the car when it was broken into. It would turn out to be a significant piece in the jigsaw of this case.

The right-hand wing mirror had also disappeared. There were seven or eight dents on the bonnet where the flailing umbrella had left its imprint. And there were bloodstains on the bonnet.

But of the occupants there was no trace. For Garda Thornton the question was, where had they gone? It soon became known from the residents of Tymon Heights that yet another vehicle had been stolen on the spot. This belonged to Finbarr Martin, who was visiting his brother-in-law, Maurice Walsh, in an adjoining house. Many years later these two would provide a small but significant nugget of information on the developing saga of the Tallaght Two. At the time, their involvement appeared peripheral.

Maurice Walsh immediately rang Tallaght Garda station, told of his stolen car, and was informed that a Garda motorcycle was on the Old Bawn Road at that moment, approaching his house and actually approaching where the thieves had headed. This motorcyclist was Garda James Broe, another principal character in the Tallaght Two saga.

Martin and Walsh were later told that Garda Broe followed the stolen car of Finn Martin up the mountains but eventually lost it. Years later, Martin and Walsh would reveal intriguing details of what they recalled being told by the Gardaí later that night; these details would tend to confirm growing doubts about the way this whole case came to be processed through the courts.

On the same Sunday night, after Eamon Gavin had been treated in hospital for injuries to his head and hands, Gardaí Thornton and Broe arrived at his house. Broe remained outside with his motorbike while Thornton went inside to talk to his key witness. Later they emerged and the conversation continued outside the house. They were talking, in all, for about three-quarters of an hour.

Gavin said in court he only gave the Gardaí 'a slight description' of his attackers. While he assured them he could identify the culprits, the Gardaí must have been disappointed at the absence of detail or distinguishing features in the description he gave them. Thornton's notes showed Gavin's description, in full, of his attackers: the first wearing black leather jacket, hat, peak, 16–17 years, light frame, dark complexion, short hair; the second, curly hair, short, thin face. It was, unfortunately, a description that could fit hundreds of local youths. So meagre was Gavin's recollection of the faces that Garda Thornton stated later in court that they had no suspects at all for the attack.

The fundamentals of what happened to Eamon Gavin, which he told the Gardaí and which he would confirm over and over again in various court cases, were as follows. Three young men stole his car; they broke into it through the back left-hand fly window; as they started it he rushed out and flung himself onto the bonnet of the moving vehicle; throughout the subsequent traumatic journey, as he stared into the car through the windscreen, two of the youths were in the front and the third remained in the back.

At no time did the person in the front passenger seat change with the person in the back; at no time did the person in the back get into the front. The only significant movements of the culprits were when the front-seat passenger climbed out the window and beat Eamon Gavin with an umbrella held in his left hand and when the person in the back sat out on the right-hand back window to threaten him with a petrol can. All this would be important many years later, as the case hinged on exactly who was sitting where.

2

Disputed Identification

For several days after Eamon Gavin's night of horror, nothing of any significance happened towards finding the young men who had abused him and stolen his car. The case, however, had quickly become a national event, and for good reason.

In early 1984 'joyriding', as it was called, had become a scourge in certain parts of Dublin, and many of the big housing areas ringing the city had earned descriptions as night-time 'race-tracks' by the Gardaí. For bored and irresponsible youth in depressed and under-resourced areas, 'joyriding' had become a form of recreation. Illegal consumption of alcohol went hand in hand with the theft of cars; the prospect of a daredevil chase with the Gardaí in hot pursuit brought some of these youngsters as near to heaven (in every sense) as they could imagine. It was dangerous and mindless behaviour, occasionally leading to violent death. To many adults, Eamon Gavin's daring attempts to thwart one such gang of young criminals made him a hero.

The story was reported with relish in the newspapers. It was clear to the public that this was no ordinary man. No-one could so describe someone who leaped, recklessly and apparently fearlessly, onto the bonnet of his car to prevent three young thieves from making off with it—a man who refused to abandon what was clearly a precarious hold on the car's bonnet, despite being beaten across the arms and head with an umbrella, all this time being driven at breakneck speed. In the media Eamon Gavin, through no fault of his own, found himself inevitably appearing as a champion for the legions of frustrated middle-class house-owners who saw themselves increasingly besieged by lawlessness and criminality.

In Rathfarnham Garda station the two Gardaí involved in the investigation, James Broe and Patrick Thornton, discussed the case among themselves, as it was discussed in many other Garda stations and in homes throughout the country. Unfortunately they had very little hard evidence to go on, despite being assured by Eamon Gavin and his young son that they would be able to identify the guilty parties if they ever saw them again. No written statement had yet been taken from Eamon Gavin, or from Paul. That would change, however, after the events that were about to unfold.

It was not unusual at the time among local Gardaí for witnesses to be brought by the investigating officers down to District or Circuit Court hearings, in the hope that they would identify some of the culprits among those present in the courtroom. The witnesses would stand around discreetly, trying to spot someone they recognised from among those in court. It was a practice born of circumstances. In a heavily built-up area, such as Tallaght, with a volatile young population, it was inevitable that there would be a frequent absence even of suspects for a given crime.

At any rate, it occurred to Garda Thornton—so he would state later in court—through discussions with colleagues in both Rathfarnham and Tallaght stations that 'a number of persons' who might fit the bill as suspects for the crimes against Eamon Gavin would be present at the regular District Court session in Rathfarnham the following Monday, 5 March 1984. He called to see Eamon Gavin some four or five days after the night of the crime and asked him to attend that court sitting, to see who he might see. 'I thought it might be in the interest of justice,' Garda Thornton said in evidence, 'if he might come down and look around the court, he might in fact see somebody … I thought that from the names I had been given that were in court that day it could be possible some of them had been involved in the incident …'

A rendezvous was agreed between Eamon Gavin and Garda Thornton at Rathfarnham courthouse for the morning of the fifth. Eamon Gavin decided to wear an improvised disguise, which amounted to a hat, dark glasses, and an overcoat. This was to avoid the possibility that the culprits might be there and spot him before he spotted them, and vanish before they could be apprehended, or even seen.

On the appointed morning, Gavin and Thornton met as arranged on the roadside near the Yellow House pub, some two hundred yards from the courthouse. Thornton had already been to the court, which had not yet started for the morning, and arranged there with Garda Broe that he would accompany Gavin into the building, hoping there to make an identification. As the investigating officer, Garda Thornton felt he should remove himself from this process. He waited outside.

The court was busy that morning, just as the Gardaí had expected. Crowds of young people and of Gardaí were in attendance. Many of the youngsters attending the court were, by definition, already in trouble. Eamon Gavin, accompanied at a discreet distance by Garda Broe, wandered among them in his somewhat conspicuous disguise. At first he could see no-one he felt he knew.

A group of five youngsters, four youths and a girl, were sitting on and around a table in the waiting-room, just outside the courtroom proper. Joseph Meleady, a seventeen-year-old, was one of the group. He was up on several charges under the Road Traffic Act. The local Gardaí had good reason to be aware of Meleady in March 1984, as they had within the previous two months secured two convictions against him, one for common assault. Joseph Meleady, despite the close and concerned attention of his parents, Paddy and Kathleen, was showing to the authorities all the signs of a teenage delinquency which, while not uncommon among his peers in Tallaght, was seriously disturbing to the wider adult community. His worried father, a heating and plumbing contractor, was present in the courtroom on that 5 March, to give his son moral support.

Joseph Grogan, also aged seventeen, sat alongside Meleady that morning in the porch area of Rathfarnham courthouse. He too was known to the Tallaght Gardaí, though at that stage he had no criminal record. In the course of 1984, several convictions would be secured against him for various delinquent acts, including motor car theft and common assault. On 5 March, like Joseph Meleady, he was simply awaiting hearing of one of the charges against him.

Although the two, Meleady and Grogan, knew each other, and had gone to the same national school, they were not in any sense close mates; largely, they hung around with different sets of friends, based in different areas of Tallaght's sprawling estates. But that morning as Eamon Gavin arrived, they sat, fatefully as it turned out, side by side, in the middle of their small group inside the courthouse.

There were, it emerged years later, two other people in the court-house that morning who would play, in very different ways, a decisive role in the eleven-year saga that had already begun. One was another Tallaght youth, Gordon (Gus) Dunne; the other was a detective from Tallaght station, Det.-Garda Felix McKenna. Neither appears to have come to Eamon Gavin's attention that morning; they were soon to emerge, however, as two of the main characters in the drama of the Tallaght Two.

Eamon Gavin came out of the courtroom after several minutes, still garbed in the dark glasses, hat, and overcoat, and told Garda Broe that he couldn't identify anyone. He was, he said himself later, quite disappointed. Garda Broe was waiting in the doorway between the court and this waiting area. He asked Eamon Gavin to have a look around the waiting-room. This was the Garda's evidence later under oath as to what happened next: 'He saw two youths out in the corridor. He saw four or five youths out in the porch at the entrance to the courthouse itself, and he pointed out these two youths to me ... I approached Joseph Grogan and Joseph Meleady and I asked them to come into the waiting-room, and I told them they had been identified ...'

Eamon Gavin, it seems, had been confronted in Rathfarnham courthouse by an extraordinary coincidence of positioning. As he came upon the two youths sitting on the courthouse table, Meleady was to the left, Grogan immediately to Meleady's right, as he looked at them. It was almost as if they were in the car, frozen still in the positions vis-à-vis each other that they were supposed to have occupied that night eight days earlier: driver (Meleady) and front-seat passenger (Grogan), with Gavin facing them.

Having been told by Eamon Gavin that these were the culprits, Garda Broe went up to the two and brought them over to Gavin, who identified them in the Garda's presence. Gavin said in the retrial that he put his hand on Meleady's shoulder and said, 'This was the driver, and this one the front-seat passenger.' They were then cautioned by the Garda. For reasons that were never fully clarified, they were not, for the moment, arrested.

At this stage Eamon Gavin had some discussions with the Gardaí present. He then left the courthouse and went off to Terenure College, where his son, Paul, was at class. He got him out of school and drove him back to Rathfarnham courthouse; it was now about 11:30 a.m.

Paul Gavin went inside, accompanied by Garda Broe, and in the courtroom he picked out Joseph Meleady as the car's driver. He did not identify Grogan. Both youths were then confronted again by Garda Broe after they left the courtroom proper, and father and son identified them, Eamon Gavin doing so now, it seems, for a second time. They were charged by Garda Thornton with malicious damage to Gavin's car and with assault occasioning actual bodily harm. They were taken to Rathfarnham Garda station and fingerprinted.

It was over a year later, in May 1985, that Meleady and Grogan were brought to trial. As they had done consistently throughout the interval, the two accused pleaded their innocence. The case against them rested totally on the identification, made in these informal and unsupervised circumstances, by Eamon Gavin and his son. Gavin was 100 per cent certain in evidence that he made no mistake. Referring to the night of the crime, he said: 'I was pretty terrified—in fact I was so terrified that I would say their faces are indelibly marked on my brain for the rest of my life.'

There was no other evidence of an incriminating kind. No fingerprints of the accused had been found, there were no confessions, and there were no corroborating witnesses. As a result, the circumstances in which the identification of the supposed culprits was made became, from the beginning, the principal issue in the whole case. Nonetheless, in May 1985 Meleady and Grogan were found guilty, unanimously, by a jury in the Circuit Criminal Court.

Almost immediately after the conviction, Meleady and Grogan heard that a new witness had emerged in their case. His name was Paul McDonnell, another youth from Tallaght and also seventeen years old. McDonnell came forward to swear on oath that he was in the car when Eamon Gavin was attacked, and that Meleady and Grogan were not.

McDonnell's surprise evidence led to a successful appeal against conviction. In November 1985 the Court of Criminal Appeal granted a retrial; but later the same month, at the retrial in the Circuit Criminal Court, Meleady and Grogan were convicted once more, again unanimously, again on the visual identification evidence of the two Gavins. To most observers the convictions appeared now not only impregnable but also totally just. Two juries had agreed on the verdict; the youths who were convicted had a record of car theft and brushes with the law. The matter, on a surface reading, seemed to have ended with justice done.

Issues raised by the identification

From the very beginning and throughout the next eleven years, controversy surrounded the Garda decision to hold an informal identification process. Why was a formal identification parade—as laid down in Garda regulations—not held? Garda Thornton maintained throughout the trial and the retrial that he couldn't hold a formal parade because he had no real suspects. He thought the culprits could be any of twelve, or even twenty, young fellows from the area. In the second trial he would say that he did have an inkling, that he had a suspicion, but that he had nothing to go on. 'Nothing worth talking about' was his own estimate of these suspicions. To hold an identification parade, he thought, he would have had to be 'fairly certain that we had the right person in the first place.'

Nonetheless, Meleady and Grogan's lawyers, right from the start, challenged the fairness of the informal identification approach adopted by the Gardaí. From their perspective the two youths had no idea an identification procedure was taking place until in effect it was over. No-one was present on their behalf to ensure that there was no bias in the way it was conducted. It all happened silently and without impartial scrutiny. Only the state's witnesses could later give detailed evidence on the matter, as only they knew it was happening. Normally a suspect could expect to have a supervised and controlled procedure for an identification; normally too the courts favoured and expected such an approach from the Gardaí.

However, the counter to this argument was that, as a tactic in a Garda investigation, it was not completely unknown for the sort of identification procedure adopted in Meleady and Grogan's case to be accepted in evidence, despite its significant drawbacks. No law stipulated that there be a formal identification parade whenever investigating Gardaí required a witness to scrutinise a possible suspect. The law also recognised that a formal parade, which the suspect's solicitor had the right to attend, might, depending on the circumstances, be neither practicable nor necessary—for example in a situation where the Gardaí had no suspects for the crime. The case of Meleady and Grogan would be accepted by both judges involved as a case in point.

Arguments from the defence side that a formal identification parade should have been held, under supervision, were rejected by the presiding judges in the first Circuit Court trial and in the retrial. The judges were convinced by the argument that if, as the Gardaí maintained, they had no suspects, how could they hold a formal parade?

Yet the question of precisely how Meleady and Grogan were identified raised important issues of law and of the protection of an accused's rights. (See appendix 1.) As an issue it dogged the case throughout the years from 1984 to 1995, until the extraordinary contents of a memo discovered on the state files gave the circumstances of the identification a devastating final twist.

In the retrial, held in November 1985, Judge Gleeson became deeply immersed in the arguments over this matter. At one such point Meleady and Grogan's counsel, Michael Feehan SC, had asked Garda Thornton why he did not arrange a proper identification parade in this case.

Thornton: I wasn't sure who—

Feehan: Of course you weren't sure: this is the purpose of an identification parade, to have someone identified. You obviously suspected somebody, or were you just dipping in the bag, as it were?

Thornton: No. From the description given and my knowledge of certain individuals, a Monday morning in Rathfarnham—

Feehan: Just a moment. You say from the description given—what in the description made you think that these two men were involved?

Judge Gleeson: He didn't say that.

Feehan: He said from the description given—

Judge Gleeson: I think I know what he was going to say: that he didn't know from the description given, but they are the sort of people who might be in Rathfarnham on Monday morning.

Thornton: The court in Rathfarnham, it's the biggest court in the week.

Feehan: Your lordship is saying he is entitled to bring someone along and dip them in the barrel of Rathfarnham court?

Judge Gleeson: He is entitled as an investigating police officer to suggest to the witness to go anywhere that the material might be.

Feehan: I accept that, my lord.

Garda Thornton told the retrial that his suspicions were not so strong as to make a formal parade 'worth while'. His colleague, Garda James Broe, was even more blunt. Asked in the retrial why there was no formal parade, he answered, 'Because we had no suspects at that stage.'

Feehan: You had no suspects?
Broe: No.
Feehan: At all?
Broe: No.

The issue was central to the whole case, yet in regard to it the Garda evidence was somewhat confusing. On the one hand, Garda Broe said they hadn't any suspects in the week after the crime; yet Garda Thornton said he did have an inkling, he had a suspicion, although nothing to go on.

For the judge, the issue was whether Eamon Gavin or his son, or both, had been told to expect the guilty parties to be there. The judge made it clear during the trial that if he felt the Gardaí had 'marked the cards' of Eamon Gavin and his son by saying that the guilty party would be there that morning, he would not let the case go to the jury. He found as fact, however, that the Gardaí had not done this.

Eamon Gavin's evidence on this important point was that he asked Garda Thornton, in advance of visiting the court, if there would be someone there he might recognise. Garda Thornton, he said, did not answer; but Gavin conceded in court that he assumed there would be someone there he should recognise, otherwise Thornton would not have asked him to go down at all.

In the second trial the following exchange took place between Eamon Gavin and Michael Feehan, counsel for the accused:

Feehan: You aren't a fool; you knew you were going down to try and identify two people in the court.

Gavin: I accept that. I knew when I was going down that the possibility was that the boys were there and in fact I was going in because I knew that I would recognise them when I saw them—which I did.

Later the counsel for the accused returned to the same line of questioning.

Feehan: I put it to you that you were there to recognise two people
   if you could?

Gavin: Yes.

Feehan: You appreciate your function there was to recognise
   people if at all possible?

Gavin: Yes.

Feehan: So that you knew if you went in there, if there were people
   in there, you would be expected to recognise them, isn't that
   correct?

Gavin: I assume.

The circumstances in which Eamon Gavin made his identification
were extensively analysed during both the trial and the retrial. But
despite this, important specific flaws in the procedure adopted seemed
to escape the attention of the court.

The identification by Paul Gavin

One problem not directly addressed either in the trial or the retrial
concerned the identification made by Paul Gavin. The issue was the
interval between the identification made by the father and that by the
son. Eamon Gavin's evidence was that after making his own
identification he left to collect his son from nearby Terenure College.
He did so, he said, 'at the Garda's request'. 'He asked me would my son
be able to identify them, and I said yes, that my son had told me that
he would be able to identify them, so I went up and collected my son
and brought him down.' It was unclear to which Garda he was
referring.

By now, on the basis of the state's own evidence, the Gardaí, in this
interval between Eamon Gavin's identification and the arrival of his
son, had definite suspects for the crime. Meleady and Grogan had by
now been cautioned by Garda Broe; they had been identified. Yet
when he was asked in court why the Gardaí had not held a formal
identification parade, Garda Thornton had replied that his suspicions
were not that strong for it to be worth while. Garda Broe had replied
by saying they had no suspects.

If these explanations were valid beforehand, they had surely ceased
to be after Eamon Gavin had pointed out the two suspects to Garda
Broe and they had been cautioned. The situation was then changed
materially: clear suspects were now known to the Gardaí, and there

was, as a result, an equally clear opportunity to create a more formal and indeed more fair identification procedure before Eamon Gavin's son would be involved. This opportunity was not availed of; no formal parade was set up for Paul Gavin.

This failure was not directly addressed as an issue either in the trial or the retrial of Meleady and Grogan. Once it became evident as an issue, many years later, it raised the question of whether as a result the identification by Paul Gavin should ever have been allowed to go to the jury.

Judge Gleeson's charge to the jury

Judge Gleeson, in his charge to the jury, said of the procedure adopted by the Gardaí, 'It bore all the hallmarks of the structure of a formal identification parade.' He acknowledged that there were 'minor discrepancies as to where in the courthouse, or in what room, the identification was made ... Maybe the guards might have taken notes as to which part of the courthouse any identification was made ... The weight of evidence indicates that the identifying witnesses were not told that the culprits or suspects would be there and that they were simply told to go along and see if they could recognise or see anybody that was involved in the incident ... I'm satisfied that propriety was observed by the guards in this case ... I'm satisfied that the guards were fair here, that they didn't say, "He's in there: it's only a matter of picking him out." I'm satisfied that wherever the precise point within the building the identification took place, there was sufficient covering of the same sort of people that would be lined up in an identification parade to make the matter fair.'

The judge's charge made no reference whatever to the stated interval between the father's first identification, leading to the cautioning of Meleady and Grogan, and that of the son approximately an hour later; in this respect the two were treated, in the judge's charge to the jury, as one. 'One of the guards gave evidence as to why he didn't hold a formal identification parade ... Whilst there was a possibility that the defendants might be under suspicion, you might think so would dozens of others and that the guard's answer might be right when he says he hadn't enough to go on.'

While this statement from Judge Gleeson might represent a reasonable account of the propriety involved in Eamon Gavin's identification, it could hardly cover the second identification that went to the jury, that of Paul Gavin. By then, the Gardaí had enough to go on.

In his charge to the jury in the retrial, it was striking that Judge Gleeson made no reference whatever to the usual entitlement of an accused person to protection of their rights in any criminal identification process. He did not refer to the desirability of their solicitor being present during the identification, if only to ensure that justice was done and to protect the accused person's interests. He made no specific reference to various other factors that might have impeded a correct identification, for example the extreme danger that existed to Eamon Gavin's life during the incident; the precariousness of his hold on the bonnet of the speeding car; the darkness of the night; and the distraction of being beaten by a heavy umbrella—all at the time when he was committing his attackers' faces to memory.

It was particularly surprising that Judge Gleeson made no reference to the fact that Eamon Gavin had never seen Meleady and Grogan before. This was one of the circumstances particularly stressed by the Supreme Court in the Casey judgment in 1962. (See appendix 1.) In such circumstances the Supreme Court felt that a statutory warning to the jury might have to be 'couched in stronger or more ample terms' to be fully appreciated by them. Not only did Judge Gleeson not couch his warning in more ample terms, he never even referred to Eamon Gavin's lack of acquaintance with the two accused. He made no reference to the fact that Paul Gavin gave no description of the attackers to the Gardaí and had had only a fleeting opportunity to observe the driver yet was able to identify Meleady by the pimples on his face.

Whatever the significance of the failure of Judge Gleeson to address these aspects might have been, within a few years a series of crushing judgments was issued by the Court of Criminal Appeal against a number of judges whose charges to the jury omitted to mention various aspects similar to those referred to here. (See appendix 1.) All cases, of course, are different, and one cannot generalise. In the end, in 1985, Michael Feehan lost the argument over the identification process, and the appeal court subsequently allowed the guilty verdict to stand.

3

The Fingerprint of Brendan Walsh

The fingerprint of Brendan Walsh represented the evidence that never was. Walsh, another seventeen-year-old Tallaght youth, played a strange, shadowy role in the trials of Joseph Meleady and Joseph Grogan. The unusual aspect of his fingerprint was that it was evidence in the Tallaght Two case yet never achieved that actual status. It was mentioned in both the trial and the retrial, but through an extraordinary series of mishaps and mistakes on all sides, the basis for the reference, the facts as known to the state, were never entered as evidence. Partly as a result of this, the trials, denied scientific findings that could have assisted the defence, were dominated by the identification evidence of Eamon Gavin and his son.

It was almost five years after all the legal avenues open to Joseph Meleady and Joseph Grogan were exhausted that Brendan Walsh's fingerprint became an important issue.

In 1984 the scientific examination of Eamon Gavin's car yielded a number of smudges but only one potentially identifiable fingerprint. This was processed on 27 February. Joseph Meleady and Joseph Grogan were identified by Eamon Gavin one week later, on 5 March; one of the first acts thereafter by the Gardaí, naturally, was to take Meleady's and Grogan's fingerprints and to check the print already in their possession against these. The case against them would have been virtually sewn up had the print matched either of theirs: it would have confirmed the accuracy of Eamon Gavin's identification by adding to it indisputable scientific findings. Disappointingly, however, the fingerprint found in the car did not match the prints of either Meleady or Grogan. As a result it had to lie, unidentified, for several days in the Garda laboratory.

Meanwhile, the night before Eamon Gavin visited Rathfarnham courthouse, quite independently of him and of Garda Thornton, a breakthrough in the case was occurring elsewhere. This was to lead to the arrest and eventual conviction of Brendan Walsh for involvement in the Gavin incident. Walsh appears not to have been a suspect for the crime; his undoing was pure chance, arising from activities completely unconnected to Eamon Gavin. He would be a central though dimly lit figure in the events of the next ten years.

The events that brought Walsh to the attention of the Gardaí occurred on the night of Sunday 4 March, one week after the assault on Eamon Gavin. An incident took place at Watergate estate in Tallaght involving an attempted car theft and a violent scuffle with local residents at the scene. The investigating officer was Det.-Garda Felix McKenna. He secured a written confession to this crime from an associate of Brendan Walsh; he then arrested Walsh himself and brought him to Tallaght Garda station for questioning. Walsh was suspected of involvement in this other crime only: his presence in Tallaght station had nothing to do with the Gavin incident. But in custody, Brendan Walsh had his fingerprints taken, and this was to prove his undoing.

In the Garda Fingerprint Section in the Phoenix Park, Det.-Garda Joseph Kinsella was unable to match these fingerprints of Walsh's with prints taken at the scene of the Watergate crime. But he had another fingerprint in his possession, relating to another crime, that had not yet been matched with a suspect—the print found in Eamon Gavin's car. When he checked this print against the fingerprints of Brendan Walsh, he stumbled on the answer to a question he had not even been asking. The fingerprint found in Eamon Gavin's car was that of Brendan Walsh. Arrested on suspicion of the Watergate crime, Walsh now found himself conclusively linked with the assault on Eamon Gavin.

Det.-Garda Kinsella reported this good fortune to his investigating colleague, Det.-Garda Felix McKenna. Around eight o'clock that evening in Tallaght station, McKenna and another colleague resumed their questioning of Walsh regarding the Watergate incident. Walsh continued to deny any involvement and made a written statement to this effect. Only at this point did McKenna tell Walsh they were also investigating the Gavin incident and the assault involved. They gave Walsh the bad news that his fingerprint had been found inside the car. They cautioned him, but Walsh again denied involvement and would say nothing more.

Next, Det.-Garda McKenna arranged an identification parade, to see if Eamon Gavin could recognise Walsh. This was another important moment, for Walsh was the only person the Gardaí could be absolutely certain was in the car on the night of 26 February. The circumstances of Eamon Gavin's identification of Meleady and Grogan were a good deal less than ideal; in fact a case mounted solely on the basis of Gavin's identification would be likely to be heavily contested and quite possibly might not even be allowed go to a jury. If Eamon Gavin could pick out Walsh in a proper identification parade, under proper supervision, it would provide vital corroboration for his evidence against the other two. It would also confirm the accuracy of his visual memory and generally enhance his claim to be believed in relation to Meleady and Grogan.

But it was not to be. When he inspected the identification parade that evening, Eamon Gavin was unable to pick out Walsh. He thus failed to identify the one certain culprit in the case. To the detectives, including McKenna, it was a disappointment—though Gavin had signalled in advance that he was unclear about the appearance of one of the three in the car, the person in the back.

If this failure to identify Walsh raised in the minds of investigating Gardaí the disturbing possibility that their witness might be mistaken over Meleady and Grogan, they would give no sign of it. Could Gavin have been mistaken? Following his failure to pick Walsh out in the identification parade, it was then crucially important that Walsh be seen to have occupied the back seat. If he turned out to have been sitting in either of the two front seats, then Gavin's identification would be undermined. Gavin had picked out Meleady and Grogan as being the driver and front-seat passenger, respectively. Walsh, therefore—by the logic of Gavin's evidence and as a vital explanation for his failure to recognise him—had to be the back-seat passenger. Anything that subsequently threatened the contention that Brendan Walsh was in the back seat of the car would threaten the whole basis of the state case against Meleady and Grogan.

These were matters for the investigating Gardaí to ponder carefully as they began to look towards a successful prosecution of the case. They had Walsh's fingerprint, found inside the car. Depending on the details, a jury might well be persuaded that Walsh was probably sitting where his fingerprint was found. If so, its position would be important. If it was found in the back it would certainly assist the state case; if it was found in the front, however, it would be much less helpful, especially so if Walsh himself were to maintain that he was sitting in the front.

While the location of the print could never in itself be conclusive as to Walsh's position in the car, depending on its nature (which hand? which finger?), its precise location and its orientation, it could affect the balance of probabilities. It was the *only* scientific evidence in a case where the prosecution rested totally on a highly disputable informal identification procedure. The state case was far from cast-iron. The jury would have to be warned by the judge, under a compulsory procedure, of the dangers involved in convicting on visual identification evidence alone. (See appendix 1.) All in all, the Walsh fingerprint could prove a far from negligible factor when the case came to court.

But the significance of the fingerprint's position was partly disguised by the manner in which Walsh himself was tried and convicted. He was tried separately from Meleady and Grogan and several months before them. This was partly because of his alleged involvement in other events that had nothing to do with Eamon Gavin's car. Because of the almost accidental way he had been connected with the crimes against Gavin, his case was investigated, processed and brought to trial by Det.-Garda Felix McKenna from Tallaght station; the Meleady and Grogan prosecution, meanwhile, was prepared in Rathfarnham station, where Garda Thornton was based.

In addition to this, Walsh pleaded guilty when the case came to court. His fingerprint had been found in Eamon Gavin's car, and any other pleas would have been pointless; also, by pleading guilty he secured for himself the relatively short sentence of two years in jail. But because he pleaded guilty there was no need for the state to present evidence in court: the trial consisted only of sentencing. The fingerprint evidence was therefore not brought out into the open when Walsh's case came up in the Circuit Criminal Court in March 1985. The relevant statement of evidence was contained in the Walsh book of evidence but it was not publicised or discussed at the time, because of the way the case was settled.

When the first Meleady and Grogan trial came up, two months later, in May 1985, it became a chapter of accidents and disasters regarding the fingerprint. The full extent of this, and the reasons for it, would only be revealed ten years later.

Some of the problems were apparent at the time. In the first place, Brendan Walsh, who appeared as a witness for Meleady and Grogan, appeared only to have heard of the trial on the very morning he gave evidence. He was brought from St Patrick's Institution to give evidence. The transcript also showed that Walsh was not an impressive witness. In fact his evidence on behalf of Meleady and Grogan in the first trial in the Circuit Criminal Court was, even his friends could see, riddled with grey areas. He may have had some vital evidence to give, but he buried the truth in equivocations and evasions.

The jury could hardly be expected to appreciate that Walsh had what seemed to him a good reason for his lack of candour. As with the two others who would claim to be with him in the car that night, he was simply not prepared to incriminate or implicate his accomplices directly. It was a kind of honour among thieves. But, of course, in court it never looked like honour: it looked like deception.

By the time Meleady and Grogan came to court, Walsh's trial was over; he had been convicted on his own plea of guilty, brought about because his fingerprint was found in the car. Now he gave evidence for Meleady and Grogan, saying they were not with him that night in the car. But he was not prepared to say who was; so he found himself giving the unlikely testimony that he didn't know the names of the other two in the car with him. He said he only knew them to see. This lacked credibility.

In addition, he wasn't prepared to admit to having stolen other cars that night, in particular one taken earlier from outside St Dominic's church in Tallaght. This had been driven by Walsh and the other two youths to Gavin's house at Cremorne, and there abandoned in favour of Gavin's more powerful car. Walsh was afraid that he could yet be prosecuted for this offence if he admitted involvement. This left him having to claim that they walked to Cremorne and to Eamon Gavin's house, which was palpably untrue. The alternative, Walsh thought, might mean risking another jail sentence, something he naturally wished to avoid.

The lurking issue was where Walsh had been in the car that night. If he could be proved to have been in the front, the state case would almost certainly collapse. However, on this important issue the defence counsel, Bernard Madden, told the court: 'Brendan Walsh will be a witness for the defence in this case, and he will say that on the night in question he drove the car ...' In the event, Walsh's evidence proved to be that he was the front-seat passenger. He said that he was the one who beat Gavin with the umbrella. During his evidence in chief, Walsh firmly denied being the driver.

> Madden: You admitted you were in the car on that night?
> Walsh: Yes.
> Madden: Were you driving the car?
> Walsh: No.

It was then left to counsel for the Director of Public Prosecutions, Eamon Leahy, to extract a fuller story from Walsh in cross-examination. This was done in an exchange that would haunt this case for years to come.

> Leahy: I must suggest you were in the back of the car, where your fingerprint was found.
> Walsh: I was in the front seat.

But Brendan Walsh's fingerprint was *not* found in the back of the car, as Leahy said. It was found in the front, high up and near the pillar of the left-hand front passenger window. Not only that but, curiously, it was a print of Walsh's right-hand thumb, not his left, as might be expected, and it was upside down. This very particular location and orientation suggested that Walsh at the time was in an unusual position: the balance of probability seems to suggest that at the time he left it, Walsh was in the front of the car and turned, somehow, directly to his own left, towards the window.

The actual details of Walsh's fingerprint were completely misrepresented by counsel for the DPP in his question. The defence had heard nothing from the state about this evidence and had no reason to seek to contradict the misrepresentation in the question. The truth, obviously, was unknown to Eamon Leahy.

While it would have suited the defence to argue that Walsh was sitting where his print was found, clearly they could not do this fruitfully if his print was found in the back. Had it been known that it was in the front it could have been used, in conjunction with Walsh's evidence that he was the front-seat passenger, to challenge Eamon Gavin's identification of Joseph Grogan as having been in that seat. This course was not open to the defence, because Eamon Leahy had said the print was in the back, and the defence side had no reason to disbelieve him or to think he might be mistaken.

Eamon Leahy's misstatement, as an event in itself, might not have mattered if the state had either entered the scientific findings about the fingerprint in evidence or otherwise informed the defence side about it. In those circumstances a misstatement by counsel on either side would quickly have been set right. But, unfortunately, the state had not disclosed the existence of this relevant and potentially vital evidence to the defence lawyers. It had neither included it in the book of evidence nor informed the defence side of its existence.

For good measure, counsel for the DPP had now inadvertently misled the court and placed the fingerprint in the back of the car. While undoubtedly an innocent mistake by counsel, this had the effect of turning the thrust of the actual evidence on its head. It eliminated any possible help the evidence of the fingerprint could bring to the defence side; it served instead to help the DPP's case. Also, the very question asked by Leahy contained an assumption—which the state would, years later, seek vigorously to discount—that the location of the print indicated where Walsh was seated.

It is an extraordinary fact that the serious matter of counsel for the DPP misinforming the Circuit Criminal Court on a matter of material scientific evidence would remain unexplained, unapologised for and unaddressed publicly for a further nine years.

The error remains uncorrected in retrial

The failure of the state to disclose the fingerprint evidence in advance of the first trial of Meleady and Grogan could be partly explained by the surprise nature of Brendan Walsh's statement that he had been sitting in the front of the car. This appeared to be the first the state knew of such evidence. It immediately increased the significance of the print's actual location for the defence, had they been aware of it; but it seems also to have come as a surprise to the defence.

The defence side in the first Meleady and Grogan trial were having their own difficulties, regardless of the state's mistakes. Defence counsel had said that Walsh's evidence would place him in the driver's seat, not the front passenger seat; yet this turned out not to be Walsh's evidence. Thereafter, Bernard Madden heard counsel for the state tell the court that the fingerprint evidence had been found in the back of the car, and so appeared to be not at all helpful to the defence case. He appears, from the court transcript, to have decided to accept this exactly as it reached him, and concluded that it would be wiser for him to avoid pressing the issue of Walsh's precise position within the car. Thus he did not seek the evidence that lay behind Eamon Leahy's misstatement, nor, unfortunately, did he challenge it.

The result was that there was absolutely no elaboration by the defence of the contention that Brendan Walsh was the front-seat passenger. Yet this contention, if true, would have broken the state case apart. Walsh's brief statement that he was the front-seat passenger was simply left there in the court proceedings, unexplored, undeveloped and, eventually, disregarded by everyone, defence and jury included.

One person in the court that day who should have known where Walsh's fingerprint had been found was the investigating Garda, Patrick Thornton. But Garda Thornton appears not to have known the full facts about the fingerprint, and failed to enlighten the court. The full transcript of his sworn evidence in this, the first trial of Meleady and Grogan, contains no reference whatever to the existence of Walsh's fingerprints within the car.

> Leahy: Was there any forensic examination carried out on the car?
>
> Thornton: There was a forensic examination done on the car. It was done by a person from the Technical Bureau.
>
> Leahy: Were the prints of either of the accused found in the car?
>
> Thornton: No. There were a number of smudges, but they were inadmissible as evidence.

This was the total of Garda Thornton's evidence in the first trial on the scientific findings. There was no reference whatever to the existence of Walsh's fingerprint, not to mention its precise position and orientation. Thornton gave his evidence before Eamon Leahy made reference to the existence of Walsh's fingerprint, in the course of which Leahy misstated its location.

Years later it would come to light that Garda Thornton was the one who gave Eamon Leahy the wrong information. Thornton stated that he himself had been misinformed on the location of the fingerprint. An internal Garda memo written by Thornton in late 1985 (see chapter 6) would show him stating clearly that Walsh's print had been found in the rear of Eamon Gavin's car.

There was another detective who ordinarily should have known where the fingerprint was and who was present in the Circuit Criminal Court at Meleady and Grogan's first trial. This was Det.-Garda Felix McKenna. It was he who had investigated Walsh's case and had personally processed the fingerprint that in turn led Walsh to confess. Unfortunately, McKenna was not called as a witness in the case. Might he not have been expected nonetheless, even privately to his colleague, to correct the mistaken claim that the fingerprint was in the back of the car? McKenna told the *Sunday Business Post* in 1993 that he wasn't actually present in court at the moment when Eamon Leahy indicated that the print was in the back. He was not in a position to help Garda Thornton set the court record straight. Did McKenna know where the print had been found? A memo written by him in December 1986 indicated that he knew the print had been found 'on the inside of the glass of passenger door of motor car 547-TZO.'

Whatever about who knew what at the time, the significance of the state's error would, with hindsight, eventually become obvious. The evidence about the location and orientation of the fingerprint tended to corroborate Brendan Walsh's claim that he was in the front of the stolen car. If, as he said, he was in the front passenger seat, then Eamon Gavin was mistaken on Grogan, and his evidence against Meleady would be immediately called into serious question. The state case would, in these circumstances, in effect collapse. But this argument was never made, and could never be made, because no-one knew the facts and everyone came to believe that the print had been found in the back of the car.

The problem appeared to have originated, and to reside, within the ranks of the Gardaí. They were in possession of the evidence yet seem to have been unable to grasp its nature or its significance, and therefore were unable to transmit it even to counsel for the DPP. Collectively,

the state side were mishandling the matter. When a retrial un-
expectedly materialised, none of those involved on behalf of the
state—the Chief State Solicitor's office, the Gardaí, state counsel, or
anyone in the office of the DPP—proved able even then to correct
their mistake.

There was an interval of six months between the two trials. In this time
the transcript of the first trial was typed and was made available to all
sides. Transcripts are essential for all appeals to the Court of Criminal
Appeal. In the transcript the errors in the first trial were, or should have
been, manifest; and yet the retrial was doomed to labour under the
same misapprehension as the first trial. Again there was no disclosure
from the state side. As a result, a new defence legal team also had no
opportunity to make anything of the fingerprint evidence. The
transcript shows them never once indicating the slightest awareness of
its significance. It could hardly be otherwise, because they were,
simply, unaware of its true nature.

Only incidentally can the state of knowledge of the Meleady and
Grogan defence team on this issue be gleaned from the transcript of
the retrial. The passage in question was when Michael Feehan SC was
seeking to challenge Eamon Gavin in cross-examination. Feehan's
questions exposed the depth of his misapprehension, as defence
barrister, of the facts regarding the fingerprint evidence.

> Feehan: Tell me something. Did you know in fact that the person
>   that was in there [Walsh], that his fingerprint had been found
>   in the back of the car?
> Gavin: I didn't, no.
> Feehan: I have to suggest that you were well aware at the time that
>   the fingerprint of the man that was in Tallaght [Walsh] was
>   found in the back of the car …

Later Feehan returned to the theme: 'I'm suggesting the reason he
didn't identify him was that already his fingerprint had been found in
the back of the car …'

As a result of all this, nothing in Judge Gleeson's charge to the jury
in the retrial alerted the jurors to the significance of the location of
Brendan Walsh's fingerprint. Having been misinformed in the first trial
by Eamon Leahy, everyone remained in the dark.

One person attending these trials who had no doubts about the truth of Brendan Walsh's key testimony was his father. His son had been convicted already, and was guilty; with a heavy heart, the father had accepted his son's involvement in this dreadful escapade. But Brendan Walsh senior also became convinced, from talking to his son, of the innocence of Meleady and Grogan.

This belief in their innocence was to lead him into trouble. When the verdict in the retrial was announced, Brendan Walsh senior made a loud protest from the public gallery, shouting, 'Rubbish! Rubbish! It's a disgraceful verdict!' The Gardaí in court were ordered to take his name. Later, the judge let him go.

But the matter came up again several weeks later in the Court of Criminal Appeal, where the appeal against conviction and sentence had been lodged by the defence. The court rejected the appeal. Once again Brendan Walsh senior, from the public gallery, let fly: the court's decision, he shouted out, 'was clearly unjust, and diminished the rights of every citizen.' The president of the court, Mr Justice Griffin, asked him to apologise. Walsh refused.

Before dealing with Walsh senior, the court announced that the conviction would stand but reduced the sentence by six months. Then it turned to Walsh and his outburst. He was brought from the body of the court and invited to purge his contempt. He said to the three judges, in front of the crowded courtroom and the two convicted youths: 'I'm not the only one here upset. There are many law-abiding people here that are upset. I would have no sympathy for these two people if I thought they had any hand, act or part in this affair, but they're innocent.'

Mr Justice Griffin responded by saying that the matter had been decided by the jury in the case. Walsh, he said, would have to go to Mountjoy prison for his contempt of the court. Before being taken off to spend two weeks in Mountjoy, Brendan Walsh senior's last spirited comment was: 'I know that I'll be in jail with at least two innocent people.'

The central role of Eamon Gavin as witness

Eamon Gavin proved a powerful and impressive witness against the two accused. He was articulate, and he was confident. The record showed he was an innocent victim who had displayed unique personal courage and determination—foolhardy perhaps, but admirable nonetheless. He was the kind of witness towards whom a jury could not fail to be sympathetic.

Most importantly, Gavin presented himself before the jurors as being certain in his own mind that he was not making a mistake. He entertained no doubt, or possibility of doubt, over the correctness of his identification. Questioned about possible doubts by Eamon Leahy, he replied, 'None whatsoever.'

Under-cross examination he was even more emphatic. 'The driver's face was not far from me, and I was in a situation where I was determined during the course of the drive that if ever I got off that car I was going to recognise both of the people who in my mind were killing me … If I thought there was one per cent of doubt in my mind I would say that I wasn't sure. I am totally and absolutely one hundred per cent sure.' In the later hearing of the perjury action against Paul McDonnell, Gavin would state that he would stake his life on the correctness of his identification, even if the crime involved were capital murder. Through the first trial, and through all subsequent court hearings on this case, Gavin stuck fiercely to his conviction and his certainty. His honesty and his sincerity communicated themselves to the jurors.

Yet the objective facts might have given a lesser man plenty of grounds for caution. The crime was committed at about 7:30 on a winter's night in February. It was dark; the lights were off inside and outside the car during the hell-for-leather journey: only the street lights overhead, and the reflected lights from passing cars, provided illumination. The witness was, on his own evidence, frightened, and certainly in danger of losing his life unless he could cling on as the car's speed reached something like 60 miles an hour. On top of this he had never seen either of the accused, or the third person in the back of the car, before that night.

In all, Gavin was on the bonnet of his car for about five minutes. With stops and starts he travelled a little over one mile. During at least part of this time he was trying to ward off blows from the front passenger; at other times he was confronting, and being threatened by, the youth in the back of the car. He conceded in the perjury hearings that he may only have been looking straight at the two youths in the front for half the time of the journey, which would be about two-and-a-half minutes. Afterwards he could only give what the Gardaí described as a 'slight' description of the two in the front of the car, and no description of the youth in the back. Yet Eamon Gavin was able to tell the second trial in November 1985: 'I don't wish to appear melodramatic, but ... when you spend five minutes of your life believing that you are being killed by two people, you do not forget them: you remember their faces.'

The jurors believed him; they believed him despite the solemn warnings, read out to them by each of the presiding judges, that there were great dangers involved in relying on uncorroborated visual identification. A transparently sincere witness, personally convinced of the accuracy of his own visual recall, was taken on trust. The jury knew nothing of Eamon Gavin's *technical* ability to remember two faces that he had seen only once and in stressful circumstances. They received the mandatory judicial warning that it would be dangerous to convict on such evidence alone; but, as was their right, they ignored the warning and did convict. They had only Gavin's demeanour, and his certainty, to go on, though each of these were quite useless in helping them with what was ultimately a starkly technical question. It must be asked, as many lawyers would ask: did the jury fully understand the nature of the warning given to them by the trial judge?

As for Paul Gavin's identification of Meleady as the driver, he had no more than about seven seconds, as the car interior light faded, to see and to remember the face of the driver. He too had never seen Meleady before the night of the incident. His initial statement showed uncertainty whether the person he later identified got into the front or the back of the car; yet later he was able to recognise him, he claimed, by the pimples on his face.

The alibi evidence and conduct of the defence

In certain respects, the force of Eamon Gavin's own certainty was strengthened rather than weakened as the trials developed. In the first trial, eight uncertain young witnesses were put in the witness box to provide an alibi for the accused. But they were so uncertain in their recall, and ultimately unconvincing, that the evidence proved disastrous for Meleady and Grogan. In the second trial a decision was taken that no evidence at all would be offered by the defence; instead there was in the retrial a total and, in the end, unsuccessful reliance on the legal argument that the identification procedure followed by the Gardaí in the case was unsatisfactory and should not even be allowed to go to the jury.

The perfect vision of hindsight shows that the two quite opposite approaches taken—in the first place to call evidence that proved unreliable and in the second to call no evidence at all—actually made a questionable prosecution case appear stronger than it really was. The defence lawyers could not, of course, be expected to know that outcome in advance; they were taking decisions in the best interests of their clients, and they were clearly operating under considerable difficulties not of their own making.

A study of the transcript of the first trial shows clearly that the alibi witnesses who took the stand were never likely to impress a jury. Their various accounts were less than credible. To an extent, a genuine difficulty of recall could have been a factor in this, for the first trial was not held until May 1985 and the incident had occurred a full fourteen months earlier. The defence solicitor, John Reidy, had been given notice of the impending trial only four or five days before the trial day; witnesses for the defence were contacted either the night before or the very morning of the hearing.

The alibi witnesses were all young—seventeen or eighteen years old; they lacked authority, they lacked composure, and, most important of all, they lacked any kind of detailed recall of the night in question. And, as the prosecuting counsel did not fail to underline, they were all friends of the accused.

In the first trial the alibis advanced by the two accused were separate, though not dissimilar. Joseph Meleady gave evidence that from 6:30 until 7:30 or 7:45 on the night in question he was with three friends drinking at a bonfire not far from his home. He then walked from there to a flat where his girl-friend was baby-sitting, and remained there with her and three others till 11:30. The crime was committed shortly before 7:45 and several miles away from where Meleady claimed to be.

Joseph Grogan's evidence was that he also was drinking with friends at a bonfire in Tallaght—though not the one Meleady was at; that he was walking up to the supermarket in Tallaght to get cigarettes about the time Eamon Gavin's car was being stolen several miles away; that he then returned to the bonfire and stayed there till he took his girl-friend to catch her bus at about 10 p.m.

The accounts of the accused lacked detail. In addition, the alibi witnesses contradicted each other at regular turns. They were all easy meat in the hands of a skilled barrister. Whereas Meleady said he was given nothing to eat in the house where his girl-friend was baby-sitting, she said in evidence that she gave him tea and sandwiches. Meleady said they were only carrying single cans of beer when they went to the flat; she said they were carrying a brown plastic bag.

All the alibi witnesses were quizzed on how they remembered that night in particular. One youth said he remembered it because Meleady told him the next day that he'd been arrested for a crime committed that night; but the prosecuting counsel, Eamon Leahy, was able to point out that Meleady wasn't arrested in Rathfarnham courthouse for another week. One young witness was asked how she had a clear recollection of that particular night. Without any elaboration she answered that Joseph Grogan had told her it was that night.

None of the defence witnesses remembered details such as what they were wearing, what kind of night it was, or what they talked about. They all provided the same kind of uniform structure to the evening, based on arrival and departure times from the bonfires, but they could not give it the detailed elaboration that alone would make their testimony sound authentic.

As a result, even supposing that the jurors entertained doubts over the prospect of convicting on Eamon Gavin's identification alone, their doubts would certainly have been to some degree allayed by observing the sheer weakness and lack of credibility in the alibi evidence. With hindsight, the defence might have been better served by no alibi at all.

The decision in the retrial to call no evidence would have appeared surprising to outsiders, since the retrial had been granted specifically as a result of the emergence of the new witness, Paul McDonnell. But the defence had their reasons. Meleady and Grogan's lawyers decided it was a better course to put no-one in the witness box: neither Meleady, Grogan, nor Walsh, not even the new witness, McDonnell. They challenged the prosecution case instead on grounds of law, arguing solely on the basis of the not inconsiderable imperfections in the identification procedure.

Of course if, as happened, the legal argument was lost, this approach held its own risks. It meant that while the second jury heard a detailed case for the prosecution, they heard no rebuttal evidence from the defence, of any sort. The jury never heard Paul McDonnell, the witness whose emergence in the Court of Criminal Appeal had actually brought about the retrial. They did not hear Brendan Walsh, nor even Meleady and Grogan themselves testifying to their own innocence. They heard, simply, no evidence at all for the defence, alibi or otherwise.

When eventually the judge rejected the very cogent legal submission from Michael Feehan SC, the die was cast. After the second jury had handed in its guilty verdict, Judge Gleeson remarked to the court, 'What alternative had they but to convict?'

Two juries, in the end, unanimously convicted Joseph Meleady and Joseph Grogan of malicious damage and of assault occasioning actual bodily harm to Eamon Gavin. It was this unanimity of view that, above all, the authorities found over the years so hard to ignore. It acted as a powerful, silent force over the decade during which the controversy over the Tallaght Two dragged on, frustrating all efforts to have the state admit to a miscarriage of justice. It appeared impossible that these juries, twenty-four citizens in all, could have been mistaken. Their verdicts had, on the surface, a devastating finality about them.

4

The Emergence of Paul McDonnell

Very shortly after the crime in February 1984, Paul McDonnell, a young apprentice electrician and the son of a local Labour Party official in Tallaght, began telling people that he was one of the three who stole Eamon Gavin's car. At the time, the attack on Gavin was a national event; it became notorious not only in Tallaght but throughout the country within hours of taking place.

One of the first people McDonnell told was his friend, the late Rory Hynes. Hynes himself, a youth of similar age to McDonnell and a witness for Grogan in the first trial, told the author in 1986 that shortly after Meleady and Grogan were arrested and charged, McDonnell produced a newspaper cutting and showed it to him. It was a report of the assault on Eamon Gavin and the stealing of his car. McDonnell was 'kind of boasting', according to Hynes, that he was involved. He said that Meleady and Grogan were not in the car with him. Brendan Walsh was there, and a third person, another friend of his, who McDonnell named at the time to Rory Hynes but would later refuse to name to the court.

This admission by McDonnell arose long before Meleady and Grogan had even entered a plea of not guilty and long before their trials and the handing down of the five-year prison sentences. No question had arisen of wanting to, or needing to, get Meleady and Grogan off these severe sentences. Over a year later, in drastically changed circumstances, Paul McDonnell swore solemnly to his own guilt in several successive court hearings and underwent three painful cross-examinations in open court. His story, it may be noted, remained the same.

The conviction of Meleady and Grogan just one year after the assault on Eamon Gavin transformed the general view taken in Tallaght of their case. They were not only found guilty but given a punitive, exemplary sentence of five years' penal servitude. Hitherto there had been, among the youth at least, a somewhat ribald view taken of their prosecution. Most youngsters had heard how others, who were not charged, had always said they were the real culprits. With the outcome in May 1985, many in Tallaght were shocked both by the verdict and by the sentence. It was not that they felt the culprits did not deserve five years, for few adults would have disagreed with the severity of the sentence: it was rather that most people in Tallaght would have heard what the dogs in the street were barking, that the wrong people were being sentenced. The guilty people, so the gossip went, were Brendan Walsh, Paul McDonnell, and the man named privately by McDonnell to Rory Hynes, Gordon (Gus) Dunne.

Among those who had heard this story and who believed it was Brendan Walsh senior. His information came from his son, who he could see was certainly in a position to know. He had told his father that with him in Gavin's car were his two mates at the time, Paul McDonnell and Gus Dunne. His story told to his father matched exactly the story told by Paul McDonnell to Rory Hynes.

Brendan Walsh senior protested in court when the guilty verdict was announced. Afterwards, outside the court, he fell into conversation with Jimmy Brady, companion of Joseph Grogan's mother, Joan Grogan. Walsh assured Brady that young Grogan had not been in the car. Then several days later two youths, one of them Rory Hynes, called to Grogan's house and told Mrs Grogan that the two guilty youths were McDonnell and Dunne.

Rory Hynes told the author in 1986: 'I couldn't believe it when they [Meleady and Grogan] were charged. But I was convinced they'd get off. I couldn't believe that two innocent blokes could get picked out and convicted. There was a lot of pressure on Paul McDonnell to own up. A lot of people were very angry. A lot of people would have said it to him.'

Within days of the guilty verdict and the five-year sentence, a meeting took place on a Sunday morning in Mrs Grogan's house in

Bawnville in Tallaght. Present were Paul McDonnell, Brendan Walsh senior, Jimmy Brady, a neighbour of the Grogans called Aidan Lawlor, Rory Hynes, and Mrs Grogan herself. Mrs Grogan remembered the conversation years later. 'McDonnell said he did it. He'd thought they [Meleady and Grogan] would get off. He said that the oul fella wouldn't get off the car—they were all cursing at him.'

Rory Hynes recalled: 'Macker [McDonnell] is the type of bloke who wouldn't own up if he didn't want to. He'd stand his ground. He wouldn't be afraid of threats or anything like that. But it was no problem to him to own up: it didn't seem a problem at all. He was honourable. Twelve months' sentence is one thing, five years is a different story. He had a sense of fair play.'

Over the next few days McDonnell again met Brendan Walsh senior, this time at the Baron John's lounge in Crumlin Road, Dublin. He dictated a statement outlining his role in the whole affair, and he signed it. McDonnell now consulted his father, John McDonnell, who was an electrician in Tallaght and also an election agent for the local Labour Party TD, Mervyn Taylor.

Whatever suspicions John McDonnell might have picked up beforehand regarding his son's involvement in this notorious crime, he now found himself placed in an unenviable situation. His own son told him, privately, that he had played a major part in a serious crime and that, under the influence of drink, he had done dreadful things to Eamon Gavin. He told his father that he was the one sitting in the back seat who had threatened to burn Gavin off the vehicle and kill him. Now, partly out of a sense of fair play and partly because of community pressure, he was proposing to make a clean breast of it and to confess to the authorities.

It was disastrous news, the sort no father could ever wish to hear. What was he to do?

One of the first questions was, was his son serious? Was this some sort of a game? Could it perhaps be that Paul was being forced by some other party to admit to something he didn't do? He may not have been the brightest boy in his class but he had done his apprenticeship under his father and was well on the road to becoming an electrician. He had been in trouble once before—nothing very serious, just a broken window and a conviction for malicious damage. He was good to his mother and made a reasonable weekly contribution to the household expenses. The idea that he was part of the gang that had brutalised Eamon Gavin was a bolt from the blue.

John McDonnell would later state in court, quite candidly, that he tried to get Paul to change his mind. But as his son's determination to proceed became clear to him, he realised that what he was saying to him was indeed true. Paul had done this thing to Eamon Gavin. He realised that he himself, and Paul, had no real options: Paul would have to go to the authorities, and he, as his father, would have to support him.

McDonnell's sworn statement and evidence

And so, exactly two weeks after the first guilty verdict against Meleady and Grogan was handed down, Paul McDonnell found himself sitting in the office of a solicitor, John Reidy, in South Great George's Street, Dublin, dictating a sworn affidavit setting out his complete role in the assault on Eamon Gavin. It was an account with a considerable amount of detail in it.

This is part of McDonnell's account of the nightmare journey with Eamon Gavin: 'He got off and stood in front of the car to try and not let us go forward. The driver put it into reverse, drove back, and he jumped on again; somebody started shouting when we turned into the estate, "Get something to get him off." I got into the boot, found an umbrella, gave it to the passenger, Walsh; he sat out on the window, swiping the umbrella at your man on the bonnet. He was lying on the bonnet in such a way that the driver couldn't see, so we were swerving from side to side on the road. Walsh started hitting around him on the bonnet; I think that he hit him once or twice on the legs. We stopped and started, going back and forth, jerking back and forth (just before that he was after losing the umbrella out of his hand), shouting, "Get off, get off." Then we took off again; he immediately hopped on again; we swerved from side to side because the driver couldn't see the road; then Walsh screamed, "Stop, stop," and on the opposite side of the road there was a Toyota Starlet coming against us. Only the passenger could see it, and he screamed, "Stop, stop," only going at about 30 miles. I don't know the exact speed but he was going slow. Your man got off the bonnet again. We pulled off to go back up the road again and he jumped back on again. We drove up the road, and the driver said, "Get something else," so I looked in the boot again and found a red tin. The driver said, "Take it out." I got out on the window, then put the tin on the roof, shouted, "Get off, get off." The driver told me to show it to him, then he said, "Let me off, let me off." We stopped, and he walked round the side of the car, and he said, "Don't damage my car." We pulled off, all looking back, shouting, "We're not going to damage your car, we're just going home in it …"'

It was a story that did McDonnell no favours, although it lacked the more lurid quotations from Gavin about the threats that the person in the back—McDonnell, according to the affidavit—had issued.

The affidavit contained the information that McDonnell had been drinking cans of beer before getting involved with this apparently simple car theft that then went hideously wrong. It also contained other significant details that could not have been gleaned from the evidence in the first trial.

One apparently innocuous detail that went unnoticed for years was McDonnell's description of the petrol can in Eamon Gavin's car as red. Nowhere in the court proceedings or in any public discussion of the case up to this time had the colour of this can been mentioned. It was a detail unlikely to be known to someone who was not the owner of the car or had not at some time handled the can. In stating its colour, McDonnell was leaving a hostage to fortune, for if the can turned out to be any other colour it would immediately expose his story as suspect.

Other aspects of McDonnell's story were less convincing. As with Brendan Walsh before him, his credibility was not helped by his stating, 'I don't know the driver's name.' There were just two people with him, driving around in the stolen car, yet he said he did not know who the driver was. This, by any standards, was an unlikely story.

Paul McDonnell's affidavit was dictated almost fifteen months after the events he described. McDonnell added to it some months later with a short additional statement, also sworn before the solicitor. In this he sought to explain why he had not come forward earlier as a witness. 'I did not believe they would be convicted,' he said, 'and I believed that if I came forward and was a witness I would then be prosecuted and would be likely to receive a prison sentence. I was also anxious to do nothing which would endanger my apprenticeship as an electrician.'

The contents of these affidavits, setting out his confession of guilt, would cause McDonnell considerable grief over the next two years; but it was not the kind of grief that he himself, or his father, expected.

In coming forward, young McDonnell was bringing down on his head both disaster and infamy. If his confession was accepted, he risked immediately the loss of his job as an apprentice electrician and possibly a lengthy jail term. If, on the other hand, he was engaged in an elaborate pretence that he had committed this serious crime just to get Meleady and Grogan off, then the consequences of his ruse might be just as grave, perhaps more so. In either case his confession never offered him anything other than grief. Few people would ever wish voluntarily to be associated with the kind of confession to which McDonnell was putting his name.

It all started to go quickly wrong when McDonnell appeared before the Court of Criminal Appeal some six months after making his statement, on 11 November 1985. In the appeal the defence were seeking a retrial for Meleady and Grogan on the basis of McDonnell's confession. His sworn statement represented new evidence. While there was little doubt that McDonnell was an important new witness in the case, his big test would be in the appeal court, where he would have to face the cross-examination of Eamon Leahy.

To the consternation of the appellants, when the Court of Criminal Appeal met to hear the case, McDonnell failed at first to turn up. The court, comprising Mr Justice Anthony Hederman, Mr Justice Roderick O'Hanlon, and Mr Justice Robert Barr, heard legal arguments, and then, still with no sign of McDonnell, went to an early lunch. In the afternoon the judges were in the process of reaching a speedy judgment on the appeal when in walked, or rather ran, Paul McDonnell.

The witness now had two problems. First of all, his breath smelt of drink. In fact he had been in a nearby pub in Capel Street, calming his nerves. This was a poor preliminary for the evidence he was about to give. But in addition, as a result of medical treatment he had received as a baby, McDonnell's normal speech was indistinct. His father years later would give evidence that had his son been more articulate the whole case would have had a different result.

All in all, McDonnell had reason to be apprehensive about what lay before him. This was obvious as soon as he began to give his evidence. His performance in the witness box came across as little short of disastrous. On the one hand, he appeared confused over the dates: though he first said he felt the incident had happened some time after Christmas (it had been the end of February), he went on to agree with Eamon Leahy's suggestion in cross-examination that it took place in September. There were extenuating circumstances for McDonnell's confusion on this point (see chapter 6), but impressive it was not.

According to an affidavit later sworn by the prosecuting barrister, Eamon Leahy, McDonnell also gave self-contradictory evidence, stating that he was the front-seat passenger in the car, though his own affidavit had maintained that he was in the back. This particular claim by the state's counsel was also repeated by the investigating Garda, Patrick Thornton, in internal Garda memorandums; however, years later it would be shown to be incorrect, as would a number of the other perceived weaknesses in McDonnell's evidence (see chapter 6).

In the appeal court, Mr Justice Hederman asked McDonnell if he realised that the sentence for perjury could be five to ten years. McDonnell said he did. Did he still want to give evidence? He did.

Despite all the inconsistencies and weaknesses in his account, McDonnell made his point. He was unquestionably a new material witness in the case. His evidence challenged the safety of the conviction. In the circumstances, however unimpressed they may have been with McDonnell's slurred speech, poor presentation, and uncertainty over key points, the three appeal court judges felt they had no option but to grant a complete retrial. It was, at the time, a major victory for the two accused.

The failure to call McDonnell's evidence

What happened next, when the retrial got under way just two weeks later in the Circuit Criminal Court in November 1985, was disastrous for McDonnell. The defence lawyers decided on the day not to call him to give his evidence. They withheld their apparent key witness; in fact they decided not to call any witnesses at all, opting instead to rely on legal arguments challenging the undoubtedly shaky identification procedure used by Garda Thornton and Garda Broe.

On the face of it, this was a decision guaranteed to raise eyebrows. Why would the defence choose to offer no evidence whatever? In fact, whether it was a wise decision or not, the defence lawyers had their reasons. At least one of these was a worry over McDonnell's continued refusal to admit that he knew the name of the person who was driving the car. There had also been a bad experience with the alibi witnesses in the first trial. In addition, the lawyers were under the impression, because of that first trial, that the fingerprint of one of their previous principal witnesses, Brendan Walsh, had been found in the car, not where he said he was sitting but where the DPP said he was sitting. But whatever the reasons, because of the way the retrial had been granted it was a decision open to be misunderstood, particularly on the state side, and one that would leave McDonnell further shrouded in suspicion, in a sense now abandoned even by those he was seeking to help.

One member of the defence team told the author in 1986: 'McDonnell was of very limited intelligence and could be a very dangerous witness. I believe he was telling the truth, but the jury wouldn't have had time enough to see this. His evidence would have been very short, and he would not have survived the cross-examination. I don't think that he has enough intelligence to make up such a story. Mr Leahy put it to him in the appeal court that he had been assaulted or coerced in some way into coming forward. He denied this emphatically. I believe I can tell if a witness is telling lies. McDonnell's evidence was a mixture of fantasy and truth.'

At the retrial in November 1985, McDonnell duly presented himself at the court as a witness for the defence—available, if apprehensive. But he was left waiting outside the courtroom, with Brendan Walsh, for a witness call that never came. The realisation that he was not being called and would not have to go into the witness box brought relief, no doubt, of a kind, for in the extraordinary situation in which the young man had placed himself it may have seemed a more palatable option that everyone should decide that he was lying, and leave him alone, than that he should be believed. But McDonnell's performance under oath in the appeal court was perceived as having been so poor that the seeds of doubt were deeply sown. If he was telling the truth—and this would remain for years a proposition that many on the prosecution side could not accept—the ultimate effect of his performance, and of the subsequent decision not to call him as a witness for Meleady and Grogan, had been to completely obscure this.

But suspicion of McDonnell's motives, while hardly totally unexpected in the circumstances, was obscuring from the watching gardaí and state prosecutors the broader picture. If, as the DPP would shortly argue, McDonnell had been lying about being in the car, the outcome of the retrial should have been an important turning point for him. It removed the alleged purpose from such lies: getting Meleady and Grogan off. The ruse, if ruse it was, had failed. The upshot of the defence decision not to call any witnesses was that Meleady and Grogan were convicted once again. If the DPP and Garda Thornton were right, McDonnell's purpose in coming forward was now completely redundant. If his supposedly perjured evidence had just been a ploy to get Meleady and Grogan off, it had not worked. Having now been convicted for a second time, nothing further in law could be done for them. From November 1985 onwards there was no reason for McDonnell to persist with his story.

Was McDonnell a sharp operator trying to hoodwink and embarrass the state, or an inarticulate youngster with an attitude problem who was simply trying to unburden himself of a deep sense of guilt? If the former, and he was telling lies under oath, the question was, why? Why would he take such risks? If the latter, and he was simply—albeit in a hamfisted way—trying to do the right thing by Meleady and Grogan, how could the state have got it so completely wrong as to seek, and secure, a perjury conviction against him?

5

The Gus Dunne Factor

They said Gus Dunne was one of the best 'wheel-men' in Tallaght, and it was meant as a compliment. In a city and county where juvenile 'joyriding' had reached epidemic proportions, Tallaght was one of the areas most heavily plagued, and Dunne was one of the most active people involved. His own recollection of those months in 1984 and 1985 is that he might steal as many as seven cars in one night; on a weekend this number would rise to perhaps ten. Typically, one car would be driven till it ran out of petrol, or until Dunne saw a car he preferred; and so the evening would go on, until he might return home at one or two o'clock in the morning.

The word that Dunne was involved in the theft of Eamon Gavin's car and the accompanying assault on him was not long in getting about. Gus Dunne's name had been the one that Paul McDonnell was bandying about privately as the person who had driven the car, with himself and Walsh as passengers. Dunne was known locally to be friendly with Walsh and McDonnell; in fact he and Walsh spent several years sharing a house together in Seskin View in Tallaght; later the Gardaí understood they went to Jersey together.

But a general awareness that Dunne may have been involved had no particular significance for the community at first, not until the shock of the five-year jail sentence on Meleady and Grogan. At that point what had been just the common gossip of the streets now became a matter of some urgency. As Dunne and McDonnell were saying they were the real culprits, many felt it was time for their admissions of guilt to be translated into some more public statement. As we have seen, various friends and neighbours put pressure on Paul McDonnell, for whom it became a moment of truth. Independently of anything happening to Gus Dunne, he went and owned up. But Dunne was less easily moved; he lay low, and said nothing.

Dawn Keegan's story

Dawn Keegan was one of those who immediately understood the full significance of the verdict against Meleady and Grogan. She had good reason to. In 1985, as a teenager in Tallaght, she was friendly with both Gus Dunne and Joseph Grogan. She became pregnant by Grogan and gave birth to a baby. At the child's christening, Gus Dunne was made godfather to the infant. So when, shortly afterwards, Meleady and Grogan were convicted and given five years' penal servitude, Dawn Keegan was caught between a man who was believed to be one of the real culprits and one who everyone believed had taken the punishment for him. As an observer of the events going on, she was uniquely placed to know the truth.

Dawn Keegan later told how, shortly after the sentencing of the Tallaght Two in June 1985, she visited Gus Dunne several times in Shanganagh open detention centre, where he was serving six months for other motor theft offences, unconnected with Eamon Gavin. She told the author in late 1986 that in his cell at this time Dunne had posted on the wall a newspaper cutting relating to the crime involving Eamon Gavin. The Meleady and Grogan convictions had occurred just three or four weeks previously. The prison governor, according to what Dunne told Dawn Keegan, had ordered him to take the cutting down.

Dawn Keegan recalled how on one of her visits to Shanganagh, Gus Dunne told her explicitly that it was he who had driven Eamon Gavin's car, and that Joseph Meleady and Joseph Grogan were not involved. The Shanganagh visitors' records later confirmed that Dawn Keegan had visited Dunne at about the time she first indicated to the author, on 29 June 1985.

This frank admission of guilt from Dunne placed the young woman immediately in a conflict of loyalty. But her primary loyalties, she felt, lay with the father of her child, Joseph Grogan, who was now languishing in St Patrick's Institution for a crime that Gus Dunne now said he had committed. She now told Grogan's mother, Joan Grogan, what Dunne had said to her.

Later, in October 1986, Dawn Keegan would repeat the story to the author in a televised interview. 'He [Dunne] knew he did it, but he was too afraid to say it. Anyone would be afraid. He didn't want to get locked up for five years ... I think he should go up and say he done it.'

In speaking out as she did on television, Dawn Keegan risked bringing about a prison sentence for Dunne. Yet her interview directly implicated someone who was more than a friend to her. Yet her account of Gus Dunne's self-incrimination was so damaging that on hearing it for the first time the author wondered whether it could be authentic. Was there some other possible explanation for why Dunne might have said something to Dawn Keegan that might not be true? Perhaps, while he may have said what she alleged he did, Dunne could have been lying to her, or just joking. Perhaps he could have said it for reasons of bravado, and she had failed to realise that it was all just talk. But, on reflection, the idea that he might have falsely told his close friend, out of boastfulness or bravado or whatever, that her lover, the father of her child, had been wrongly jailed for something he had done stretched credulity beyond breaking point. Dawn Keegan herself never had any doubt that Gus Dunne's story as told to her was the truth.

Gus Dunne's television interview

Dawn Keegan's evidence was one part of a wider pattern uncovered by a 'Today Tonight' television team in late 1986. When the Tallaght Two case was first discussed in the offices of RTE's main current affairs programme, scepticism was the predominant attitude. However, the author was eventually assigned by the programme editor, Eugene Murray, to produce a television report on the subject.

A researcher, Brendan Leeson, had completed some initial inquiries in Tallaght. He had come back to the office with the view that there could well have been a miscarriage of justice. He reported that one man, who had never been charged, had actually admitted in court that he was in Eamon Gavin's car; the same man had also sworn under oath that Meleady and Grogan were not. This, of course, was Paul McDonnell. Another person, Leeson said, was widely known in Tallaght to have been involved in the crime, yet he too had never been charged. This was Gus Dunne. The victim, however, Eamon Gavin, was insisting that he had correctly identified Meleady and Grogan as culprits.

Leeson prepared a short report on the case in May 1986, just a week after Meleady and Grogan had failed in their appeal at the retrial. It set out the salient facts of the matter, and suggested that there was a good case for the state to answer. However, it was then May, and television current affairs programmes, as is their annual pattern, were winding down for the summer. The matter accordingly rested for several months, until the 'Today Tonight' team reassembled to prepare programmes for the autumn schedule. Leeson then received the go-ahead for further research.

By now the trials were over almost a year. Grogan was locked up in St Patrick's Institution, while Meleady had escaped and gone on the run, possibly, though no-one knew, out of the country. To a television producer the story looked complicated, uncertain, and unpromising. Two juries had found against the young men: how could the producers of a television programme, or anyone else for that matter, challenge such a weight of evidence?

Clearly the only way for the programme-makers to proceed was to find the principals and try to talk to them, on the basis that nothing clarifies an investigator's mind so quickly, whether journalist or policeman, as confronting key witnesses and assessing their credibility face to face. The RTE producer and researcher were not policemen, but between them they had twenty-five years of experience in distinguishing between the chancers and the trustworthy.

Not everyone was helpful. Paul McDonnell, who had appeared under oath in the Court of Criminal Appeal but had then not been called as a witness in the retrial, was not keen to speak to the television investigators. When the author called to his house he hid behind the front door and shouted out that he would not talk about it. It was an unpromising start.

Brendan Leeson meantime had had more success. He made contact on the phone with Gus Dunne, then living temporarily in County Kerry. Dunne told him, at some length, how he had driven Eamon Gavin's car on the night in question. Later, a discussion took place between Dunne, his girl-friend and Brendan Leeson in the lounge of the Royal Dublin Hotel in O'Connell Street, Dublin, on Saturday 18 October 1986. The researcher listened as Dunne explained what had happened on the night in question, how he had been in Gavin's car, along with his two accomplices.

Leeson's notes of the conversation contain a statement by Dunne that Eamon Gavin's daughter had looked out the upstairs window and had seen them as they tampered with the car. This was significant, for a number of reasons. First of all, if Gus Dunne had been present at either trial, or was familiar with the sworn evidence, he would have known that Gavin's daughter was downstairs with the rest of the family, watching television, while the car was being stolen: she could not have been seen at the upstairs window. The remark could suggest that the man was lying, or certainly was to some degree unreliable. What, if anything, could have been seen at the upstairs window? Not Eamon Gavin's daughter, that was certain. The significance of this curious reference would, however, become apparent within a few days.

Dunne's story was otherwise impressive in its eye-witness detail. It was unequivocal on the key question: he had taken a key part in the crime. He was acknowledging his own guilt, though he was doing so strictly off the record. (Years later, Gus Dunne would tell the Gardaí about this meeting with Brendan Leeson.) He said that he had given Gavin five or six opportunities to get off the car but that Gavin would not oblige.

Brendan Leeson's notes of this conversation recorded this self-declared driver of Gavin's car as saying that he had been afterwards approached in such a hostile way by Joan Grogan and her companion, Jimmy Brady, over his involvement in the crime that he was not inclined to own up publicly or officially. Later research would confirm the truth of this. At some point after the initial verdict of guilty against Meleady and Grogan, Gus Dunne was in fact accosted by Joan Grogan and Jimmy Brady as he returned from work into the Bawnville estate. They told Dunne they wanted him to own up to the crime. They had an argument; Brady remembers Dunne saying, 'There's no fucking way I'm going forward. I'm not going to do five fucking years, and I don't want to lose my job.'

Dunne likewise was wary of doing a television interview, despite his admission to an RTE researcher, as he felt he might be prosecuted as a result. He was told that the programme was being made anyway and that several of those to be interviewed intended mentioning Dunne by name. He said he would discuss this with his solicitor.

This, at least, was progress. It was face-to-face contact with—apparently—a central witness. The only problem was that the producer of the programme, the author of this book, had not participated in the hotel interview. If the witness was who he said he was, the producer, with such a sensitive and difficult programme to prepare, would also have to hear it from the horse's mouth.

Some short time afterwards Brendan Walsh, who had pleaded guilty to stealing Gavin's car and had been convicted for it, helped the production team organise another meeting, this time with Gus Dunne. Walsh and Dunne, it was clear, were the best of friends, a fact not lost on the RTE team. They agreed to come along to meet Brendan Leeson and the programme producer. The meeting was set for a Saturday afternoon in November 1986 at Morton's pub in the Firhouse Road in west County Dublin.

The two duly arrived. Dunne was exceptionally edgy; it was clear he would prefer to be somewhere else. The reason, it quickly became apparent, lay in the seriousness of what he had to say. Yes, he confirmed, it was he who drove Gavin's car that night. No, Meleady and Grogan were not there. Dunne was repeating for the producer's benefit what he had weeks earlier told Brendan Leeson. Was McDonnell there? Dunne was not prepared to name McDonnell directly; however, he did not challenge or raise objection to various explicit references to Paul McDonnell's involvement. It was clear to the two journalists that Dunne, by his attitude, was agreeing that McDonnell had been in the car as well.

What about the story of the girl at the upstairs window—had he seen someone there? No, it was Brendan Walsh who had spotted her. Walsh had given a warning, saying 'Watch out,' as Dunne continued hot-wiring the car. Walsh had told him at the time that it was just a little girl. Walsh, now sitting alongside as Dunne told this story, shook his head regretfully, saying he had no recollection of saying this to Dunne, as he had been too drunk at the time of the theft.

Would Dunne do an interview? Would he say on film what he had just said in conversation? He hedged; his response was unwilling. He was unhappy at the thought of such an interview. It wasn't that easy, he said. But he didn't leave; he remained in the pub, still talking about it. It was made clear to him that the programme was going ahead anyway and that it was possible, even probable, that he would be named in it.

There followed lengthy discussions about the community pressure on Dunne to own up. He explained earnestly why he hadn't owned up and why he felt he shouldn't, or couldn't, do an interview now. He said he had no intention of going to jail for this crime. He said that even if he was talking frankly it was off the record, and it didn't mean he was prepared to put his head on the block and give sworn evidence in court. He was only going this far, he said, because he was getting a bad time from people in Tallaght who knew he was the driver. He wanted to get them off his back.

Throughout all this, Brendan Walsh was present, acting as a sort of intermediary in the dialogue. Walsh's whole demeanour suggested a feeling on his part that Dunne needed to do something to clear a burden of guilt from his shoulders. Dunne, however, was not budging on the idea of an interview to camera. It was pushing him too far. Eventually it was suggested that he might do a silhouette interview. Did that mean he wouldn't be identified? Yes; and his voice could be distorted. But could RTE still give his name to the Gardaí? Could he be jailed over such a public confession? The dialogue continued. Dunne was not at all easy in his mind over it. It was pointed out to him that a television interview, even one where he remained anonymous, could break the Tallaght Two case open and perhaps lead to Meleady and Grogan being acquitted.

Eventually the RTE personnel offered a written undertaking that Dunne would not be identified in the programme and that they would not reveal to the Gardaí the identity of the person being interviewed. A copy of this undertaking was given to Dunne and a copy retained by the author. The interview was then set up in the car park at the back of the pub.

(This undertaking was honoured to the letter in the resulting programme and the inquiries that followed it. However, several years later the author discovered how Dunne himself, not long after the transmission, revealed to Det.-Insp. Paschal Anders that he was the person interviewed on screen and that he was the driver of the car. This revelation by Dunne himself made the interviewee's identity no longer confidential and was felt by the producer effectively to release him from the undertaking he had made. It became clear years later that Dunne had told the Gardaí himself of the encounter, though in a totally inaccurate way.)

Jumpy and nervous as Dunne had been during the several hours of negotiation, it was as nothing compared with his agitation during the filmed interview that followed. In this he described how he, Brendan Walsh and a third person, whom he would not name but would not deny was Paul McDonnell, first stole a Ford Escort and then drove in this to Eamon Gavin's house. There they abandoned the car and hotwired Gavin's Datsun Stanza, which was parked on the roadside.

Dunne told of starting up the car and of how, as he reversed, Eamon Gavin leaped onto the bonnet and refused to get off. He recalled that Gavin, later in the incident, was weeping on the bonnet as despair overcame him. He told of turning on the windscreen wipers to try to dislodge the owner's grip on the edge of the bonnet. Dunne said he was laughing at Gavin: he thought it was a rare sight to see a forty-year-old man hanging on the bonnet of a speeding car.

Dunne told how he personally had stolen hundreds of cars in his time. He explained, with more firmness now, that he didn't do crime to own up or get caught. He did crime to get away with it. He was sorry for Meleady and Grogan; they had nothing to do with the theft that night. They should be released from prison. But it was no fault of his that they had been identified.

It was a performance of compelling authenticity. Throughout, Dunne registered conviction and a genuine sense of apprehension. He was nervous of the possible consequences for himself of what he was saying, even though it had been agreed that he would be anonymous on screen. (For Dunne's own highly coloured account to the Gardaí in 1991 of this television interview see chapter 9.)

His account contained some revealing details. One was a passing description of the car he had stolen before reaching Gavin's house. It was, he said, a Ford Escort. In neither the trial nor the retrial of Meleady and Grogan had any of the details of such a stolen car been revealed. The first reaction of the author was to consider the question, had such a car been stolen in the way he described? It would turn out, again years later, that indeed a Ford Escort had been stolen that evening outside St Dominic's church in Tallaght and had later been found abandoned outside Eamon Gavin's house. Dunne's throwaway remark was accurate.

The other revealing detail was where Dunne told of the young girl supposedly watching them from an upstairs window. The sworn evidence was that all the members of Gavin's family, including his young daughter, were downstairs when the robbery took place. Was this then a lie, an indication that Dunne was making the whole story up? It was clearly something to be checked. Several weeks later, in conversation with the author, Eamon Gavin himself provided a possible explanation. Without realising the full context in which the idea of a young girl being seen at the upstairs window had arisen, Gavin explained that around the time when his car was stolen his children had placed the top half of a tailor's dummy in the window upstairs, with a wig on it, as part of a game with the neighbours' children. This revelation immediately transformed the significance of Dunne's story; unwittingly, Eamon Gavin's statement had invested Dunne's curious account with a new appearance of truth. Later, when the possible significance of the story was explained to him, Gavin's response was to say that while the dummy had been there in the upstairs window at around this period, it was not there on the night in question. He said he had checked with his son.

The question not easy to explain away was how Dunne had come to make this unlikely reference at all. If, as Eamon Gavin's evidence implied, Dunne was not outside the house that night, he certainly would not have known anything about a figure, tailor's dummy or otherwise, at the upstairs window. The fact was that no-one else in the whole saga, before or since, made any reference to a figure at the window. It was Dunne's story, and his alone. He had told it first to Brendan Leeson, then repeated it on camera four weeks later. The reference may have been, technically, an error, but it was the kind of error that eventually seemed to the author, and later, more significantly, to Det.-Insp. Paschal Anders, to have a ring of truth about it.

Returning to the television interview outside Morton's pub, why did Dunne agree to do it? If he really had not been involved in the crime, in what way could it have been to his advantage to admit on television, even anonymously, to such a thing? There was no question of any big payment from RTE: the payment he would get for this performance would more likely be grief, possibly jail. His mood suggested that he was doing the interview simply because he had no option. He was under pressure to be seen to do something to help Meleady and Grogan; this was the very limit of what he would do in that regard. He was always free to walk out of the pub that afternoon, but chose not to.

Face to face with Gavin

The programme was scheduled for broadcasting in early November. Eamon Gavin was invited to appear, but he had detected the programme-makers' scepticism regarding his identification of Meleady and Grogan and refused to be interviewed.

The filming of the Dunne interview represented a major new development in the case. How might Eamon Gavin react to this account? There was an outside chance that once he saw and heard Dunne he would be persuaded that he had been mistaken after all. He might be persuaded at least to give his reaction in an interview, which would be important for the programme's credibility. He was invited by the author to come to the studios to view the Dunne interview. He agreed.

What happened next became the subject of minor controversy at the time. In the interval between issuing the invitation to view the Dunne interview and the arrival of Eamon Gavin at the studios, the author found himself with an opportunity to arrange for Gavin to meet Dunne face to face. When Brendan Leeson had met Dunne in mid-October in the Royal Dublin Hotel, Dunne had offered to meet the victim. Gus Dunne himself came to RTE at this time, as a result of a separate undertaking given to him, to view the edited version of his interview. To the author's surprise he said that morning that yes, he was prepared to confront Eamon Gavin, face to face, when Gavin arrived later to see the interview. Dunne indicated that he was prepared to wait until Gavin arrived and then introduce himself to him, to see the reaction.

It would be a unique opportunity to see if Gavin would be able to identify the man who claimed to have driven his car that night. If Gavin recognised him, there would be a breakthrough; if he did not, no harm would be done. In case the former happened, it was decided to film the encounter. Conceivably, it could turn out to be the pivotal moment in the whole saga. Eamon Gavin, of course, was completely unaware that he would be filmed when he agreed to attend to view the interview. At that stage, the idea of filming the encounter had not arisen.

As Eamon Gavin was leaving the studios after viewing the interview, Gus Dunne stepped forward and introduced himself to him, and asked him if he recognised him. Gavin gave no sign of doing so. Then, as he saw the film camera in the background, he turned and stalked away.

It was unfortunate that Dunne at this time had a quite heavily damaged left eye, giving him a squint, because of his involvement in another hair-raising motor escapade that he had participated in since the Gavin incident. His appearance had been markedly affected by injuries to his face, jaw, teeth, and eye. The date of this accident, significantly, was later confirmed by Det.-Insp. Anders as February 1985—that is, between the time of the assault on Gavin and this encounter at RTE. The records of Dr Steevens' and the Meath Hospitals confirmed that Dunne was treated for these injuries at the time, some twelve months after the assault on Eamon Gavin. He was also attending an eye specialist at the Meath Hospital. Given that it was the driver's eyes that had left the most marked impression on Gavin's memory, according to his courtroom evidence, it was an unfortunate complication. Would it have made a difference had Dunne not been temporarily disfigured? Eamon Gavin was to tell the newspapers in the following days that the man who had approached him at RTE couldn't possibly have been the driver of his car, because he was 'squinty-eyed'. This seemed to be a clear reference to the temporary disfigurement.

In the event, the decision to confront Gavin with Dunne was not a success. The film of the encounter was discarded by the producer and never transmitted; the incident left the producer exposed to not unreasonable criticism for filming Gavin without his consent. At the time it had seemed that a breakthrough could come from a bold approach; this belief turned out to be mistaken.

Meanwhile it became known that Paul McDonnell was about to be charged by the Director of Public Prosecutions with perjury. This move by the DPP was to have dramatic consequences. One of the most immediate of these was that the DPP, Eamon Barnes, sought to block transmission of the 'Today Tonight' programme twenty-four hours before it was to go on the air. The grounds for this drastic action were that it would allegedly prejudice the McDonnell hearing. But the President of the High Court, Mr Justice Liam Hamilton, rejected the call for an injunction. The programme was allowed to go ahead, but with all references to Paul McDonnell cut out.

The 'Today Tonight' programme

The 'Today Tonight' programme made a considerable impact when it was transmitted in December 1986. Its centrepiece was the interview with Gus Dunne, who was not named but seen only in silhouette, with his voice electronically distorted. The anonymous, hunched figure on the screen said he had driven the car, that Meleady and Grogan were not there, that they were innocent. He described in detail breaking into the car, the journey with Gavin on the bonnet, and the aftermath.

Heney: He [Gavin] got a good look at you?

Dunne: He was more or less looking at me all the time, you know, because he would have liked to know what was going on in my head at the time.

Heney: You were laughing at him?

Dunne: I was. Well, it's not every day a forty-year-old man jumps on the bonnet of a stolen vehicle. I wouldn't do it myself if I was forty.

Heney: Why were you laughing?

Dunne: I was drunk. And I thought it was great fun—you know, if I wanted to kill the man I would have killed him, put it that way.

Heney: But he had a good look at you, and a good look at the passenger.

Dune: That's right, he had.

Heney: So you'd have thought he'd have been able to identify you.

Dunne: He should have identified me ...

Asked if he would come forward and admit his involvement formally, Dunne answered no. You didn't do crime to turn yourself in, he said: you did it to get away with it. He was sorry it ever happened to Meleady and Grogan. They should be let out. A lot of people thought it should be him that was in prison. But it wasn't his fault that they were identified.

It was put to him that people watching might think he was lying about the whole thing, just boasting; who could say he was there at all?

> Dunne: Well, I'm after putting myself through a lot of pressure to do this [interview]; like, I wouldn't be sitting here lying and risking a couple of years of my life here. I wouldn't boast about this, put it that way.
>
> Heney: So you're not lying; you're telling the truth that you were the driver of the car?
>
> Dunne: I was the driver.

Also interviewed in the programme in a hotel room in London was Joseph Meleady, who had escaped from St Patrick's Institution and was in hiding in England. Meleady insisted he was not in the car that night. It was put to him that Eamon Gavin was a hundred per cent certain that he was in the car. 'How can he be a hundred per cent certain? I know I had nothing to do with it. No matter what he says or does, I know I wasn't in the car. I know I'm telling the truth.'

Brendan Walsh, identified in the programme by name but with his face obscured from the camera, talked about the failure of Eamon Gavin to pick him out in the identification parade in Tallaght Garda station on 7 March 1984.

> Walsh: He looked closely at me, but he failed to pick me out. He obviously can't remember my face. I don't know why he didn't, because of all of us he got the best look at me.
>
> Heney: He says you weren't in the front seat.
>
> Walsh: He's wrong, then, because I was.

Others in the programme included Dawn Keegan. She told how Dunne had admitted his guilt to her, although she did this without naming him.

Brendan Walsh senior told how soul-destroying it had been for him to learn that his son was guilty of the crime, but he was convinced that Meleady and Grogan were innocent. Eamon Gavin had made a genuine mistake, he thought. But because Gavin had been so positive about it he had by now backed himself into a corner, and even if he had any doubts now, by this stage it would be impossible for him to back out.

Joan Grogan told how she and Jimmy Brady had confronted Dunne after her son's trial. 'You were in the car,' she had said to Dunne accusingly. 'Yes, I know I was in the fucking car,' the reply had come, 'but I'm not going to say that in court.' Joan Grogan felt he didn't want to go to prison for it. That was understandable, she conceded grudgingly.

Kathleen and Paddy Meleady said on the programme that Dunne should come forward to the authorities, publicly. Their son was innocent. They wanted the Minister for Justice to review the case, and as it could not go back to court they wanted the minister to grant the boys a pardon.

The programme, however, had one big lack. It made nothing of the location of Brendan Walsh's fingerprint within the car. At the time the programme team presumed, as had the defence lawyers before them, that the trial had been given accurate information by Eamon Leahy, that the fingerprint had been found in the back of the car. No inkling had yet reached the public that the truth might be different. And yet the message of the programme could not have been clearer: there had been a miscarriage of justice, and it would require political intervention to redress it.

To the programme-makers, and to the Meleady and Grogan campaigners, it seemed that the corner had been turned and that justice for Meleady and Grogan could not be long delayed. It was to prove a forlorn hope. In addition, the state was already embarked on a very different course: its master-stroke to nail down the Meleady and Grogan convictions. This would be the prosecution of Paul McDonnell for perjury. Before this would happen, however, issues raised by the 'Today Tonight' programme would have to be looked into.

The Anders investigation

One significant consequence of the 'Today Tonight' programme in December 1986 was that at last the state was provoked into a kind of action. The Garda Commissioner immediately assigned an investigation team to look into the programme's contents. This led eventually to two reports, the first from Det.-Insp. Paschal Anders of Tallaght station, the second, a 'consolidated report', from Anders's superior officer, Supt William McMunn of Rathfarnham station.

For years the contents of these Garda reports would remain a secret. Throughout this time they were the object of intense speculation among those interested in the case. Their contents, revealed below for the first time, contained fascinating glimpses into the official mind.

Det.-Insp. Anders had been first into the field, reporting to Supt McMunn. Anders interviewed all those who had appeared on the programme, including the author. He was given a copy of the unedited RTE interviews with Gus Dunne, Brendan Walsh, and Dawn Keegan. Under the commitment of confidentiality given to Dunne and still operating at the time, Dunne was only described to Det.-Insp. Anders as Mr X; inevitably, though, Anders had no difficulty acquiring Dunne's name from people in Tallaght. He then set out to interview Dunne himself; before long, his Garda colleagues found Dunne, lying low in his uncle's house in Killarney. But Dunne, who had had little enough enthusiasm for the interview he had given on 'Today Tonight', was not in the mood to talk to top brass in the Gardaí. He refused, at this first encounter since the programme, to tell detectives whether he was or was not the anonymous man in the RTE programme.

However, Dunne did tell Gardaí that he had come face to face with Eamon Gavin 'on the day the programme was made,' and that Gavin had told him he was a liar when he said he was the driver of the car. It was Dunne's first effective admission to the Gardaí of his role in the affair.

After this visit Dunne's father, Oliver Dunne, now became interested in his son's role in the affair. He asked him what the truth was. The father would later tell Gardaí that his son would not answer directly; he seemed to him to be 'beating about the bush' and failing to say whether he had been involved or not. Oliver Dunne now advised his son that if he was in Gavin's car he should contact the Gardaí and tell them the truth.

Before that could happen, a report in the *Sunday World* on 8 February 1987 named Dunne as being at the centre of the crime, and printed his photograph. Dunne was reported by the *Sunday World* correspondent, Dave Mullins, as having admitted his guilt to him. This story marked the first time that Dunne was publicly identified with, and actually named as, the driver of Gavin's car.

Two days later, on 10 February 1987, Det.-Insp. Anders met Dunne again, this time in Tallaght Garda station. Here a remarkable exchange took place, recorded by Det.-Insp. Anders for his superiors. At this meeting Dunne told Anders, voluntarily, that he was the person who had been interviewed on 'Today Tonight' as the driver of the car. He also agreed he had spoken to the *Sunday World* but said that he had not said everything they reported him as saying, nor had he posed for a photograph. However, everything he had said on 'Today Tonight' was the truth.

Anders, sensing a breakthrough, immediately cautioned Dunne; he told him that anything further he said might be taken down and used in evidence. Dunne asked the inspector if he could be charged and taken to court; Anders replied that if he made a statement it would be forwarded to the law officers, and it would be a matter for them to decide.

Dunne asked to be allowed to see a solicitor before he did anything further. He left the Garda station but returned within five minutes, saying that the solicitor was not in. Anders told him that he could contact him when he got hold of the solicitor. Dunne then left, and Anders never heard from him again.

The inspector had listened to Dunne endorse the television interview he had given, and stand over it. He was impressed. Not only had Dunne identified himself as the interviewee in silhouette but he had reaffirmed as the truth what he had said in the interview. Anders still had no evidence to offer in court, as what had taken place before he cautioned Dunne was useless as evidence. Nonetheless he had confirmed at first hand that Dunne was saying that he, and not Meleady, was the driver of the car. Details of this meeting with Dunne would accompany his report, and his superiors would be able to see the extent to which the programme's contents had been confirmed by the Garda inquiries.

The Anders investigation continued, with every person interviewed on the programme being seen. Each of them, including Dawn Keegan, Joan Grogan, and the Meleadys, repeated what they had said in the interviews they had given on the programme. Anders was also able to confirm a number of significant details. He confirmed that Dawn Keegan had visited Dunne in Shanganagh open detention centre at the time she said she did; she repeated that Gus Dunne had said he was the driver of Eamon Gavin's car. He also confirmed the existence of the tailor's dummy in Gavin's upstairs window. As a professional detective with long experience, Anders had himself been struck by this reference in Dunne's recorded interview. From hospital records he confirmed that Dunne had had his face disfigured, including his left eye, in a car accident that had occurred between the date on which Eamon Gavin was assaulted in 1984 and the time Dunne came face to face with Gavin in November 1986 at the RTE studios.

But Anders's most significant discovery was something else entirely, something of which the RTE programme-makers had known nothing. It was he who discovered that the wrong information had been given to the courts about the position of Brendan Walsh's fingerprint. He established that the fingerprint, far from being in the back of the car, was high up on the front of the front passenger door window, and upside down. This, he could see instantly, was a clear irregularity in the case.

Although he had discovered this error by the state in the trials, and had also confirmed that the 'Today Tonight' programme appeared to stand up, Det.-Insp. Anders's report to the Assistant Commissioner, Crime Branch, was guarded in its language. He concluded that there was no evidence to rebut any of the interviews given on 'Today Tonight' by Dunne, Walsh, and Keegan, or to rebut the confession made by Paul McDonnell. He had interviewed these and other witnesses, he said, and 'as a result of these statements, it would appear that Meleady and Grogan were not in the car.' However, he went on, 'no evidence can be found to support these statements.' And, for good measure, he added that neither was there any evidence to rebut the evidence of Eamon Gavin.

The Anders report tentatively underlined the problem that had arisen over Brendan Walsh's fingerprint. 'Brendan Walsh's story,' Anders wrote, 'that he was the front seat passenger, cannot be ignored by the fact that his fingerprint was developed on the inside of the front passenger window.' Anders had not got access to the transcripts of the Meleady and Grogan trial; there was no direct reference in his report to the way those proceedings had been given inaccurate information about the location of the print. His report also included his own account of how Gus Dunne had admitted to him that he was the person who had appeared on the 'Today Tonight' programme, and Dunne's acknowledgment that everything he said on the programme was the truth.

The Anders report, of its nature, had a very limited and classified circulation. It was seen only by those directly involved in the case on the state side, by senior Gardaí, officials in the Department of Justice, and, presumably, the Minister for Justice. While it lacked emphasis, it clearly suggested that something was not right with the case.

The McMunn report

By way of contrast, the subsequent 'consolidated report' from Supt McMunn of Rathfarnham station dismissed all Anders's concerns about the case. McMunn was required by his superiors to conduct a review of Anders's investigation, shortly after that report had been received. Having reviewed the issues raised by both Anders and the television programme, McMunn concluded: 'I respectfully suggest that not enough credence can be put in same to warrant any further action.'

The Anders report had suggested the clear possibility that Meleady and Grogan were not in the car. McMunn's repudiation of this view, very shortly after the authorities received it, was a critical moment in the eleven years of the Tallaght Two saga. It is worth looking in some detail at the superintendent's report.

Supt McMunn made no reference to the fact that Det.-Insp. Anders had heard Gus Dunne informally admit his guilt to him in Tallaght Garda station. The McMunn report stated at one point: 'Gordon Dunne has told all and sundry that he was the driver of the car on the night in question, except where it matters—i.e. to the Gardaí, and to his family.' It was true that Dunne had not provided Anders with a formal statement after he was cautioned, but he did, immediately before this caution, in effect tell the inspector that he was the driver of Eamon Gavin's car.

McMunn made a detailed critique of the content of Dunne's televised interview. In this he employed a memo submitted by Eamon Gavin to the Gardaí that sought to contradict Dunne's account of events. He noted that Dunne would have had 'ample opportunity to acquaint himself with the general facts of the case' since the night in question. Many young people had attended both trials, he said, and 'were familiar with the evidence given by Mr. Gavin.' Eamon Gavin had made eight particular criticisms of aspects of Dunne's account. Supt McMunn added to this what he called 'certain corroboration in support of Mr. Gavin's version of events.'

The report noted in passing that Dunne had described the first vehicle stolen that night as a Ford Escort; it did not note that this description of the make was correct, nor did it note that this detail had not been mentioned in evidence at either trial. It did not question how Dunne could possibly have known of such a detail. If Supt McMunn, like Det.-Insp. Anders before him, had no access to transcripts, the significance of Dunne's reference to the Ford Escort would not have been apparent to him.

On the question of the dummy in Mr Gavin's upstairs window, which Det.-Insp. Anders had seen as corroborating Dunne's interview, Supt McMunn was less impressed. He was not struck by the remarkable coincidence here but instead emphasised Paul Gavin's statement that the dummy was not in the window on the night in question. The young man had said that he remembered this detail particularly because he had remarked to friends the next day that had the dummy been in place it might have deterred the robbers.

While Supt McMunn made reference to the new evidence regarding the position of Brendan Walsh's fingerprint, unlike Anders he did not see it as warranting further action. He did not refer to the misleading information given by Eamon Leahy some two years earlier in the first trial, nor to the fact that this remained uncorrected in the retrial. Again he could only have done so had he had access to the trial transcripts, which appear not to have been provided.

Of Paul McDonnell's sworn statement admitting involvement, McMunn stated: 'It is apparent from a copy of his statement [i.e. his affidavit] made to Mr. Reidy that he could not have been present on the occasion of the theft of Mr. Gavin's car.' He did not explain his reasons for this bald assertion. He made no reference to McDonnell's description of the petrol can in Gavin's car, nor did he question how McDonnell could have known about this.

Supt McMunn's report appeared to err in one particular instance concerning Eamon Gavin's memo to the Gardaí. In this he had challenged a purported statement of Dunne in his television interview that after colliding with a Granada car, he got out of the Stanza 'and ran away.' Gavin said that this was clearly untrue, as Dunne had immediately stolen another car on the spot and had not 'run away'. In offering his own corroboration of this and other points made by Gavin, Supt McMunn did not state that this was in fact a misquotation. Dunne did not say in the interview that he 'ran away': he said that they hit the Granada, 'and I just ran out of the car and that was it.' Dunne simply chose to end his story at the point where he left Gavin's car; he did not wish to recount further self-incriminating deeds involving the car of Finbarr Martin, stolen shortly afterwards.

Buried in the transcripts and statements accompanying McMunn's report to the Assistant Commissioner was one intriguing statement from Det.-Garda Felix McKenna. McMunn made no direct reference himself to this document, yet it had some importance in relation to Gus Dunne's various admissions of guilt. McKenna stated: 'On 13.3.84 [eight days after Meleady and Grogan had been identified by Gavin], I questioned Gordon Dunne in connexion with Mr. Gavin's car, outside Rathfarnham District Court.' This statement introduced a hitherto completely unknown aspect into the case. The memo from Det.-Garda McKenna showed, for the first time, that Gus Dunne had been regarded as someone who possibly could help with inquiries in March 1984 into the crime against Eamon Gavin. The date was interesting too. At the time, both Meleady and Grogan and Brendan Walsh had been charged with the crime. Det.-Garda McKenna may not have been aware at this early stage that Eamon Gavin's evidence would be that there were only three in the car, and of course with three already charged, that had to exclude Dunne. How Det.-Garda McKenna thought Dunne could help with inquiries was not explained. There was no sign in the memo that he was ever contemplating arresting or charging him in relation to Eamon Gavin's car. Supt McMunn, though he included this memo as an appendix to his report, did not comment on this aspect of its contents.

All this information, of course, including the various conclusions by Anders and McMunn, remained confidential to the state for years. Though they were on file from as early as 1987, they would stay buried in the state records for another seven years and are being publicised for the first time in this book.

6

The Perjury Trials

From the start, Paul McDonnell was a thorn in the side of the authorities. When he first publicly announced his involvement in the Tallaght Two case, and thereby presented himself as a key witness, his action heralded for the state the trouble and expense of a complete retrial. So it turned out. The Court of Criminal Appeal obviously decided that it had no option but to send the case back for trial once more. The interests of due process demanded it, despite the fact that everyone present when McDonnell first testified under oath in the Court of Criminal Appeal, lawyers for the state as well as lawyers for Meleady and Grogan, could hardly avoid observing how unimpressive a witness McDonnell was.

Then, two weeks after the retrial had been granted, those involved in the prosecution of Meleady and Grogan were given what must have seemed like confirmation of any initial suspicions they harboured towards McDonnell when Meleady and Grogan's lawyers decided, to everyone's surprise, not to call McDonnell as a witness in the new proceedings. Indeed they decided to call no evidence whatever. Had McDonnell not given his evidence in the Court of Criminal Appeal, the retrial would never have been ordered. Now, with the retrial about to take place, McDonnell's evidence, against all expectation, would not be submitted to it. The decision came as a shock; and though it was one entirely within the rights of the defendants and their lawyers, in the circumstances it was bound to raise eyebrows.

The decision not to use his evidence inadvertently fed a suspicion that McDonnell's purported confession had in reality just been an attempted confidence trick. Why else would the defence decide not to call him? From the outside it looked as if the lawyers had belatedly realised that McDonnell was not telling the truth. He had successfully secured a second chance in court for Meleady and Grogan, and seemed now to be about to vanish from the scene, taking his story with him, before he was found out. This certainly was the thinking of Garda Thornton. And the impression that Meleady and Grogan's lawyers themselves had decided that his evidence was, at best, unreliable only confirmed the sceptics in their jaundiced view of McDonnell.

With thoughts like this firmly entrenched, the official mood hardened against McDonnell. As soon as the retrial resulted in another unanimous conviction of Meleady and Grogan, and a further appeal against conviction was dismissed, the state prepared to close in on the hapless young man.

Garda Thornton initiates the perjury action

The move against McDonnell began with Garda Patrick Thornton. Just two weeks after the retrial of Meleady and Grogan, on 12 December 1985, he sent a memo to his superiors in Rathfarnham Garda station urging that McDonnell be tried for perjury. He believed that McDonnell had a 'corrupt intention' in coming forward as a witness. 'The intention was to allow Meleady and Grogan the facility of a retrial, and if possible to pervert the course of justice.' Thornton had spoken to Frank Aylmer, a barrister in the office of the Director of Public Prosecutions, during the previous week, and Aylmer had instructed him to submit the available evidence to the DPP's office for specific instructions. Urging that McDonnell be prosecuted, Thornton said: 'I believe that a prima facie case has been established in this matter, and that a charge of perjury at common law be considered against Paul McDonnell.'

In his memo, part of Garda Thornton's justification for the perjury action was the mistaken view that McDonnell had sworn that he was in the front of the car. 'Paul McDonnell swore on oath,' he wrote, 'that he was the front seat passenger in the car.' This would later be effectively disproved by the evidence of the Registrar of the Appeal Court, Columba Ward. In this memo Garda Thornton stated twice that Brendan Walsh's fingerprint had been found in the back of Eamon Gavin's car, and this also, as we have seen, was mistaken.

On 5 March 1986 instructions came from the DPP's office, through Frank Aylmer, that proceedings for perjury be begun against Paul McDonnell. Aylmer conveyed this to the Chief State Solicitor's office. As a result, Garda Thornton applied on 3 June in the Dublin Metropolitan District Court for a summons for perjury against McDonnell.

Nothing happened for some months. In late October or early November it became known that a 'Today Tonight' television programme was being prepared on the case. On or about 17 November, Garda Thornton went into the office of the Clerk of the Metropolitan District Court to ask where the summons was and when the case was coming up for hearing. He was told he would have to take his place in the queue, that there was an enormous quantity of summonses waiting to be listed for court. Thornton asked how he could get the case before the court more quickly. He was told he could make out a summons himself, which he duly did. After he brought this personally to the Clerk of the District Court, the summons was issued.

On 26 November, a week before the 'Today Tonight' programme was due to be broadcast, the summons was served on Paul McDonnell, returnable to Rathfarnham District Court on 12 December.

Two days later Frank Aylmer phoned the editor of 'Today Tonight', Eugene Murray, to tell him that a prosecution by the DPP was pending in the District Court against a person who had given evidence in one of the hearings in the Tallaght case. He told Murray that in his view any programme dealing with the guilt or innocence of Meleady and Grogan would be a serious interference with the course of justice: the programme should be postponed.

However, after an amount of cautious sparring over the next few days, Aylmer received a letter from Murray on 2 December saying that the programme would be going ahead as planned. As a courtesy, the DPP's officer was invited to view the programme in advance, which, that afternoon, he did. After watching it with the author, the programme's producer, Aylmer's worst fears seemed confirmed: the programme asserted that Meleady and Grogan were wrongly convicted. This was the essence of McDonnell's evidence; the state case against him in the forthcoming perjury action would, Aylmer concluded, be prejudiced by the showing of the programme. He protested accordingly. But RTE would not budge. It was confirmed that the programme was going ahead.

As far as the DPP was concerned, it had to be blocked, and on the morning of the proposed transmission, 3 December 1986, an application was made in the High Court for an interlocutory injunction to restrain RTE from showing it. Video equipment was installed in Mr Justice Liam Hamilton's court in the Four Courts so that the programme could be viewed. The commentary, which had not been recorded at this time, was read in the courtroom by the producer. The barristers then made their submissions.

It took only a short break before Mr Justice Hamilton reached his decision. He ruled that references to McDonnell should be excised from the programme; for the rest, he did not 'for the life of him' see why it could not be transmitted. And so the programme went out, with its main message intact: that Meleady and Grogan were innocent, Eamon Gavin's identification was mistaken, and there had been a miscarriage of justice. Only McDonnell's role in the affair was missing.

Not a retrial of Meleady and Grogan

Why did Mr Justice Hamilton allow the programme to proceed? His reasons were important, if only because they contained assumptions that the state would seek to further contest in 1995 in an attempt to uphold the convictions against Meleady and Grogan.

The judge took the view that the McDonnell perjury case did not hang on the guilt or innocence of Meleady and Grogan but on a different issue: the credibility under oath of Paul McDonnell. The guilt of Meleady and Grogan was, in the eyes of the law, already proved and not in question, and therefore a programme querying it was entirely incidental to any pending proceedings. Superficially, as the DPP had implied in his submission to the court, the McDonnell action might look like a retrial of the Tallaght Two, but Mr Justice Hamilton decided that it was nothing of the kind.

The decision was important, because the essential argument before Mr Justice Hamilton, decisively lost by the state, was one that the DPP would seek to reopen in different circumstances in the Court of Criminal Appeal in 1995.

The charge against Paul McDonnell was that he, 'on the 11th of November, 1985, at the Court of Criminal Appeal … being a competent witness to whom an oath was administered, did make an assertion in evidence upon oath … which to his knowledge was false, to wit that Joseph Grogan and Joseph Meleady were not involved in the commission of offences … on Eamon Gavin and of malicious damage to a car, property of Eamon Gavin.' From the state's point of view, of course, it was simply a matter of fact that McDonnell had said on oath what was now alleged against him as perjury. In addition, Meleady and Grogan had been found guilty of the crimes against Eamon Gavin and had no further redress open to them. The perjury action seemed an open-and-shut case.

Later, in his charge to the second McDonnell jury, Judge Michael Moriarty would emphasise the stark facts that underlay the prosecution. Firstly, there had been only three people in the car. Brendan Walsh had been convicted of being one of these; Meleady and Grogan had also been convicted, twice, of being in the car; and Meleady and Grogan had exhausted all possible appeals against their conviction. This was the background of fact against which the jury would be asked to decide if McDonnell's sworn evidence that Meleady and Grogan were not in the car could be seen as anything other than perjury.

Obviously, the legal fact of the Meleady and Grogan convictions had loaded the dice heavily against McDonnell. Put crudely, there was no room in the car for him, either in the front or in the back. A perjury conviction seemed inevitable, a formality. The logic, from the authorities' point of view, was impeccable.

On the face of it, there was a good chance that McDonnell would not even contest the action but would enter a plea of guilty. The advantage of such a plea, from his point of view, was that it could well lead to a reduced sentence. It would mean, of course, admitting he was lying when he said Meleady and Grogan were not in Gavin's car; but if that *had* been a lie, there was no value whatever in persisting with it at this stage.

McDonnell surprises the state

Paul McDonnell confounded Garda Thornton and the lawyers representing the DPP and the Chief State Solicitor by entering a plea of not guilty to the charge of perjury. He was sticking to his story. The perjury prosecution was to be contested.

From the point of view of the state, for McDonnell to take this course appeared to be against all logic, and against his own self-interest. His original supposed motivation for lying, as described by Garda Thornton in his memo of December 1985, was, as everyone could see, now redundant. This had been 'to allow Meleady and Grogan the facility of a retrial, and if possible to pervert the course of justice.' The retrial was over; Meleady and Grogan had been convicted, and nothing could now stop them completing their sentences. Yet McDonnell and his lawyers were persisting with the story that he had been involved in the vicious assault on Eamon Gavin. That was what his 'not guilty' plea added up to. Pleading not guilty to perjury meant in effect insisting that he was guilty of the much more serious crime against Gavin.

The perjury charge had now nothing to do with Meleady and Grogan's fate. Why was McDonnell adding to his own agony in this way? The situation had become crazy. It must have appeared virtually incomprehensible on the prosecution side. Convictions having being secured against Meleady and Grogan, the logic was that McDonnell could not be guilty of the crimes against Gavin, no matter how much he insisted he was. A conviction against him for perjury, on the other hand, would neatly tie up the loose ends of the case. Or would it?

Preparations for the case proceeded. The state prepared to call once more on its star witness, Eamon Gavin, proven and case-hardened before several juries and three judges. The DPP could also rely on the apparent incoherence of McDonnell's own evidence given before the Court of Criminal Appeal. This time there could be no avoiding putting him into the witness box.

The McDonnell trials and the fingerprint evidence

The perjury case came to court on 21 July 1987 in the Circuit Criminal Court in Dublin. It lasted three days. Against all the odds, it ended not with a conviction but with the jury failing to agree on a verdict.

Again there was a retrial. This was held in November 1987. Once again the jury had difficulty bringing in a verdict; eventually, late on Friday afternoon, the jury divided 10–2, in favour of convicting

McDonnell. Once again this looked like a victory for the state case, as if the coping-stone had been placed on the whole prosecution against Meleady and Grogan. But the reality was somewhat different.

There were several moments of particular significance in the perjury hearings that should have given the state pause for thought. One was when McDonnell's father took the witness box.

John McDonnell was in an impossible situation. His son, in one view, had done the honourable thing in confessing to a terrible crime, in order that two innocent people would not suffer. Yet his reward now was to be accused by the state prosecutor of a different crime altogether: of lying about his guilt, and committing perjury. Perjury, of course, was an offence that carried much less public opprobrium than assaulting and threatening to burn someone. In the Alice in Wonderland situation that had been created, it would in one sense be more damaging to McDonnell if he won the perjury action than if he lost it.

In the witness box in the first perjury hearing, John McDonnell was asked if his son had consulted him before he made his sworn admission of guilt to his solicitor, John Reidy. Yes, he replied; Paul's conscience had been troubled, and he was feeling regret. He said his son had been very aware of the dangers to himself in choosing to come forward with such evidence. But he, as the boy's father, stood by him in the action he had taken.

The other moment of significance was of a different order altogether and marked at least a factual correction of the mistake made by Eamon Leahy two years earlier. This was the public revelation by Det.-Garda Felix McKenna that Brendan Walsh's fingerprint had not been found in the back of Eamon Gavin's car, as had hitherto been understood by all, but close to where Brendan Walsh had claimed to be sitting, on the front passenger window. Det.-Garda McKenna revealed this in the course of cross-examination in the first perjury trial; he repeated it in the second. He had used the scientific evidence three years earlier to get a conviction against Brendan Walsh, being then aware that the fingerprint was found on 'the inside of the glass of passenger door.' The fact that the fingerprint was in the front of the car had not reached the investigating Garda in the Meleady and Grogan case, Patrick Thornton. Now, finally, the truth was out.

However, even at this stage the fingerprint evidence, misrepresented as it had been in the previous hearings, was not included in the

McDonnell book of evidence. It did not come out in McKenna's evidence in chief but only under cross-examination, in reply to a direct question from the defence barrister, Séamus Sorahan SC.

It was unfortunate that even at this late stage—it being now 1987— Det.-Garda McKenna's evidence did not detail the precise position and orientation of the fingerprint. He did not refer to the fact that it was a print of the right thumb, nor that it was found high up on the glass near the front left window pillar, nor that it was upside down. These relevant matters even at this stage did not see the light of day. What they suggested was a most unusual posture for Brendan Walsh when he deposited the print. There was also, perhaps surprisingly, no reference made to the errors in the previous trials. The judge and jury in the McDonnell case heard Det.-Garda McKenna's evidence but heard nothing about how the same facts had been misrepresented in the trials of Meleady and Grogan or how the fingerprint was never formally entered as evidence.

There is no suggestion in any of this that Det.-Garda McKenna or anyone else was deliberately obscuring information. Nonetheless the full facts were not yet evident—not even, it seems, to prosecution counsel in the McDonnell case. Several years later, counsel for the DPP, Erwan Mill-Arden, would state that he had acted throughout both McDonnell trials without having had brought to his attention all the facts regarding the previous irregularities.

In the state files released privately in 1994, Mill-Arden stated that he had been instructed by Garda Thornton, in advance of the McDonnell hearings, that there had been a problem in the first trial over the fingerprint evidence. But counsel had no recollection of being told that it remained uncorrected through the retrial, or of it being stated to him that the issue had never been resolved, or even raised, at any of the appeals. Mill-Arden told investigating Gardaí that he had been, at the time of McDonnell's trials, under the misapprehension that the fingerprint evidence had been adduced in the Meleady and Grogan proceedings to challenge Eamon Gavin's identification. As a result, he said that he specifically decided not to give it to the defence in the McDonnell case, because he thought it had already been divulged in the earlier proceedings.

When counsel for the DPP discovered three years later, from the 1990 'Wednesday Report' television programme, that the fingerprint evidence had *not* been divulged earlier, he was, he said, astonished. His recollection was that he had been informed of a problem relating to the first Meleady and Grogan trial, but nothing thereafter.

This statement from Erwan Mill-Arden was in itself a remarkable, not to say astonishing, one. He gave evidence in the Court of Criminal Appeal in 1995 that he had not had available to him any transcripts of the Meleady and Grogan trials. This meant that he could not read there for himself that Eamon Leahy's error had not been corrected either before or during the retrial. The person who had given out the misinformation in open court, Eamon Leahy, was himself a prosecution witness for Mill-Arden in the perjury case. Mill-Arden, however, had no consultation with his Law Library colleague in the context of the case. He felt, probably quite rightly, that it would be inappropriate for the two barristers, in circumstances where one was a witness for the other as prosecutor, to confer. This was unfortunate, if unavoidable, as Leahy could hardly have been better placed to see that Mill-Arden was informed of how prosecution errors regarding fingerprint evidence had marred the previous proceedings. He had no means of so doing.

In the event, Mill-Arden, by his own account, went through two trials of the perjury action against McDonnell and never learnt the full history of the fingerprint evidence. (For the Garda inquiry's treatment of this issue see chapter 11.) As a result, the perjury actions proceeded as if there had been no irregularity outstanding from the earlier proceedings. This would leave them vulnerable to the charge that they were conducted on a false basis.

The truth was that by the time of the McDonnell perjury trials, because the guilt of the Tallaght Two was by then a legal and seemingly unalterable fact, it was too late to effectively challenge Eamon Gavin's identification with this fingerprint evidence. The fingerprint evidence should have been used to challenge Gavin's evidence in the earlier trials; indeed Mill-Arden went through the proceedings believing that it had been so used.

It was also notable that in his charge to the second McDonnell jury, Judge Moriarty at no time actually stated that the Walsh fingerprint had been found in the front of the car. Nor did he at any time refer to its possible significance in corroborating Brendan Walsh's claim to have been in the front. When the jury had gone out he was then asked to do exactly this, by Séamus Sorahan, counsel for McDonnell. He refused. The judge indicated that he felt he had already made the reference Sorahan was seeking; but the transcript, when it became available many years later, showed clearly that he had not. (See chapter 11.)

There was one person at the McDonnell perjury trial who realised the full significance of Det.-Garda McKenna's evidence. A week after the first perjury trial, a letter from Paul McDonnell's solicitor, Oliver O'Sullivan, arrived at the home of Paddy Meleady, Joseph Meleady's father. In his letter, O'Sullivan pointed out the new nature of McKenna's evidence and the fact that the earlier trials had been under a false impression on the matter. 'I do not know', O'Sullivan wrote, 'how it came to be that your son's legal advisers were apparently under the impression that the fingerprint was found in the back of the car, but my purpose in writing to you is to point out that a piece of evidence has now been given in court which may not have been available to your son's legal advisers previously.'

O'Sullivan, a solicitor practising in Castlepollard, County Westmeath, appears to have been the first to fully grasp what had happened. His letter included photocopies of the relevant evidence from both trials of Meleady and Grogan. These emphasised how the defence team in each case had laboured under the mistaken impression that the print was in the back of the car, not the front.

However, if McDonnell's solicitor was aware of the important implications of McKenna's evidence, his barrister, Séamus Sorahan, chose to make no reference to this in the McDonnell trials. The defence side knew of the infirmity in the earlier proceedings but appear to have decided that it was not in the specific interests of their client to introduce this as part of his defence. McDonnell's lawyers may also have presumed, not unnaturally, that Erwan Mill-Arden, for the state, was already informed on these matters, so it would not have occurred to them to bring it to his attention. Mr Mill-Arden told the Court of Criminal Appeal in January 1995 that he did not know the full facts on the irregularity in the fingerprint evidence until more than three years later—October 1990. The date of the letter from Oliver O'Sullivan was 27 July 1987. It was then twenty months since the second trial and over three years since the evidence had first come into the state's possession. It was to take many more years before the state faced up to the seriousness of what had occurred in its name.

Brendan Walsh returns to the witness box

A third significant development when the McDonnell case came to trial was the evidence given by Brendan Walsh at the retrial. Walsh did not appear as a witness in the first perjury trial; at the time he had recently been released from prison, and he said later he had wanted to have nothing to do with courts. However, in the second hearing he returned once more to the witness box and gave extensive evidence, a good two-and-a-half years since he had come up from St Patrick's Institution to testify at Meleady and Grogan's trial. His evidence on this occasion amplified his earlier testimony: he said he was the front-seat passenger in Gavin's car, and that Meleady and Grogan were not present. He said, explicitly, that Paul McDonnell was in the back.

But the importance of Walsh's testimony at this time lay less in its detail and more in why he chose to testify at all. He could easily have avoided appearing as a witness had he wished to do so. Yet he chose to come. The question was, why?

Officials, lawyers and Gardaí clearly believed that Walsh had been lying about Meleady and Grogan's innocence when he gave evidence in 1985. Yet now, surely, as with Paul McDonnell, any reason he might have had on the previous occasion for lying about Meleady and Grogan no longer existed. Meleady and Grogan were now convicted, and the outcome of the current proceedings could not change that. They had exhausted all means of appeal then open to them. So why was Walsh sticking to his story? In fact he was now adding to it, in that he was now acknowledging McDonnell's presence in Gavin's car, something that he had refused to do in his previous court appearance.

From the state side it would have appeared clear that Walsh must have known that McDonnell was not present with him in the car. After all, Walsh himself was definitely there and so must know the truth. So if McDonnell was not in the car, and Walsh knew this, why was he persisting with his story that he was? If it made no sense for McDonnell to be saying he was in Gavin's car when he wasn't, it made even less for Walsh to peddle the same story. Why would he do such a thing? Not to embarrass the Gardaí: that theory no longer made sense, if it ever did.

Walsh, it should also be remembered, at this point had already served two years in jail for the offence against Eamon Gavin and was now free. Now, in supposedly committing perjury on McDonnell's behalf, he was risking, for no apparent reason, a further term in jail. His evidence held the further risk that if accepted it could result in Paul McDonnell, for whom he was appearing, receiving up to five years in jail through a possible subsequent prosecution for his role in taking Gavin's car.

The truth is that the very fact of Brendan Walsh's evidence showed that the state case made no sense whatever. The perjury action against McDonnell was misconceived and should have been abandoned as the impeccable but ultimately distorted logic behind it became evident.

McDonnell under fire

In the perjury action, Paul McDonnell had to take the witness box again, and, as in the Court of Criminal Appeal, he had a bruising time, on this occasion at the hands of he DPP's counsel, Erwan Mill-Arden.

The main assault on McDonnell related to his evidence before the Court of Criminal Appeal. He had gone drinking, and arrived late in the courtroom. Counsel for the DPP alleged that in the first perjury trial this showed what little importance he placed either on the business of the court or on his own evidence. McDonnell had then attempted to explain away discrepancies in his evidence as being due to his drinking. He attempted to argue that if he did really say he was in the front seat in Gavin's car it was accidental and he had not meant to say that.

Counsel for the DPP was sceptical. McDonnell had said that he didn't know who the driver of the car was. The only conclusion to be drawn from this was that he was not in the car at all. If, on the other hand, as Joan Grogan had testified, McDonnell did know who the driver was, then he was not a credible witness. Either way, McDonnell should be disregarded.

The state was also unhappy about McDonnell's evidence regarding how many times Eamon Gavin had got off the car bonnet. Gavin's evidence had been that it was twice, but McDonnell had sworn that it was four times. This, the prosecution submitted, was clearly unreliable. And although he was given plenty of time in the Court of Criminal Appeal to recall when the assault on Gavin had taken place, McDonnell had still managed at one point to say it had happened in September, when in fact it had happened in February. It all showed how unreliable and untruthful McDonnell's evidence was—in the prosecution submission. It was with all these arguments, used to considerable effect, that the barrister for the state attempted to undermine McDonnell's credibility.

But, damaging as these arguments may have seemed, and clearly they did damage McDonnell in the eyes of the jury, a contrary interpretation could be put on the same facts.

While it was obvious, for example, that McDonnell was stressed and frightened in the witness box, and undeniable that this may have appeared to reflect shiftiness and insincerity, it could be argued that anyone would feel highly nervous in a similar situation, given the enormity of McDonnell's own decision to come forward. His drinking and his late arrival in court were not necessarily inconsistent with the view that his account was genuine. It could be said that in one sense McDonnell heartily wished to be anywhere on that day other than where he was—in court; there was no gain for him in the admission of guilt he was making.

As far as the question of the driver's name was concerned, McDonnell at least clarified in the second perjury action that he did in fact know the driver's name. But he still would not give it in evidence. He would not say it in court, nor would he write it down for the judge. He was not prepared, he said, to 'rat' on the person concerned. It was not out of fear, he insisted; it was not out of bribery. It was, from one point of view, a credible enough explanation, yet from another it was conduct that could seem just another example of the witness's evasiveness and unreliability.

McDonnell was subjected to rigorous cross-examination by Mill-Arden on the details of Eamon Gavin's journey on the car bonnet. His account clashed in several respects with that of the victim. This did not help his credibility; yet was it realistic to expect minute recall of detail from someone inside the car that night? All the young men claiming to be involved had been drinking heavily; indeed their wild and reprehensible behaviour showed all the signs of a loss of normal control. In such a state of intoxication their precise recall was unlikely to be fully accurate.

One aspect of the evidence in the Court of Criminal Appeal in 1985 had proved particularly—and in the end somewhat unfairly—damaging to McDonnell. This was when he accepted from Eamon Leahy, presenting the DPP's case at the appeal, a suggestion that the incident took place in September. But this exchange only occurred *after* an obviously confused and uncertain McDonnell had said correctly that it happened 'after Christmas'. And, as we will see, there was a good deal more to the confusion that day in the appeal court than McDonnell's uncertainty.

Appeal Court registrar contradicts Leahy's evidence

It emerged in the second perjury trial that Eamon Leahy—appearing now as a witness rather than as counsel—had made a mistake in his evidence on a particular point in both the McDonnell trials. This had nothing to do with his misinformed question in the first Meleady and Grogan trial. The mistake now was over alleged discrepancies in McDonnell's evidence in the Court of Criminal Appeal in 1985.

As a witness, Eamon Leahy swore an affidavit that he had heard McDonnell give evidence at one point in the Court of Criminal Appeal that he was sitting in the front of Eamon Gavin's car. This was damaging evidence to the accused. If true, and even allowing for confusion through alcohol, it would have meant that McDonnell contradicted himself even on his own claim to have been in the back of the car; it was evidence that suggested that McDonnell was either completely insincere or completely unreliable, or both. Leahy gave this account both in his evidence in chief and under cross-examination.

It was not until the former registrar of the Court of Criminal Appeal, Columba Ward, heard his evidence during the second perjury trial that Leahy's version of this was contradicted. Ms Ward had already given her evidence but was still in court; she was disturbed by what she heard Leahy say, because it did not tally with her own recall. She immediately left the court to consult the notes of McDonnell's evidence she had taken in 1985. After checking her records she asked, unusually, to be recalled to the witness box. She then stated that Leahy was mistaken, that her notes said that McDonnell had said he was in the back of the car, not in the front.

The judge, in his charge to the jury, accepted that, on balance, Ms Ward's evidence on this had to be preferred to that of Mr Leahy, as she had taken notes and he had not. But he said it was not a crucial point, nor, he felt, could Mr Leahy be faulted for his error, as, being on his feet for cross-examination at the time, he could not be expected to take notes.

But accepting the judge's point on this, Eamon Leahy's mistaken recall had been accepted in the first perjury trial as fact. Prosecution counsel, Erwan Mill-Arden, had used it with such force in his cross-examination that McDonnell had even conceded that he might himself have said he was in the front (though it eventually appeared, from Columba Ward's evidence, that he had not).

In the second McDonnell trial Ms Ward gave striking evidence about another aspect of the first hearing that had helped discredit McDonnell. This was the defendant's confusion over the date of the incident. She gave this a whole new perspective by recalling that this had only arisen after McDonnell's counsel, Paul Carney SC (now a High Court judge), had put the wrong date to McDonnell in the course of his initial evidence. Carney himself was confused, according to Ward, and referred to the crime having occurred in September. This, she felt, had induced a general confusion in the proceedings over the issue of the date. Not only that but, according to Ms Ward, she also remembered that one of the counsel had later acknowledged his own error over this matter and had actually apologised to Mr Justice Hederman in the Court of Criminal Appeal for having created the confusion.

What was unfortunate about this was that in the first perjury trial Eamon Leahy had made no reference to Carney's role. He had clearly forgotten the exact context in which McDonnell's mistaken reference to September had occurred. At the end of the day, of course, the witness had to take responsibility for his own evidence, evidence that, as Eamon Leahy rightly testified, was faulty on this point. However, the full story, as recounted by the former court registrar during the second trial, substantially qualified McDonnell's culpability. Eamon Leahy's evidence in the first perjury trial had subsequently been used with considerable force by counsel for the DPP, Erwan Mill-Arden, to challenge McDonnell's credibility. In all of this, McDonnell's case appeared to suffer under an assault based, inadvertently, on a partial recall of the facts.

Although Columba Ward's evidence went unchallenged at the second perjury trial on the issue of how Paul Carney had accepted responsibility for his client's confusion over the dates, Judge Moriarty's charge to the jury did not deal with this point. Overall, one can say that while McDonnell may have been an unimpressive witness, being

Eamon Gavin (Eamonn Farrell/Photocall)

Demonstration outside Mountjoy Prison looking for the release of the Tallaght Two (Eamonn Farrell/Photocall)

Joseph Meleady in December 1986 (Gavin McClelland/*Sunday World*)

Frank Connolly, author of the 1988 *Magill* article on the Tallaght Two (Tony O'Shea)

Paddy Meleady (John Carlos/ *Sunday Tribune*)

Greg O'Neill, solicitor (Derek Speirs/Report)

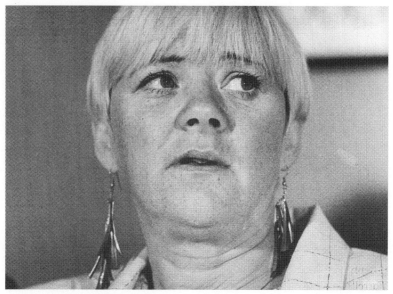

Joan Grogan (John Carlos/*Sunday Tribune*)

Brendan Walsh, *c.* 1990

Gus Dunne with *Sunday World* reporter Dave Mullins, February 1987 (Gavin McClelland/*Sunday World*)

Joseph Meleady at home (Eamonn Farrell/Photocall)

Joseph Grogan in the Dublin Mountains after his release (Eamonn Farrell/Photocall)

Joseph Meleady on his release from Mountjoy (*Irish Times*)

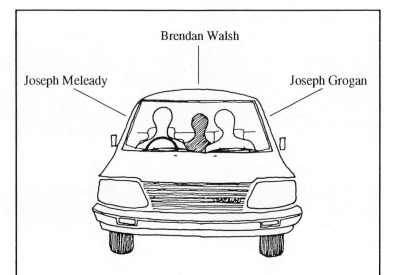

Positions in Eamon Gavin's car as argued by the State.

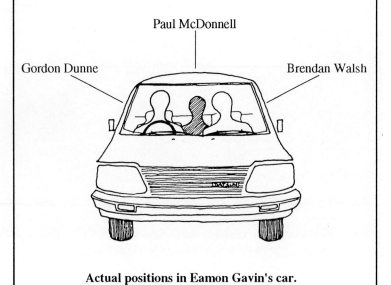

Actual positions in Eamon Gavin's car.

Position of thumb print on front passenger window in relation to B. Walsh's claimed position.

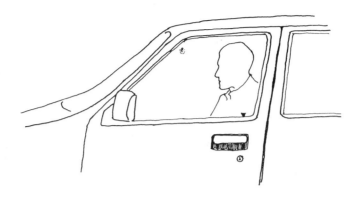

Artist's impression showing the State's explanation of precise position and orientation of Walsh's fingerprint.

Artist's impression of alternative explanation of fingerprint position and orientation.

1. Window is wound down.

2. Walsh grips window with right hand while holding umbrella in left.

3. Walsh begins to lever himself out of window.

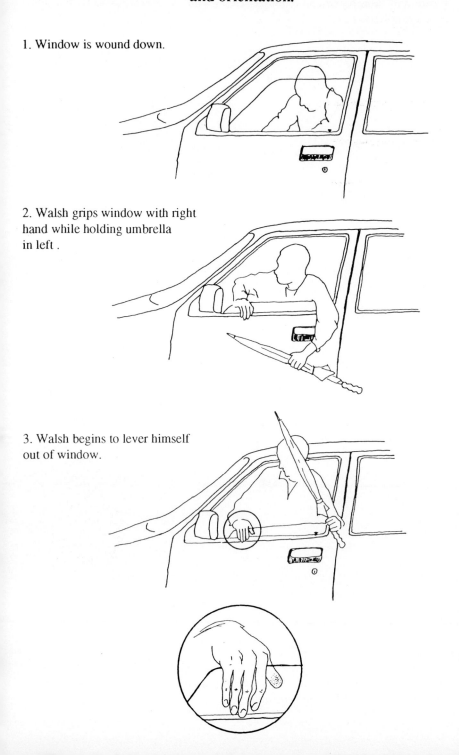

imprecise, inarticulate, devious, and at times truculent, his testimony was also weakened by a number of avoidable errors for which he had no responsibility.

The jury seeks extra information

It was after midday on the fourth day when the jury retired to consider their verdict. Before they went out, Judge Moriarty pointed out a part of the evidence where there was 'a reasonably clear conflict' between defence and prosecution. This related to the first car that had been stolen on the evening of the attack on Eamon Gavin. Brendan Walsh and Paul McDonnell had given precise information in relation to this car, including its make. The state had given no such information in its evidence. What was the truth of this? At about 3 p.m., at the jurors' request, Garda James Broe was recalled to the witness box to give further evidence on this point; the jury trooped in again from their jury room deliberations to hear him.

Garda Broe was asked whether he could confirm or deny the various references by McDonnell and Walsh to this first car. Unfortunately, he was unable to confirm that the car was a Ford Escort. He said he could not say whether Walsh and McDonnell's descriptions of that first car would coincide with his own recollection of it, because he didn't remember much about the car except that it was a small car, and it was stolen. The jury, as a result, never got the clarification they had sought, never heard that the car had indeed been a Ford Escort and that the defence evidence was accurate.

At about 5:35 p.m. the jury came back to the judge once again looking for clarification, this time relating to evidence from another state witness, Carolyn Smyth. She was a resident of Killakee Way, the road where Eamon Gavin's car had been abandoned. She had stated in evidence that, contrary to McDonnell's account, all three raiders, as far as she could recall, had driven off in the third car stolen, after Gavin's car was dumped. If true, this would mean that McDonnell had been lying about running off and leaving the other two to steal the Opel Rekord. The jury chairman said they were 'troubled' and uncertain about Ms Smyth's evidence. The issue had direct implications for both McDonnell's and Walsh's credibility.

A transcript of that evidence, however, was not available, so the judge read to the jury his notes of what the witness had said. There had been an element of uncertainty in her account. She said she had not seen the three men get into the second car: she had seen two men in one car and one man in the other, as she pulled up to her own driveway. The three were then out of her vision for a moment as she and her husband parked their own car. Thereafter, 'as far as I can recall,' she saw three in the car as it drove away. Was there any possibility that she might have made a mistake about the numbers? She doubted it. Was it possible she might be mistaken? No, she said.

But when the transcript became available years later it contained a revealing answer. The precise evidence was as follows. When Ms Smyth was asked why she was definite about the numbers, she said: 'They were blocking our way, making it impossible for us to get into the gate of our house, so I'm definite about the numbers of people.' But this was confirmation not that three people drove off in the Opel Rekord but that when she first pulled up she saw two people and one person, making a total of three, in two separate cars. What Ms Smyth's evidence was definite about was in fact virtually common sense. It did *not* confirm that McDonnell, contrary to his evidence, 'definitely' was in the Opel Rekord as it drove off.

The jury came back twice seeking clarification on exactly this point. But the absence at the time of a transcript meant that the judge was unable to clarify exactly what Carolyn Smyth had been definite about. Through no-one's fault, the jury were denied the precise sentence quoted above. And the transcript showed that when the witness had referred to three people being in the Opel as it sped away, she said simply that this was 'as far as I can recall.'

The jury were having some difficulty in reaching a verdict. Judge Moriarty told them there was still some point in trying to reach unanimity. Thirty minutes later, at about 6:05, they returned to say they could not reach a unanimous verdict. The judge advised them then that they could return a majority verdict if ten could agree. If there was to be an acquittal, no numbers need be reported; if a conviction, then the numbers should be made known. Was a unanimous verdict not possible? No, replied the foreman. But he said they would only require five minutes to reach a majority verdict.

At 6:15 p.m. the jury returned and announced that McDonnell had been found guilty of perjury by 10 to 2. The court then adjourned to the following day to pass sentence.

When the court resumed, Paul McDonnell's father stood up in the body of the court and addressed the judge. He told him that he disagreed with the verdict and believed in his son's innocence of perjury. He said that he had totally supported his decision to go forward and tell the truth about the case. He described the previous four years as a nightmare, because of the trauma caused both to his family and also to the families of the others convicted for the offence against Mr Gavin.

One final twist was to come. Paul McDonnell had been found guilty of perjury; his supposedly perjured evidence had specifically caused one hearing of the Court of Criminal Appeal, one Circuit Criminal Court case against Meleady and Grogan (the retrial), and two Circuit Criminal Court prosecutions (one of these being inconclusive) against himself for perjury. On the face of it, Paul McDonnell had sought to pervert the course of justice. Conviction for the serious offence of perjury carried a possible jail sentence of five to ten years. The judge, after initially contemplating a custodial sentence, eventually gave him approximately twenty-seven days' *community work*: a total of 210 hours.

This left hanging a final question arising from this extraordinary prosecution. Why was the sentence for such a serious and prolonged and, apparently, totally mischievous charade so lenient? Was it perhaps that the judge had understood more about the case than the ritual of the adversarial courtroom procedures had revealed to the jury?

The McDonnell verdict's significance

Eamon Gavin informed the author in later years that as the perjury trials were given the precise fingerprint evidence and yet eventually found against McDonnell, this showed that the fingerprint evidence did not raise a sufficient doubt, or indeed, in his mind, any doubt, about the guilt of Meleady and Grogan. It was an argument the DPP and Eamon Leahy would also seek to use in the later years of the campaign. (See chapter 11.)

How should the outcome really be viewed? In the first place, as we have seen, it was no retrial of Meleady and Grogan. Their conviction and guilt were not an issue in the case. On the contrary, it was already established, and was part of the evidence. Beyond that, a disagreement among the jury in the first trial, and a 10–2 majority against McDonnell in the second trial, seemed to show that the juries were less sure of the balance of the evidence than the Meleady-Grogan juries had been. This was despite the fact that they had to take into account the guilt of Meleady and Grogan as a given and unalterable fact, which must have heavily influenced their view of McDonnell.

In the end, the question before the perjury jury was a different one from that before the Meleady-Grogan trials. Paul McDonnell's credibility was the central focus, not Meleady and Grogan's innocence. And McDonnell's credibility was difficult to defend, especially when he admitted that he had not been truthful about some central matters, such as knowing who the driver was. His evidence was full of holes; it would have been very difficult for any jury to know where his lies and confusion stopped and his truthfulness began. The proposition that he had told the truth under oath was, overall, a harder one to defend than the proposition that Meleady and Grogan were not in the car.

In spite of all this, the outcome was a 10–2 majority verdict for conviction. This division among the jurors might suggest that when the fingerprint evidence was opened to the jury, new elements of doubt entered into play, despite McDonnell's obvious unreliability and the different basis of this case.

In fact the first perjury jury, which could not reach a verdict, appears to have been divided 8–4 for *acquittal* of McDonnell. This was the jury that had been accidentally misled by Eamon Leahy's evidence over what McDonnell had told the Court of Criminal Appeal. Did this error influence the divided jury sufficiently to mean the difference between a possible acquittal of Paul McDonnell and the hung jury that emerged? It was another intriguing question to add to the others building up in the saga of the Tallaght Two.

7

The Campaign in the Lean Years

For the Meleadys, the Grogans and their supporters the three years between July 1987 and October 1990 were the worst of times. It was a time when the ice surrounding the case might have been showing some signs of a thaw, but instead the official attitude towards those questioning the convictions was as frosty as before.

For Paddy Meleady, the driving force behind the campaign to clear the two boys, the official attitude was perplexing and frustrating. The fingerprint evidence was now known to the authorities in a way that it had not been when Eamon Leahy made his misstatement in court in May 1985. Yet the authorities' attitude had not changed. It seemed that someone—whether the Director of Public Prosecutions, the Chief State Solicitor, or senior Garda officers—had determined that the new evidence was of no consequence. If this were so, the Meleadys and the Grogans needed someone to explain it to them. But explanations were not forthcoming.

The Department of Justice and its two successive Fianna Fáil ministers, Gerry Collins and Ray Burke, appeared, at least to those on the outside, to have every opportunity to respond to the argument over the scientific evidence in the case. Surely they must be aware of it? Did they know that both Meleady and Grogan trials had been conducted on an incorrect basis? What would it take to bring about a full-scale review of the case?

Each side was seeing the case from its own perspective. As far as officials on the state side were concerned, the conviction of Paul

McDonnell for perjury appeared to have sent a very strong signal that no miscarriage of justice had taken place. In fact the case, and its outcome, had been misunderstood from the start, as we have seen. But even if the prosecution had been misconceived it had nonetheless secured a guilty verdict, and this was helping to stymie all efforts to have a root-and-branch review of the case.

The collapse of the official position began in earnest as a result of a second television programme, broadcast in October 1990. (See chapter 8.) Yet, as will be apparent, this did little more than state facts that had been on the public record for years. The only difference was the full spotlight of public attention that television, at one stroke, could create. The effect, however, would be electric.

In the meantime, the years from 1987 to 1990 were virtually lost years. Scattered through the newspaper pages of the period and its radio tapes, a tiny voice of dissent can today be only barely detected. It emanated from a house in Tallaght; against a background of civil servants and Government ministers moving to redress miscarriages of justice in England, the voice insisted that a case in their own country was being ignored. It was the voice of Paddy Meleady. Meleady found it difficult to restrain his resentment at the readiness of the authorities to detect miscarriages of justice abroad, even such spectacular ones as the case of the Birmingham Six, while seeing nothing amiss with the Tallaght Two case at home.

But the Tallaght Two campaign ground on. Although the commitment of the small band of helpers caught up in the agony of the Meleady and Grogan families did sometimes falter, and although they were often discouraged and dispirited, they never gave up belief in their cause. There poured out a remorseless string of press releases, of letters, petitions, and invitations to public meetings, most of them from the pen of Joseph Meleady's father. These documents contained all the information that would later provoke a top-level two-year inquiry by the Attorney-General and the Director of Public Prosecutions. At the time, they were, in public at least, roundly ignored by the authorities.

Meantime, on the other side of the argument, it was also a time of stress and personal difficulty for Eamon Gavin. Deeply offended by media and in particular television coverage of the case, he had become obsessed with the whole episode in exactly the way Meleady senior had. His marriage had come under strain, as had his employment. The innocent victim of the events of February 1984 saw himself being portrayed in the media as mistaken in his evidence against Meleady and Grogan, and it hurt. The proposition that the two young men had been wrongly jailed was one that he could not and would not entertain. His resentment at sections of the media matched that of Paddy Meleady against the authorities.

The new evidence: Paddy Meleady spreads the word

While the facts about Brendan Walsh's fingerprint had startling implications for this case, these were by no means fully apparent to the public. The idea that the state might have failed to vindicate the right of two citizens to a fair trial was far from obvious from the press coverage of the various trials. The reports on the perjury trial were brief; the story had lost its news currency, and there was a dearth of informed analysis to bring out the significance of what had happened.

So it fell to Paddy Meleady, the now out-of-work plumbing contractor, a man without money, influence, or legal advice, to preach the gospel from his home in Tallaght. His first press statement recounting the significance of the fingerprint evidence was issued in the first week of October 1987. This was sent to a large number of TDs and senators of all parties, as well as all the national papers. It began:

> Dear —,
>
> I would like to bring to your notice a piece of very important evidence that has come to light in the perjury case of Paul McDonnell, that was not available to our legal advisers at the trials of Joseph Meleady and Joseph Grogan.
>
> Detective Serg. Felix McKenna stated in evidence in reply to a question put to him in cross-examination by Mr. Séamus Sorahan, counsel for Paul McDonnell, that a forensic [test] was carried out on a car x, and that a print belonging to Brendan Walsh had been found on the inside of the front door passenger window.
>
> At the first and second trial of Meleady and Grogan, each jury was told that Brendan Walsh had to be in the back of the car x,

where his fingerprint was found, [as in] the visual identification evidence given in court by Eamon Gavin and his son.

The D.P.P. did not put the correct information before the court. We have to say that if counsel for Meleady and Grogan had known the correct whereabouts of the fingerprint found in car x, they would have suggested to either jury that Brendan Walsh was in the front passenger seat, where his fingerprint was found, and that would have shattered the visual identification from Eamon Gavin that was heard in court.

This statement was issued three years before the television programme (see chapter 8) reported virtually the same information, with dramatic consequences. At the time, only the local TD Mervyn Taylor, the Labour Party's spokesperson on justice and himself a practising solicitor, saw the seriousness of the issue.

Four weeks later, in mid-November 1987, a meeting of Dáil deputies and senators with an interest in the case was called in Dublin by Mervyn Taylor. The newspapers carried reports next day. Taylor said at this gathering that a serious miscarriage of justice had occurred in the Tallaght Two case. He listed the new fingerprint evidence and pointed out that the original trial had been given wrong information on this matter. The new evidence showed that Brendan Walsh had been telling the truth about being in the front of the car, he said. The Minister for Justice should review the case.

At the meeting, Taylor was supported in his call by Pat McCartan TD, spokesperson for the Workers' Party, and Donal Carey TD, spokesperson for Fine Gael. The following month, however, the campaign for Meleady and Grogan was jolted by the verdict in the Circuit Criminal Court, convicting Paul McDonnell of perjury. This came as a shock as, suddenly, it appeared to close off the last opportunity to keep the case alive in the courts. And yet to Paddy Meleady it was only one in a long line of reverses, going back three-and-a-half years to March 1984; he and his wife, Kathleen, and Joan Grogan, the mother of Joseph Grogan, had learnt to withstand them.

Nonetheless it took another six months before Meleady could gather his energies and his conviction sufficiently for another assault on what looked like an impregnable fortress. On 23 June 1988 he sent a detailed four-page letter to TDs and senators and to the national newspapers. In effect this was a review of the McDonnell perjury trial. It reads today as an impressive critique of what had happened there.

Meleady's 1988 letter recorded, for the first time in print, how the Registrar of the Court of Criminal Appeal, Columba Ward, had felt obliged to take the witness box the previous year to contradict the prosecuting barrister Eamon Leahy's evidence on supposed discrepancies in Paul McDonnell's evidence. It was far from clear that Meleady's report of this was accurate, as no proper record of the trial was to hand. Confirmation in fact that it was accurate would have to wait a further six years, until the state released the verbatim transcript of the McDonnell trials to the Tallaght Two's lawyers. This authenticated Meleady's claim made in 1988.

Paddy Meleady's letter also asserted that the leniency of the sentence eventually given by Judge Michael Moriarty in the second McDonnell trial was significant. Mr Justice Hederman had stated that five years could be the sentence, as McDonnell had a number of previous convictions. Instead the judge gave him four-and-a-quarter weeks' community work. 'Everyone in Tallaght knew that Paul McDonnell committed that crime, even his own father, who told the judge he disagreed with the verdict of the jury as he knew for certain his son was in Mr. Gavin's car. It has to be the biggest disgrace this country has witnessed in recent years—the jailing of two innocent youths for a crime three other people stated they committed ...

'Any decent person hates to see an innocent person suffer for another person's crime, so please do something about this injustice that has gone on for far too long. You have the power, for God's sake use it. What we want is an independent public inquiry, and the case to be re-opened. We urge you as a T.D. or Senator to use your position to see that justice is done in our country.'

The Magill article

In August 1988, *Magill*, the now defunct current affairs monthly, gave five pages to Frank Connolly's detailed review of the Tallaght Two case and its significance. On the new fingerprint evidence Connolly wrote: 'If revealed to the jury during earlier trials, [it] would have substantiated Walsh's claim [to be in the front of the car], and undermined seriously the apparently clear identification evidence of Gavin.' He said he had interviewed at length 'a third man', who said he had earlier appeared on the 'Today Tonight' programme and admitted his guilt there. This clearly was Gus Dunne, though the *Magill* article did not identify him.

This man had told Connolly that he had been interviewed by Gardaí in Tallaght station and that he had acknowledged while in the station, 'off the record,' that he was indeed the driver of Eamon Gavin's car on that night. He also told Connolly how he had refused an invitation to make a signed statement to that effect. All this, of course, had been known to the authorities since the spring of the previous year, when Det.-Insp. Paschal Anders delivered his (still classified) report.

The article also reported a striking incident witnessed by its author while researching the story. Connolly was in the process of interviewing Dunne in the Cherry Tree pub in Walkinstown, Dublin, when the mothers of the two convicted youths, Kathleen Meleady and Joan Grogan, came up and confronted Dunne about the case. 'The third man [Dunne] took the opportunity presented by the meeting to apologise for the damage caused by his past errors, but repeated that he saw no point in going forward to confess to the Gardaí.'

This was a first-hand, eye-witness account by a professional journalist of Gus Dunne apologising to Kathleen Meleady and Joan Grogan for having, indirectly, got their two sons into jail. Dunne's remorse, of course, had its limits. It was never intended to be used as evidence. But no-one reading this record could fail to wonder at its implications for the convictions of Meleady and Grogan. The circumstances of the encounter left scant room for doubt that this was anything other than a bona fide apology from a guilty party. The reader could only wonder why this 'third man'—or anyone for that matter—would eat humble pie in front of two distressed and angry mothers if he had not done what he said he had.

It remained a fact, of course, that unless Dunne were to go further and make a sworn statement acknowledging his guilt, this sort of incident could never be admissible in court. It was left, therefore, to the discretion and commitment of the officials and Gardaí who had brought about the prosecution of Meleady and Grogan to take note of the revealing contents of this article. It is known to have been studied in the office of the Chief State Solicitor. No action resulted, presumably for lack of real evidence.

Gareth Peirce is rebuffed by the Government

During all these years, the Government was campaigning to secure the release and vindication of the Birmingham Six. Strenuous political and diplomatic energies were being devoted to the task of persuading the British authorities that their courts had made serious mistakes in the matter of the six Irishmen. The fact that no mechanism of any kind existed in Ireland to bring a case such as the Birmingham Six, if it existed, back into the courts for review was not allowed to stand in the way of political and legal sermons.

The media played the game also. In November 1987 the *Irish Times* devoted top billing to the Birmingham Six appeal: a story on page 1, and inside, eight columns of news. In the same edition it devoted just twelve column-inches on an inside page to Mervyn Taylor's call for a review of the Tallaght Two case.

The attitude of the newspapers and RTE to the Tallaght Two campaign was fitful, uncertain, and at best slightly sceptical. Editors were reluctant to devote time and space to this alleged miscarriage of justice. The case for review appeared unconvincing; the fact that the issues had been consistently decided by the courts in favour of the state every time it was heard seems to have been enough to deter most editors and reporters. This attitude closely mirrored the media's original lack of interest in the Birmingham Six case in the long years before Yorkshire Television's documentaries made that case a front-page story.

The contrast between the Government's enthusiasm for the case of the Birmingham Six and the Guildford Four and its indifference for years on the Tallaght Two was to have a nice irony with the brief entry into the Irish case of the London solicitor Gareth Peirce. She was one of the British legal figures most admired and respected in Ireland, because of her work in these other cases. Her outright championing of the cause of the Birmingham and Guildford accused, at a time when their cases had attracted little popular interest, had won over many people in Ireland. But in August 1989 Gareth Peirce became drawn into the Tallaght Two case to play a cameo role. It happened quietly and without publicity.

Joseph Meleady had finally been arrested in London, after spending over three years on the run from St Patrick's Institution in

Dublin. He was convicted in Thames Magistrates' Court on 4 August 1989 on charges of driving without insurance or licence at a time when he was disqualified, and an order was made for his extradition to Ireland. Gareth Peirce was contacted by Paddy Meleady. Inevitably, she inquired into the background to Meleady's presence in England. Having listened to what Meleady senior and junior had to say, and having studied the files, she was struck by the significance of the new fingerprint evidence that had emerged. She sent the following letter privately to the Minister for Justice, Ray Burke, on 16 August 1989:

Dear Sir,

Re. Joseph Meleady:

We have been asked to represent the above named who is presently due to be extradited to the Republic of Ireland from England. A number of matters have been drawn to our attention which appear to give serious cause for concern about the safety of the convictions of both Mr. Meleady and his co-defendant Mr. Grogan.

You are no doubt fully aware of the background to Mr. Meleady's case, and we do not go into the ground that has already been covered. It does seem to be the case, however, that a material irregularity may have occurred at both Mr. Meleady's original trial (together with his co-defendant Mr. Grogan), and upon his re-trial. It would appear that relevant forensic evidence was not only not disclosed to the defence, but indeed the suggestion was left with the court that the prosecution was actually in possession of forensic evidence contradictory to that which did in fact exist.

You are no doubt aware that at the heart of the case of Mr. Grogan and Mr. Meleady is the issue of whether they were present in a car as driver and front seat passenger, or whether they were not. At their original trial a man also charged with being party to the offence and present in the car gave evidence, a Mr. Walsh. At that trial he said he was the front seat passenger. If his evidence had been accepted, the identification of Mr. Meleady and Mr. Grogan by the civilian witness, Mr. Gavin, must have been fatally dented, in that he identified them both as being in the front of the car.

It was put to Mr. Walsh in cross examination by the prosecution that his fingerprint was found in the back seat of the car. Both prosecuting counsel, and the defence, as we understand it, made the assumption that Mr. Walsh's fingerprints must have been found in the back of the car. However, it appears that evidence has subsequently come to light to the effect that Mr. Walsh's prints were found in the front of the car. The non-disclosure of this must constitute a material irregularity in relation to both trials.

The evidence given by the only prosecuting witness, Mr. Gavin, was of the most worrying kind. You will be well aware of the concern that there has been in many jurisdictions that wrongful convictions have occurred on the basis of mistaken identification evidence. Mr. Gavin would appear to be that most troubling of witnesses, an honest but mistaken witness, convincing to a jury, undoubtedly convinced himself, but wrong. Without evidence to disprove his account, no doubt any jury would have tended to believe Mr. Gavin rather than two young and much less articulate men, whose main witness (Mr. Walsh) appeared to have been discredited by forensic evidence. We also understand that none of the relevant safeguards surrounding identification, in particular the holding of a parade, with proper protection for the suspect, and a right of representation, were followed in this case.

We hope it is not discourteous of us to make mention of the fact that we have worked long and hard and out of deep conviction on cases of a number of people wrongly convicted in English courts,—in particular, the six men known as the Birmingham Six, and now in relation to one of the defendants in the Appeal known as the Guildford Four. We would not lightly bring to your attention a case which has gone wrong in your jurisdiction when we are only too painfully aware of cases that have been flagrantly brought about by failures in our own system.

However, we have seen Mr. Meleady and we believe him; we have spoken to his father, and we have had brought to our attention this new evidence. We do not think that someone could sustain a convincing position over so many years if their account was bogus.

We respectfully request either that you might appoint a judicial inquiry to look into the further material now available, or that urgent consideration should be given to the case's further scrutiny by the Court of Appeal. We are aware that Mr. Grogan is now released, is very much affected by the experiences of imprisonment, and has been in touch with Joseph Meleady to lend his support to whatever actions might be taken to re-open their case.

We would be grateful for your urgent consideration of this matter.

Yours faithfully,
Gareth Peirce,
B. M. Birnberg and Co.

At the time in Ireland, Gareth Peirce's moral authority on matters of legal dispute could hardly have been higher. Her letter, however, appears to have been disregarded by the Minister for Justice and by his civil servants. One can gauge its impact in the corridors of power from a Dáil debate six months later, when Ray Burke was forced to respond publicly to the precise arguments made by Gareth Peirce. The occasion was an adjournment debate forced on the Minister by Mervyn Taylor on 28 February 1990.

Taylor spoke first. He dealt briefly with the distress caused to all the families involved: the Meleadys, the Grogans, and the Gavins. He challenged the identification procedure followed by Gardaí in the case. He pointed out that three young people had admitted to being in the car on that night. He invited the minister to study the 'Today Tonight' documentary transmitted in December 1986 and the *Magill* article of August 1988. He reminded the minister of the new fingerprint evidence that had emerged. Acknowledging that several different juries had pronounced on the matter, he noted that the Guildford Four had also been found against by many juries. 'The authorities in the UK, to their credit, took it upon themselves to recognise that something had gone wrong in the administration of justice in that case, and they did something about it. It required a tremendous act of strength on their part, and I would beseech the minister to show the same strength in the case of the Tallaght Two.'

The minister's response was brief and dismissive. He reminded Taylor of the various jury decisions on the matter, and, in the briefest of answers, concluded: 'In all the circumstances, I do not consider that a public inquiry into this case could be warranted. I am not satisfied that any new evidence has been adduced in this case which would provide any grounds for reasonably assuming that the verdicts of the three juries were wrong, and accordingly, I do not propose to authorise a release in this case.'

The mysterious girl in the car

In early 1990, Eamon Gavin made an appearance on the 'Late Late Show', an appearance that would have some unforeseen and intriguing consequences. He confirmed his continuing certainty that he had made no mistake in his identification. On the same programme, but speaking from the studio audience, Joseph Grogan, having by now completed his five-year sentence, offered his sympathy to Eamon Gavin for what he had been through. He said that, in their different ways, both he and Gavin were innocent victims of the same crime. After the programme, Grogan offered his hand to Gavin, who accepted it.

But it was what followed from this broadcast that was significant rather than the broadcast itself. Present on the panel alongside Eamon Gavin had been a Dominican nun, Sister Veronica, who was resident in Tallaght. She put the view that there had been a miscarriage of justice in the case and that Meleady and Grogan were innocent.

Some days after the broadcast, Sister Veronica's phone rang. The caller identified himself as Maurice Walsh, ringing on behalf of his brother-in-law, Finbarr Martin, the man whose car had been stolen on that eventful night in February 1984 after Gavin's car was abandoned in Killakee Way. He had just received a leaflet about the Tallaght Two campaign, pushed through his letterbox by Paddy Meleady. In addition he had seen Sister Veronica on television, and he was ringing to tell her something that Gardaí had told them six years earlier, on the occasion on which their car was taken. A Garda had told them, he said, that their car had been followed up the mountains by a Garda on a motorcycle. Eventually the Garda had lost his quarry, but not before he had got close enough to see a girl or young woman in the back seat, whom he recognised.

The car had gone into a lay-by, and the Garda had radioed for assistance; but meantime the stolen car had got away. When they recovered the car later in Tallaght, there was heather attached to the car's underbody. The Gardaí had been reassuring while the car was being sought; they told Walsh and Martin that it might only have been used 'for romantic purposes.'

The next morning, Walsh told Sister Veronica, he and Martin had got their car back. The Garda confirmed to them that the girl's identity and her age were known, and some personal comments were passed about her in a very specific way. The impression had been given that it was only a matter of the Gardaí going to the young woman's house and arresting her.

But after this the two men, to their surprise, heard nothing further. No statements were taken from them, and their fingerprints were never taken to check with those found in the car. There was, in fact, no further communication from the Gardaí on this matter. They had noticed that there had not been any mention of this mysterious girl in any of the court hearings or on the 'Today Tonight' documentary, nor on the 'Late Late Show' they had been watching. And they wondered if somewhere in all they had been told at the time there might be information to assist with the truth.

This was the first time there had been any mention of a girl in any of the cars that night. It was now being related to Sister Veronica by Maurice Walsh—but it had emanated from the Gardaí themselves, and not from anyone seeking to construct alibis for Meleady and Grogan.

The motorcycle Garda on the night in question was in fact Garda James Broe, one of the two Gardaí involved in the critical identification of Meleady and Grogan eight days later in Rathfarnham courthouse.

Shortly after taking the call, Sister Veronica met Joseph Grogan at a public meeting for the Tallaght Two campaign. She told him what had been said to her. He said it was the first he had ever heard about any girl being in the car. He went shortly afterwards to Brendan Walsh, who was at the time home in Tallaght from London on a visit. Grogan had never discussed the details of the case before with Walsh.

Now, he asked him, fishing for information, what about the girl in the car?

The reply from Brendan Walsh was matter-of-fact. Yes, he said, they had two girls in the car that night. He gave Grogan their names: one of them had been a girl-friend of Gus Dunne, the other was his girl-friend at the time, ST. The information from Maurice Walsh was beginning to prove valid.

Some days afterwards Joseph Grogan ran into Paul McDonnell in Tallaght and again brought up the subject of the alleged young women in the car. Grogan introduced the subject casually by remarking that he hadn't been aware that there were girls in the car. Once again he got a matter-of-fact reaction; McDonnell expressed surprise that Grogan hadn't known about them. He said that Walsh and Dunne had gone on to pick up their girl-friends after he had left them, when Gavin's car was abandoned. He had the same names that Walsh had given for the two girls, ST and one other.

The author became aware of this story of the mysterious girls in the car some months later, in the autumn of 1990, while researching the second television documentary on the subject. On hearing it, he contacted Brendan Walsh by phone in London. Walsh confirmed that he and Dunne had picked up the two girls, ST and her friend, after abandoning Gavin's car and after taking the Opel Berlina from outside the house in Killakee Way. Walsh remembered going into some car park up the mountains with the girls; he thought it belonged to Killakee House restaurant.

The next obvious course was to check this story with the two young women themselves. When contacted by the author, one of them simply refused to discuss the matter. She had since married and clearly did not wish to be reminded of any such events. ST, however, confirmed almost immediately that she had been present in the car that night; she also confirmed that the other girl named by Walsh and McDonnell had been there too. More importantly, she stated clearly that the two young men in the car were Brendan Walsh and Gordon (Gus) Dunne. She recalled how during the time she was with them the two had spoken about a man who had been hanging on to the bonnet of a car they'd stolen earlier in the evening.

ST was not prepared to do a television interview, because, she said, she did not want her father to know she was involved in such an escapade. But she had no objection to her name being given to the Gardaí, and she said she would be prepared to swear to the truth of what she had said. She said that she had never been approached by the Gardaí at the time about the case.

Once again a small, seemingly unimportant detail in the Tallaght Two story appeared to confirm doubts about the convictions. If this young woman was there with Walsh and Dunne, then Meleady and Grogan were innocent. If she was not in the car, then who was? What girl did the Gardaí think they had seen, this person some Garda allegedly thought he had recognised?

8

The Closing Stages, 1990

By the late summer of 1990 almost four years had passed since Gus Dunne had admitted, anonymously, on television that he was the driver of Eamon Gavin's car. Yet the campaign to have the Meleady and Grogan convictions reviewed appeared to have hardly advanced an inch since. The television and radio coverage, the press statements, the Dáil debates and the newspaper articles had all failed thus far to alert the authorities to the need to review the case thoroughly. Meleady and Grogan still firmly remained, in the eyes of the law, the convicted culprits.

Returning as television producer to the Tallaght Two case that August, the author's attention was brought swiftly to the changed situation over the fingerprint evidence. This had been hidden, completely unsuspected, during the making of the first documentary, in November and December 1986. Now, a fresh reading of the transcripts in the light of the knowledge that the fingerprint had been found in the front, not the back, of the car brought the startling realisation that both juries had in fact been inadvertently misled. It was not just that the proper evidence was not put before them but that directly opposing and wrong information had been given to the jury and the defence in court. When the transcript of the retrial was checked it was clear that the misinformation had not been cleared up but had persisted: the defence barrister could be observed in the transcripts referring in a matter-of-fact way to the fingerprint being in the back of the car.

But could it really be that this mistake had happened all those years ago and that no-one had attempted since to put matters right? On the face of it it seemed, in a lay person's view, that the two accused had not received a fair trial; yet the authorities, with access to the complete files, were clearly taking a different view. The detailed official thinking had not been explained. In fact little was being said; all that was clear was that the emergence of the fingerprint issue had not led to any obvious change in official attitudes.

The author's first requirement, as a journalist, was to get confirmation from expert sources that a serious error had occurred. It would be necessary also for an authoritative legal source to confirm the author's strong but strictly lay person's impression that if evidence *had* been misrepresented, the trials had been unfair.

At first, informal soundings were taken from two senior judges. One of these was retired after distinguished service in the High Court, the other was still sitting on the bench, though not involved in current cases. It should be emphasised that the consideration of the issues by these experienced legal experts was brief and, in the nature of things, informal.

However, presented with the stark facts of a conviction based solely on a disputed visual identification, with the only scientific evidence in the case (*a*) not presented to the jury and (*b*) then distorted and misrepresented in prosecuting counsel's cross-examination, so that instead of tending to favour the defence the effect was to favour the state—in this situation, as described to them, the two judges were clear that serious doubts must exist over the safety of any such conviction.

One judge, again basing his comments purely on the facts as presented to him by the author, said it would have been outrageous if the events were as suggested to him, that is, that the fingerprint evidence was not presented to the jury. No jury, he thought, hearing such evidence could have avoided having a reasonable doubt about the guilt of the accused. The judge's opinion was that such evidence could well have led to the acquittal of Grogan as the front-seat passenger and would thereby have raised doubts over the identification of Meleady as the driver.

These off-the-record, quite unofficial opinions were tending to confirm the author's concerns over the conduct of the case. However, if the verdict of the courts on the Tallaght Two case was to be successfully challenged, a more formal, more precise, more public assessment of the issues would be required. In short, a criminal lawyer would have to be briefed on the matter and asked to survey it, given all the documents and all the transcripts and asked to give a formal opinion. This would clarify the legal situation; it might also provide the bedrock of analysis for a future television programme. Paddy Meleady, of course, being without money or any regular solicitor, had never been able to fortify his argument in this way. It was quickly apparent that in the three years since the truth about the Walsh fingerprint had come out, no barrister appeared in any formal way to have assessed the full implications of the new evidence. All this would now change, as the RTE production team required as a matter of priority an authoritative opinion on the issues arising in the case.

After some consultations, Barry White SC, an eminent advocate with an extensive practice at the criminal bar, was commissioned to give his expert assessment of the case. The specific question posed concerned the state's mishandling of the evidence, and asked: was the weight of the actual evidence sufficient to raise doubts about the safety of the convictions? It asked whether, in the circumstances of the case and in the light of the transcripts of the two trials, it might have affected the defence case and possibly influenced the jury towards an acquittal.

It was clear to all concerned that what was under consideration was not conclusive evidence. However, it was evidence that appeared to favour the defence; if so, to what extent could this be gauged? Might the weight of the new evidence be such as to require the state—given the absence of other legal remedies—now to implement a presidential pardon? Were the convictions unsafe?

While RTE was waiting for the opinion, one of the detectives who had been involved in the investigation of the crime was contacted. When told by the author of a planned television programme based on the fingerprint evidence, he remarked, 'It'll be a short programme.' This person insisted that the courts had convicted the right men; he thought nothing would reopen the case, and the convictions would stand. And yet this detective agreed that the state should, on the standards of 1990, have included the scientific evidence on Brendan Walsh's fingerprint in the book of evidence. He thought that if the defence lawyers had asked for the evidence they would have got it. He pointed out that the facts on the fingerprint evidence had been included by the state in the book of evidence for Brendan Walsh's own case.

The suggestion that an injustice might have been done was something that this detective would not accept. Under questioning, he could throw little light on aspects of the case that were intriguing the author. Why did he think Gus Dunne had told a senior detective in Tallaght station that he was the driver of Gavin's car? He couldn't say. Why would Brendan Walsh, having done his time for the offence, for no apparent reason supposedly risk a perjury charge himself in two successive cases over who was with him in the car? Couldn't answer that. Why would Paul McDonnell supposedly tell lies under oath and risk five years in jail by swearing, voluntarily, that he was one of the three people in the car? The detective had no response.

Meanwhile, other researches indicated that Det.-Insp. Paschal Anders, more than three years after his own investigations were completed, remained unhappy about the whole case. Clearly out of sync with his bosses, Anders felt the handling of the scientific evidence had been unacceptable. His guarded attempts to suggest this in his 1987 report had been brushed aside, and his opinions had not been subsequently sought.

Then there was the situation of the barrister Eamon Leahy. It was now the autumn of 1990; these incidents regarding the fingerprint had occurred in 1985. Did Eamon Leahy know that he had misinformed the Circuit Criminal Court? There had been no public comment by him on the issue. If he accepted that he had misinformed the court— inadvertently, of course—it seemed reasonable to ask if he had done anything about it since. Had he any reason to disagree with the view that the fingerprint evidence in the Meleady and Grogan case should have reached the jury? Did he agree that this evidence, and his misstatement of it, could have made a difference to the jury's decision?

The author spoke to Eamon Leahy by telephone in October 1990. He was aware of the misstatement he had made earlier. He said by way of explanation that he might have been given wrong information by the Gardaí. He could possibly, he thought, have had a quick consultation with a Garda who would have been sitting behind him and that this had led to the misinformed question he had asked Brendan Walsh.

Apart from the mechanics of how he came to give wrong

information to the court, did he think the proper fingerprint evidence could have made a difference to the jury? He replied that he would not say that it would have made a difference. Pressed on this, however, he would not say that it would *not* have made a difference. He thought any possible effect on the jury's attitude would have depended on whether they were on a knife edge or were totally convinced by Eamon Gavin.

Correspondence between the author and the DPP, Eamon Barnes, in the autumn of 1990, four and-a-half years after the initial error, raised doubts whether the office of the DPP was then fully aware how the Circuit Criminal Court had been misinformed by the DPP's own counsel in 1985. The Director was asked in writing by the author in October 1990, several days before the transmission of the 'Wednesday Report' documentary, if he was aware how his own counsel misled the Meleady and Grogan trials on a question of crucial material evidence—the location of the fingerprints of Brendan Walsh. He gave a one-word answer: No.

Counsel's opinion

After six weeks, Barry White delivered his opinion. It was short—just three pages—but it was to the point. The scientific evidence in the Meleady and Grogan case ought to have been disclosed by the state. There was no obligation to include it in the book of evidence, but, he said, 'they cannot suppress material evidence, or evidence that may be relevant to a trial, and in the interest of fairness of procedure, they must make known to the defence the existence of all such evidence which otherwise may not be known to them. Thereafter, it is a matter for the defence as to what use, if any, they make of such evidence.

'In my opinion, evidence of the presence of Brendan Walsh's fingerprint on the interior of the front passenger window is capable of being corroborative of his account of having been the front seat passenger, and is a matter which may well have influenced the jury in determining the veracity of his testimony, and in reaching their verdict herein. However, it should be borne in mind that there may well be some other explanation as to the circumstances in which his fingerprint came to be where it was found, but that was a matter that ought to have been considered by the jury.

'I am particularly concerned that on the first trial herein counsel for the prosecution's cross-examination of Brendan Walsh was based on the premise that his fingerprint had been found in the back of the car. There is no way of knowing what influences a jury in their deliberations, and the jury may well have accepted that the fingerprint had in fact been found in the back of the car, and that may well have been the determining factor in their rejection of the defence case.

'It must be borne in mind that it has been the experience of our courts that one, or more witnesses, whose bona fides is not in question, and whose opportunity of observation has been adequate, have made identifications which have subsequently been proven to have been erroneous.

'Nobody has ever questioned the bona fides of either Mr. Gavin or his son, and properly so, and I have no doubt that both Mr. Gavin, and his son, honestly believe in the correctness of their respective identifications; nevertheless, in the light of the forensic evidence, the possibility exists, in my opinion, that Joseph Meleady and Joseph Grogan may not have committed the crimes of which they were convicted.'

It was a breakthrough. In the barrister's terse and professionally cautious formulation there was the basis for a turn-around in the long history of the case. Counsel was not required to offer a definite opinion on the guilt or innocence of the two convicted: the issue was the fairness of their trial and whether a jury might (not necessarily *would,* because no-one could know how a jury would act) have been swayed by the evidence that was denied to them. The answer was yes.

The doubts were at two levels. In the first instance, might the jury have been swayed towards an acquittal by the facts, had they possessed them, regarding the fingerprint? Secondly, having been denied these facts, were they then swayed in the very opposite direction by the nature of the misinformation from the state side? White's answer seemed to suggest that the answer at both levels was yes: the jury could well have been so swayed.

This opinion now represented crucial legal underpinning for a television treatment of the issues. Yet Barry White, whose views would be amplified for the programme during an extended filmed interview, did not promise a quick end to the saga of the Tallaght Two. His view was that the Court of Criminal Appeal should be invited to hear an appeal against the conviction. The outcome would almost certainly mean that the conviction would be set aside. In the hypothetical situation of a further retrial being ordered (which he regarded as unlikely) he felt a jury would then be presented with all the evidence: the scientific findings, the evidence of Brendan Walsh that he was the front-seat passenger, and the evidence of Eamon Gavin. And the verdict in such a trial, 'in all probability,' would be that Joseph Grogan, supposedly sitting in the seat Brendan Walsh claimed to be in, would be found not guilty. As for Joseph Meleady, there would be a consequential effect for him, in that if Eamon Gavin was mistaken over Grogan, the possibility of a mistake over Meleady was also there, and so Meleady 'may well also be found not guilty of the crime.'

Barry White felt it was a very unusual thing to find a jury misled in the way that had happened; he had never come across anything like it before. It was, he thought, 'a matter of grave concern' that a cross-examination that was designed to discredit a witness should have been based on wrong information, albeit innocently so. He also felt that if a second retrial were not granted, then, in view of the 'real possibility that there has been a miscarriage of justice in this case,' the Government ought to grant Meleady and Grogan a pardon, with appropriate compensation.

In the nature of television production, Barry White's view, although recorded on tape and presented formally on paper to the client— RTE—could not be broadcast for several weeks. The slow-moving process of making a television documentary would have to be endured until editing and post-production had been completed. It was still far from clear that the lawyer's opinion would prove sufficient in itself to overcome the extreme official resistance to any review of this contentious case. It was time to get the politicians into the picture.

The politicians enter the frame

Politicians, with a few honourable exceptions, including Pat Rabbitte TD of the then Workers' Party, had taken little interest in the Tallaght Two case. Six years of campaigning had given representatives of all parties ample opportunity to take up the issues, but very few had responded. Now they were to be presented, years later, with new evidence. Would they accept it?

An all-party panel of politicians was arranged for the documentary. Included were Alan Dukes TD, a former Fine Gael Minister for Justice, who had been unhappy with the original conviction but had failed to do anything about it while in office; David Andrews TD, a barrister by training, who would become a Fianna Fáil minister shortly afterwards and who attended the Birmingham Six hearings in England as a Government representative; Mary Harney, a Progressive Democrat TD who was then a junior minister in the Government and would later become leader of the Progressive Democrats; and Mervyn Taylor, the Labour Party TD and later Government minister who for years had been the sole political voice expressing concern at the case.

Each of these four politicians was shown the relevant portions of the trial transcripts, as well as the scientific evidence that the juries did not get and the opinion of Barry White. The effect was instantaneous. All were seriously concerned at the implications of what was presented before them; all felt that action by the Government was required.

'To convict people we have to be certain they were guilty,' said Mary Harney. 'Looking at this evidence one could not be certain; if anything one would be most uncertain, and certainly I would be worried about these convictions. I think it's time to try and undo some of the damage that was done.'

After reading Barry White's opinion and the relevant parts of the transcript, David Andrews said that the presidential pardon option should be considered by the Government. He said that Meleady—who was still serving his sentence—should be immediately released from Mountjoy. He felt the fingerprint evidence was 'so serious, so pertinent to the whole question' that it should certainly have been made available to the defence.

Alan Dukes felt that the new material cast serious doubt over the safety of the convictions; he thought the cases should now be reopened. White's opinion he described as 'persuasive'. He added that if there had been a miscarriage of justice in the Meleady-Grogan case, then there must equally have been a miscarriage in the McDonnell perjury case. If Meleady and Grogan were not guilty, then clearly neither was McDonnell, whose supposed perjury had been to swear to the other two youths' innocence.

Mervyn Taylor, who had a long record in supporting calls for the reopening of the case, felt that Joseph Meleady should be immediately let out of prison and that the Minister for Justice should set about clearing the two men's names, in whatever way seemed appropriate.

Speaking with unusual animation, Taylor stressed how urgent it was that the state should rectify its mistakes. To him, the fingerprint of Brendan Walsh represented 'a very heavy piece of evidence that should have been an essential part of the evidence produced by the prosecution in court or, at the very least, should have been made available to the defence.' To Taylor the case was unique: like Barry White, he knew of no case that bore any resemblance to what had happened in this one.

Even before the programme could be transmitted, the state began to act. A courtesy tape of the programme was delivered to the Minister for Justice on the morning of transmission. He immediately summoned the Attorney-General, Harry Whelehan SC, who ordered an inquiry through the DPP. The inquiry was announced as the programme went on the air that evening. Within two days, Det.-Supt Gerard McCarrick was summoned to Garda headquarters, handed the Meleady and Grogan files by the Commissioner's private secretary, and told to investigate all aspects of the contents of the television programme. Over the next several months Det.-Supt McCarrick would report directly to the DPP, keeping him closely informed on the progress of his investigations.

Joseph Meleady, meanwhile, was in Mountjoy prison, serving his sentence. Within two weeks he was being offered early release by the Government. After some resistance he accepted, but only after he had been given a personal commitment by the Taoiseach, Charles Haughey, that the inquiry ordered by the Minister for Justice would be expedited.

In the event it took almost a further three years before any statement about an outcome was made. The reason for this extraordinary delay would only become clear in 1994, when the extensive state files on the case were released. They were seen to contain material that raised totally unthought-of and very serious issues; aspects of the official records seemed to contradict sworn testimony from state witnesses. These entries, uncovered in late 1990 and early 1991, were inexplicable to the authorities. As a result, behind its formal mantle of silence the state side was thrown into disarray.

Publicly all was quiet. Meleady and Grogan took on new legal representation, with Greg O'Neill as their solicitor. The barristers Barry White SC and Tony Sammon were briefed on the case. A formal petition for a presidential pardon was prepared and submitted by Greg O'Neill to the Government.

After much further delay, in the middle of 1993 the Government announced that, on the advice of the Attorney-General, it saw no grounds for a pardon for Meleady and Grogan but that it was going to create an opportunity, through new legislation, for the case to be reopened and to be returned to the Court of Criminal Appeal. A statement from the Attorney-General indicated that he felt this would be 'in the interests of the administration of justice.'

This announcement meant that there would be a reopening of the case. But the significance of this was partly obscured at the time by the Government's simultaneous statement that it saw no grounds for a pardon. This had the appearance of a reverse; in fact the Government announcement represented the most significant advance for Meleady and Grogan since they were convicted in 1985.

The Attorney-General also announced, significantly, that he would release to the legal representatives of Meleady and Grogan 'every element of the case' that led him to the view that it should be made possible to reopen it. This he would do, he said, after the legislation had passed.

It took a further nine months for the Criminal Procedure Act, 1993, to pass all stages in the Oireachtas, fulfilling the first part of the Government's promise. This allowed cases to be returned to the Court of Criminal Appeal on the basis of 'new facts' that had come to light. In the spring of 1994 the Chief State Solicitor, acting on the instructions of the Attorney-General, delivered to Meleady and Grogan's solicitors a large bundle of files. The light was finally being let into the state's conduct of its affairs as the Tallaght Two case moved into its final chapter.

9

The State Lets In the Light

The documents spilled out onto the table. There were witness statements, Garda reports, transcripts, documents from the Chief State Solicitor's office, and a report from the Director of Public Prosecutions himself. There was no index, just a jumble of documents.

Greg O'Neill, Meleady and Grogan's solicitor, stood and stared at them. Where would he begin? It was a daunting prospect to start picking his way through the piles of unclassified material. But the sense of anticipation was intense. Here at last was the state's response on the Tallaght Two—not just the response of the moment but its responses over years: how the state had reacted privately at every twist and turn of the ten-year saga when outwardly it remained silent and unbending. Here was the secret story of the case, and perhaps the key to its resolution.

Looking at the material in front of him, Greg O'Neill knew that something new and dramatic was likely to be contained in it. Why else had the Attorney-General, Harry Whelehan, taken the extreme course of handing it over to Meleady and Grogan's legal advisers in this way? Such a course clearly held great risks for the state. The possibility was that some complicated tussle had been going on among the top echelons of the criminal justice administration, something Greg O'Neill could only guess at; but there was clearly something in these files to explain the Attorney-General's unique decision to release such sensitive material 'in the interests of the administration of justice,' as he had written to the Government eighteen months previously.

O'Neill settled down to the job. At first glance the state's position was unchanged: the two men were guilty; the courts had been right. The new evidence proclaimed in the 'Wednesday Report' programme in 1990 was being rejected by the Director of Public Prosecutions: he had told the Attorney-General it was of no value. An extensive inquiry under Det.-Supt McCarrick had, it seemed from the documents, concluded likewise. The documents appeared to hold little joy for the defence lawyers. Reading his way through the files, O'Neill wondered if this was it, if he had been wrong to expect something more.

Then he saw the two memos on the files of the Chief State Solicitor. It was clear immediately that these would have thrown the state into disarray. They were deeply embarrassing to the state case and would almost certainly prove fatal to its attempts to preserve the convictions against Meleady and Grogan. All this Greg O'Neill took in quickly. He calculated that it was three years since the state had uncovered these solicitors' notes: three years of worried discussion behind closed doors, three years when hardly a hint of the unsettling truth was given in public, three years while officials must have sought desperately to explain or come to terms with a development that was likely to transform the case once it became public. Reading it, O'Neill knew why the state had felt obliged to hand the documents over. The case was won. The details might take some time, but the outcome was guaranteed.

It was February 1994, ten years since the dramatic events on a winter's night in Rathfarnham that had changed a number of people's lives irrevocably, and just under nine years since Meleady and Grogan had been convicted.

Handed over were four thick volumes, comprising secret Garda reports, reports from the DPP himself, Eamon Barnes, from senior officials in the Chief State Solicitor's office, and many other hitherto classified statements. Among them were the Anders and McMunn Garda reports, conducted in early 1987 into issues raised by the 'Today Tonight' programme the previous December; the McCarrick Garda report, produced following an inquiry in 1990 and 1991 into issues raised by the second television documentary; a report from the senior solicitor in the Chief State Solicitor's office on related issues; and finally the report of the Director of Public Prosecutions himself, made to the Attorney-General on foot of the other reports. Numerous witness statements taken by the investigating officers over the years, internal Garda memos, transcripts of the television programmes and transcripts of the various court cases made up the bulk of the rest of the material.

In a sentence, the documents showed that up to February 1994 the DPP and the Gardaí, behind closed doors, were rejecting the arguments made on the second television programme. After much inquiry and endeavour, the state agencies continued to insist there had been no failure of due process. Central to this position was the state's denial that the mishandled fingerprint evidence, if it had been known to the defence in all its detail and not distorted by the prosecuting barrister, could have helped Meleady and Grogan's case. It was not even conceded that it might have improved the arguments for the defence. In the end the DPP, having reviewed the whole saga, had privately advised the Attorney-General that he saw no basis for him to make representations 'to the appropriate authority' that justice had been denied to Meleady and Grogan.

The most important document handed over was the report by Det.-Supt Gerard McCarrick. He had been assisted by Supt Seán Camon and a small team of Gardaí. Almost half of this 160-page report was devoted to the subject of the mishandling of the fingerprint evidence. The role of Gus Dunne was also extensively, if belatedly, considered, in particular Dunne's various statements, made at different times to different people, including on television, that he was the driver of the stolen car. McCarrick's accounts of these and related issues made for riveting and at times extraordinary reading. A great deal of attention had also been given to the evidence of Maurice Walsh and Finbarr Martin and their story of the mysterious girl in the car up the mountains.

A striking and quite unexpected element in the documents was a claim by the DPP, Eamon Barnes, that a charge of deliberate suppression of the evidence had been made in the 'Wednesday Report' programme. The transcript of the programme was included in the files. Eamon Barnes several times made reference to an allegation that the evidence had been deliberately withheld; but nothing in the transcript itself appeared to support this view of the programme's content. It was clear that a great deal of the activity of the Garda inquiry had been directed towards investigating this allegation, which in fact was never made. The other aspect, the consequences of the misrepresentation of the evidence, was addressed by Eamon Barnes himself and, to some extent, in a report from the Chief State Solicitor's office. The opinion of Barry White SC, on which the programme was based, was countered only by the DPP, while avoiding explicit mention of White himself. No other legal opinion assessing the weight of the fingerprint evidence was referred to.

Another feature of the wealth of reports, statements and memos was a lack of focus on what had been done to investigate the fingerprint issue in the years between 1987 and 1990. No mention was made of any inquiry or analysis having been made in the middle of 1987, the time when the state knew, beyond all equivocation, that the evidence had been mishandled and had been wrongly used to discredit a key defence witness in the first Meleady and Grogan trial.

In fact the combined reports of Det.-Supt McCarrick, the Chief State Solicitor's office and the DPP, while exhaustive in many respects and indicative of a deeply serious inquiry, left unanswered a large number of questions on the way the Tallaght Two case had been handled. Several apparently impeccable witnesses, whose bona fides were beyond question, were in the end assumed to have variously misunderstood or misinterpreted important communications that reached them.

While the documents also showed that some dramatic material had been uncovered during the prolonged investigation, there was less attention on the fact that the controversy over the case had been going on for at least five years before the memos in question were discovered. This in itself raised questions about the level of official scrutiny that had been bestowed on the case in the five years from the convictions in 1985 to late 1990. It seemed that had Det.-Insp. Anders been given the appropriate resources in 1987, the same discoveries could and would have been made four years earlier.

The entries on the Chief State Solicitor's files

Two separate entries on the files, made by two separate solicitors in the Chief State Solicitor's office, leaped from the pages. They had been discovered by Barry Donoghue, senior solicitor in the Chief State Solicitor's office, when he was asked in 1990 by Det.-Supt McCarrick to check the files on the Tallaght Two.

One of the entries was a note made by John Rohan, a solicitor in the Chief State Solicitor's office, on the outcome of a legal conference that took place on 18 November 1985, a few days before the retrial of Meleady and Grogan. Present at this conference were John Rohan; the prosecuting counsel, Eamon Leahy; Garda Patrick Thornton; Garda James Broe; and Eamon and Paul Gavin.

John Rohan's note stated: 'He [Det.-Garda Felix McKenna] had a fellow called Walsh charged also. Fingerprint in front passenger door? inside of window. Got two years. Brendan Walsh, McKenna by way of rebuttal.'

'Fingerprint in front passenger door?' What did this mean? Taken at face value, this note appeared to show that at least one lawyer in the state team was becoming aware, before the retrial, of the mistake that had been made. The further implication in the note was that this possibility had been raised, and discussed, at the conference. If so it should have been known to the various state witnesses who were in attendance, and to their counsel.

This was an incredible, almost inexplicable development in view of the failure to correct the mistake after this conference. John Rohan himself was quite new to the case, which was undoubtedly a complicated one; perhaps he had confused something said in the discussion because of a lack of familiarity with the details of the case. It was certainly surprising, in view of his note, that nobody who was present at the conference thereafter confirmed the reality, that the fingerprint was on the front door, not the back. The retrial proceeded just over a week later with the defence left under the same misapprehension as in the first trial; this remained the situation throughout the proceedings. How could Rohan's note, and the absence of any action following it, be explained?

The second entry that raised eyebrows was from Richard Walker, also a solicitor in the Chief State Solicitor's office. This was a handwritten note on the document known as form 8, attached to the cover of the District Court file relating to Meleady and Grogan's prosecution. It was made by Walker and dated by him at the time, 16 May 1984. It read: *'Garda Thornton mentioned to me that Eamon Gavin had asked to see a book of photographs to see if he could identify any of the people who had taken his car—he saw a book containing 50 photographs and identified one of the accused. This was prior to the court identification. Should additional evidence in relation to this be brought? R.W. 16.5.84.'*

This was even more startling than the Rohan memo. If the contents of this contemporaneous note by the state solicitor were accurate, then the state case at the trials of Meleady and Grogan was a sham and had been based on totally false foundations. There had been no suggestion by any of the state witnesses that, before the identification in Rathfarnham courthouse, Eamon Gavin had been shown photographs of the accused, still less that he had actually identified one of them. The memo flew in the face of the prosecution case accepted by the courts in 1985. In the second perjury trial of Paul McDonnell, Garda Patrick Thornton had specifically denied showing photographs to Eamon Gavin.

The fact that there was, and is, no suggestion that Garda Thornton or any of the other Gardaí concerned with the investigation gave false evidence in relation to the identification only made the Walker memo all the more mystifying.

If either Meleady or Grogan had been picked out by his photograph before the identification in the courthouse, a formal identification parade would have been required, as, by definition, he was then a real suspect. As no formal parade *had* been held, the whole case against Meleady and Grogan would have been in danger of collapse. The state's evidence that they had no real suspects at the time Eamon Gavin visited Rathfarnham courthouse would be fatally undermined. If the Walker note were accurate—and there was nothing else on the file to confirm or indeed to refer in any way to its explosive contents—then the question would arise why Eamon Gavin, in the course of extensive evidence in several court hearings, had made no reference to it. No more than Garda Thornton or Garda Broe, no-one has ever suggested that Eamon Gavin was anything other than a sincere and honest witness, whether or not he was misguided in his supposed identification. The idea that he would have withheld important evidence such as this seemed inconceivable; all of which just added to the mystery of the Walker memo.

After considering first of all the note made by John Rohan, the Garda report concluded that it was based on a misinterpretation by the state solicitor of what was being said at the conference. None of those present—Leahy, Thornton, Broe, or the two Gavins—could recall any mention being made at this conference of the fingerprint being in the front of the car when they were questioned about it (over five years later) by the investigating officers. All felt that had it been mentioned they would have remembered it, as they were at the time under the impression that the print was in the back of the car, not the front.

John Rohan, it turned out, had no previous experience of the Meleady and Grogan file until that very day; he had not got the transcript of the first trial. This suggested at least the possibility that he could have been confused over the details of the case. In support of this possibility, the report of Det.-Supt McCarrick pointed to the question mark after the reference as indicating uncertainty on Rohan's part; the report also noted some confusion over detail in other parts of his note. McCarrick felt that Rohan must have been confused and mistaken when he made the note.

The obvious difficulty with this was the fact that Rohan's note reflected the truth about where the print was. The other difficulty was that, a note having being written that the print was or appeared to be in the front, this in itself might have been expected to lead to the point being clarified one way or the other. Det.-Supt McCarrick decided that the solicitor was not sufficiently conversant with the case for the note to mean what it appeared to mean.

However, the senior officer in the Chief State Solicitor's office who had investigated the matter, Barry Donoghue, had not doubted the accuracy of his colleague's note. In a separate report on the matter he seemed to place the onus back on the Gardaí who were investigating Meleady and Grogan's case in 1984–85. He interpreted Rohan's note very simply and directly: 'This note indicates that a question arose at the consultation as to whether the fingerprint was on the front passenger door or not ... It would clearly have been a matter for the Gardaí to resolve the issue, as neither ourselves nor Counsel had any means of ascertaining the answer.'

If John Rohan's note meant what Barry Donoghue said it meant, it should have sparked an inquiry into the factual situation regarding the position of the fingerprint. Had this happened, the Gardaí involved could hardly have failed to unearth its true position and realise and establish that an error had been made. There was no evidence in the files that Garda Thornton or Garda Broe were ever asked to make such an inquiry.

Despite the nature of his note and the fact that it appeared to contradict Eamon Leahy's reference in the first trial, John Rohan appears not to have considered that anything untoward was involved in the contents of the note he had made. In the Court of Criminal Appeal in January 1995 his evidence suggested that he did not think there was anything there that required further inquiry from him.

Richard Walker's memo about Eamon Gavin having been shown photographs was the cause of extensive inquiries by the Garda investigators. As with the Rohan note, everyone concerned denied all knowledge of any such incident. Garda Thornton was 'very adamant' that he never showed Gavin any photographs nor ever discussed any such showing of photographs. Eamon Gavin denied all knowledge of such a thing. Faced with these denials, the Garda inquiry stated: 'The origin of Mr. Walker's note has not been established … One can only speculate about its origin. Yet the solicitor involved, Richard Walker, confirmed that it was his note and in his handwriting and furthermore that he believed its contents were an accurate account of what he had been told by Garda Thornton. Although he stood by the note, he could not, after six years, recall the specific circumstances in which he made it.

Eamon Leahy, counsel for the DPP in the case, said he knew nothing of photographs being shown to Gavin. (He then went on, in his report on all these issues to Eamon Barnes, to state, erroneously: 'Indeed, I believe that at the first trial, he [Gavin] was asked this very question in cross-examination, and answered that he had not been shown any photographs.' The transcripts, which it appears Leahy did not have, show that Gavin was not asked any such question in either the first or the second trial. In any event, Eamon Leahy knew nothing of this supposed photograph incident.)

The authenticity of the Walker note and its contents was accepted without question by Walker's superior, Barry Donoghue, who took a severe view of its implications. At the time he made his own report, 4 February 1991, he appeared to accept the note as factual. He stated: 'Two issues arise in relation to this note. Firstly, were the defence made aware of the fact that the injured party had seen a book of photographs prior to his identification at Rathfarnham District Courthouse? Secondly, what are the implications of the note for the evidence offered by the state at the various trials?'

On the first issue, Donoghue could not establish to his own satisfaction whether the defence were informed or not. In fact they were not. However, on the second issue he noted that the prosecution case had depended solely on identification evidence. There had been no identification parade. 'The clear impression given was that neither accused was a firm suspect, and therefore could not be placed on a parade. The note on file indicates that one of the accused had already been identified by Eamon Gavin from a photograph. Furthermore, during the first and second trial of Mr. McDonnell, Garda Thornton stated categorically that the injured party was never shown the photograph of either accused prior to the identification at Rathfarnham Courthouse. This is clearly contrary to the note on the file.'

The particularly strange aspect of the Walker memo was that there was no hint in the files, or in the testimony of the principals, of any kind of follow-up inquiry. The entry was there, on the file cover; yet there was not the slightest trace that it was ever pursued, or even mentioned again. The solicitor in charge of the Circuit Court section at the time, John Corcoran, tried as best he could to explain the matter to the investigating Gardaí. 'The following possibilities occur to me and cannot be discounted. The first is that the note was over-looked and not acted on, because its contents were not included in the Garda file, nor confirmed subsequently in a written report, as would be the correct practice ... The second possibility is that the note was adverted to, and acted upon, in that the Garda was asked about it orally, and indicated that no photographs were shown to Mr Gavin prior to the identification.'

Of these two possible explanations, the second raised particular problems. The showing of photographs to Eamon Gavin, if it ever happened, would have been a most significant event. Had this possibility ever been raised with any of the principals by way of investigation, so serious a matter was it, on such a highly publicised case, that one could reasonably presume they would have remembered it. If the contents of Walker's note had been put to either Eamon Gavin or Garda Thornton at the time, would everyone involved not have recalled it? The possibility it conjured up would, as noted above, have constituted a direct threat to the whole prosecution of Meleady and Grogan.

Yet nowhere in the statements of Eamon Gavin, Patrick Thornton,

Richard Walker or any of the relevant solicitors in the Chief State Solicitor's office was there a hint that this matter ever came up subsequent to Richard Walker recording his note. Except for one law clerk in the Circuit Court section, Tadhg O'Neill, who remembered seeing the memo at some stage, no-one specifically remembered it at all, either asking about it or being asked to ask someone else about it, or hearing its contents denied. Logically, therefore, if neither Gavin nor Thornton were ever asked about this matter until it arose years later in 1991, John Corcoran's second possibility had to be discounted.

Richard Walker's note was simple and to the point: *'Garda Thornton mentioned to me … he [Eamon Gavin] saw a book containing 50 photographs and identified one of the accused.'* The nature of the entry appeared to be such that it could not be dismissed without first approaching Gavin, Thornton, and indeed the note's author, Richard Walker himself. He could hardly have been spared some detailed questioning about how he came to write such a damaging memo, especially if it turned out to be misinformed. This could then have led to a correction or revision of what he had documented. But this did not happen.

The logic of this would leave the first, not the second, of John Corcoran's two possibilities as the more likely, i.e. that the matters raised in Richard Walker's note were actually overlooked and not acted on. This would not mean that the note necessarily represented the truth, just that somehow, perhaps from pressure of other business, it got ignored, as the state solicitor in charge of the area acknowledged was possible. The report from the DPP himself would add further credence to this possibility.

Det.-Supt McCarrick, however, opted for the second of Corcoran's two possibilities: that the memo was acted on and, after consultation with the Gardaí, found to have no basis in fact. He stated: 'Bearing in mind the integrity of the staff of the Chief State Solicitor's office, and of the members of the Garda Síochána involved, and of their dedication to their chosen professions, the possibility of this course of action having been taken is most likely.' McCarrick concluded his treatment of the issue in this way: 'No evidence has come to hand which would refute the statements of Mr. Eamon Gavin and Garda Patrick Thornton [in 1991] that photographs of suspects were not used in this case … No evidence was unearthed which would verify or corroborate the contents of the note on the Chief State Solicitor's file.' (See chapter 12 for more on this.)

The Garda inquiries did establish that a recent photograph of one of the accused did exist at the time in local Garda hands. Two Polaroid photographs of Joseph Meleady had been taken by Det.-Garda Felix McKenna of Tallaght station only eight days before the car theft and the assault on Gavin. His name was handwritten on the back of the photographs. McKenna, the report stated with some precision, 'now recognises his writing on the back of each photograph.' These photographs of Meleady were kept in an album in a steel filing-cabinet in the Detective Unit of the old Tallaght Garda station. This was a prefabricated cabin at the rear of the building. Det.-Garda McKenna and all seven other unit members who had access to the filing-cabinet were interviewed on this issue, and all denied showing any photographs to Eamon Gavin, or knowing of anyone else who did.

The Director of Public Prosecutions, Eamon Barnes, in his overall report to the Attorney-General was perplexed by the Walker note in particular. He was, in fact, completely unable to explain it. Various possibilities occurred to him, but all of them seemed to him unlikely.

The first possibility he considered was that the note was accurate and that the communication had taken place as described, from Garda Thornton. If this were so, he said, 'then it follows inexorably that Garda Thornton (and possibly several other members of the Garda Síochána) was prepared to suppress evidence in the case from 26.2.84 to 11.4.84, that from some time after 16.5.85 until the present he has been prepared to suppress the same evidence, to lie about it, and to give incorrect evidence on oath about it, but that on at least one day between those periods, the 16.5.84, he makes for no obvious reason a total disclosure of the facts which he had theretofore suppressed, and which he afterwards continued to suppress and indeed falsely testified about. This appears to me to be highly improbable, if not indeed incredible.' It would mean that Garda Thornton allowed the case to proceed 'on a seriously incorrect and misleading basis,' despite knowing that one solicitor in the Chief State Solicitor's office was aware of the true state of affairs. It meant that there was no follow-up on the file seeking a further Garda report, no statement from Thornton, and no communication with the defence, with the DPP, with counsel, or between officers in the Chief State Solicitor's office. It meant also 'that Mr. Gavin gave extensive and detailed evidence at four separate trials touching his identification of Messrs. Meleady and Grogan without referring to the photographic identification which preceded it.' The DPP found this proposition incredible.

The second proposition he considered was that the note was an accurate record of a conversation with Garda Thornton but that Thornton turned out to be wrong about the photographs and had in some way, 'for some reason about which one can only speculate,' made a mistake. But how could Thornton be wrong about such a matter, the DPP wondered? And also, how was it that there was nothing on the file indicating that the Gardaí had found the reference to be inaccurate, if this was what happened? And again, how was it that there was no documented follow-up of any kind from the Chief State Solicitor's office? Highly improbable, Barnes thought.

The third possibility examined by Eamon Barnes was that Richard Walker's note did not accurately reflect any message received from Garda Thornton but was in some way the result of a mistake or misunderstanding by Walker himself. He had either confused two cases or else fundamentally misunderstood a communication from Garda Thornton, and then took no documented steps, other than the file note, to advance or dispose of the matter. 'I am aware', said Barnes, 'that some prosecutors have been under the erroneous impression that the correct time for disclosure to the defence of material possibly helpful or relevant to the defence is at the trial rather than before or during the preliminary examination, and that Mr. Walker may well have considered that he had fully discharged his duty by addressing his note to the Circuit Court Section. That said, I find the basic proposition in this third hypothesis that Mr. Walker made a fundamental mistake as to the import of whatever information was in fact communicated to him to be in itself very unlikely.'

The DPP then went on in his report to the Attorney-General: 'However, the Office of the Chief State Solicitor was at the time seriously understaffed, the work of the District Court Section in particular was to a great extent being done by young barristers on a day to day basis and the permanent staff were under severe and constant pressure. Accordingly, the circumstances in which a misunderstanding or breakdown in communication could easily occur then existed.

'Each of the three propositions seems to me to contain an inherent improbability. I find it impossible to come to a firm conclusion as to the truth which lies behind the note of 16.5.84 ... The third hypothesis seems, marginally, to be the least improbable of the three, but I remain far from convinced that it, rather than either of the other two, is the correct one.'

And he concluded: 'It is scarcely necessary to add that if in fact the courtroom identification had been preceded by a photographic identification, the failure to disclose that fact to the defence constituted a most serious flaw and irregularity in the conduct of the prosecution.'

But Eamon Barnes did not consider in his report to the Attorney-General a different and much simpler proposition: regardless of whether there had or had not in fact been a photographic identification, the failure to disclose the existence of the Walker memo to the defence in 1985 in itself could constitute a serious flaw and irregularity in the prosecution. It was a relevant and material piece of information that the defence could have used in the trial to challenge the prosecution case.

Also not referred to by Eamon Barnes in his detailed analysis was the second proposition considered by John Corcoran: that the note might simply have been overlooked. This would explain the absence of follow-up or inquiry. The circumstances described by the DPP in his last paragraph would suggest that this was at least possible. It might, in fact, be the only proposition that fitted the facts. Again, this would not necessarily mean that the note's contents were accurate, nor even that it was likely they were accurate. What it would certainly have meant, however, was that the Chief State Solicitor's office had on file, at the time of the Meleady and Grogan trial, an official document containing matters challenging the heart of the state's case, matters that had neither been discounted nor disproved at that time. In these circumstances the document would normally have had to be disclosed to the defence. It was not. The DPP did not address the implications of this.

In his report to the Attorney-General, Eamon Barnes proposed no action as a result of the Walker memo. He had been unable to explain how it came into existence and unable to explain why no action appeared to come on foot of it; he had been unable to dismiss it. Yet its contents were unproved. Those referred to strenuously denied the claims made concerning them.

Ultimately, the DPP was not prepared to act on the basis of an uncorroborated allegation, even if it came from an authentic, official memorandum, the work of a solicitor in the Chief State Solicitor's office. The memorandum did not seem to him to be of such a nature, nor its non-disclosure to be of such a nature, for him to feel obliged 'to make representations to the appropriate authority' that the convictions of Meleady and Grogan could, on the basis of this discovery, be thought to be unsafe. This was the bottom line: the DPP felt the convictions were safe.

The McCarrick and the Gus Dunne factor

Det.-Supt McCarrick in his report to the DPP devoted some considerable time to the statements and activities of Gordon (Gus) Dunne, the man who said he was in the driver's seat of Eamon Gavin's car. For four years the authorities had apparently taken little interest in the stories implicating Dunne in the crime. Now, however, the DPP's interest in this aspect of the case was stimulated; his report to the Attorney-General described the sections of the Garda report dealing with Dunne as being 'obviously of very great importance indeed.'

The story the Garda report contained, so far as Dunne was concerned, was a simple one. It was a story of denial by Dunne of a series of statement he had made about himself over a period of several years to some twelve or thirteen different witnesses, including his friends, to reporters, and even to Gardaí. The report established that Dunne had indeed made the self-incriminating remarks attributed to him, consistently describing himself as the driver of Eamon Gavin's car. However, when he was faced after the second television documentary, in October 1990, with the formidable presence of Det.-Supt McCarrick and his deputy, Supt Camon, and having been cautioned by them that anything he said could be used in evidence, he changed his tune. A written statement was required from him, in which Dunne decided to disown his utterances. The story that resulted was described in great detail in the Garda report.

Over the period from January 1987 to April 1991, Gus Dunne was interviewed a total of seven times by the Gardaí. Five of these sessions took place between November 1990 and April 1991, immediately after the 'Wednesday Report' programme. The inquiry team wanted Dunne to sign his name to a statement; Dunne had eventually obliged.

In his several signed (but not, apparently, sworn) statements to McCarrick and Camon, Dunne did exactly what he had said in his television interview he would do: he refused to own up to the crime. He stated instead that he had never been in Gavin's car. He said in his signed statement that he had been lying all the times he said he had driven the car. One by one he disowned his many and various statements over the years: on television, to *Magill,* to people on the street in Tallaght, to Det.-Insp. Anders in Tallaght Garda station, to Joan Grogan and Kathleen Meleady and Frank Connolly in a pub in Walkinstown, to Dawn Keegan in Shanganagh prison—all of these and more he disowned in his statement for the Gardaí.

The McCarrick report then dealt with the obvious question: why did Dunne ever say that he was the driver if he was not? The report concluded that 'a systematic barrage of verbal and physical abuse' persuaded him eventually to do as Joan Grogan and Jimmy Brady wanted. The 'physical abuse' complained of from Joan Grogan and her companion amounted to a series of verbal altercations and one incident in the Belgard Inn when some buttons were torn from Dunne's shirt when Jimmy Brady grabbed him. On the basis of this, Dunne said he was so frightened that he felt compelled to admit he had taken part in a crime in which he really had no part. While this must have seemed a fanciful story, it was also clearly one that the Garda investigators had to take into account.

The treatment of Dunne's story thereafter in the McCarrick report was less than comprehensive. Why had Dunne in the first place been allegedly singled out for this very special coercion? The Garda report did not explain this. There was then the problem of the television interview. Dunne, a supposedly innocent man, had given a television interview, for no payment, taking responsibility for some dreadful deeds. Why was this? The answer, in his final statement given to McCarrick and Camon, built on the supposed coercion already alleged against Joan Grogan, alleging now coercion by RTE journalists. Explaining away his interview, Dunne said that he was given drink by the RTE team and made drunk; he was bullied and blackmailed by the staff of 'Today Tonight'; he was told it would end his troubles if he just did the interview; he was provided with the answers to each question asked, and only had to parrot them back to Michael Heney.

This proposition was described in great detail in the McCarrick report, quoting Dunne himself liberally; it appeared not to have been challenged or queried. It was, by any standards, a damaging set of allegations against the two RTE employees involved. If what Dunne said was true, the conduct of the journalists was so reprehensible that it might well have merited dismissal from their employment. The argument made in effect was that the interview was a sham; the journalists knew it was a sham but deliberately conjured it up, using alcohol and blackmail to advance their story.

The importance of this revised account by Gus Dunne, of course, was that it purported to explain something that otherwise might have seemed inexplicable: how an innocent man could have gone on television and proclaimed himself to be guilty. But was it true? Could it be verified or corroborated in any way? Det.-Supt McCarrick undoubtedly had good professional reasons for proceeding in the way he did. But no contact with the author or with Brendan Leeson was made in relation to Dunne's remarks. The journalists were not asked whether, as alleged, they had presented a concocted charade of an interview as real evidence and thereby misled the public.

The report of Det.-Supt McCarrick described Dunne's disowning of his own words as 'being of significant value'. The DPP himself, on whose behalf the McCarrick report was prepared and to whom it was sent on completion, described the superintendents' handling of these matters, including the Gus Dunne saga, as being 'obviously of very great importance indeed.'

Had they been asked, however, the RTE personnel involved could and would have emphatically repudiated both the generality and the detail of Dunne's account. They first became aware of it in 1994, when the McCarrick report was issued to Meleady and Grogan's legal advisers. In the three years since Dunne made his statements, neither McCarrick nor Camon, nor anyone else on behalf of the DPP, ever sought a response from them. As a result, significant documentary and other evidence in RTE's possession relating to the Dunne interview was not available to the investigators. This material would have rebutted the claims that Dunne's television interview was concocted for him. It consisted of contemporaneous journalists' notes of remarks made by Dunne to RTE a month before his interview.

One matter he dealt with was the story of the girl at the upstairs window in Eamon Gavin's house. Dunne said in his television interview: 'One of the lads turned round and said to me, watch out, someone looking at me, you know—a little girl in the top bedroom window, I was told.' (See chapter 5.) Dunne told McCarrick and Camon by way of explanation: 'They told me to say that, the TV people. Brendan Walsh said that to them.' But Brendan Leeson's notes of the conversation he had with Dunne four weeks earlier in the Royal Dublin Hotel, on 18 October 1986, showed Dunne telling him exactly this story. The notes say: 'He described how Mr Gavin's daughter looked out a bedroom window and saw them.' Brendan Leeson had never heard this story before; it was the first occasion on which anyone in the case made such a reference. It originated with Dunne and with no-one else, as did all of the interview conducted in Morton's pub, in which Dunne acknowledged his role as the driver of Eamon Gavin's car. In addition, the author's own notes of Dunne's comments at this meeting include extra details about the sighting of the girl at the upstairs window.

Brendan Leeson's notes from the October interview state also: 'Asked him did he know who the third man in the car was. He said it was him.' The author's notes of the Morton's pub encounter tell of Dunne talking about hot-wiring the car, of starting to reverse it, of turning on the windscreen wipers to dislodge Gavin's grip, and of laughing at Gavin as the wipers went from side to side.

Elsewhere, the McCarrick report hinted that criminal charges might be brought against the author when it specifically considered 'whether Michael Heney knowingly interviewed a wanted felon.' This was in reference to the television interview with Joseph Meleady, filmed while he was on the run in England and included in the 1986 'Today Tonight' programme. The report recounted evidence suggesting that this was indeed the case, mainly by reference to the script and contents of the programme. The report stated, somewhat ominously, that 'a copy of the tape of this programme is retained by the present investigating officers.'

The Garda report, as we have seen, repeated Dunne's claim that he was harassed and intimidated into making supposedly false admissions of guilt, but showed no attempt to question or to challenge the assertions. But there were other serious complicating factors in such a theory. One was that Dunne had met one important witness, Dawn Keegan, at a time and place where none of this supposed intimidation was possible. The place was Shanganagh prison, the time was 29 June 1985. (See chapter 5.) Dunne had been in prison from April; only on 8 May were Meleady and Grogan convicted and sent to St Patrick's Institution. In Shanganagh prison, Dunne could not have been harassed or abused by any of those implicated. Why then would he tell his close friend, privately, that he was responsible for the assault on Eamon Gavin if he had nothing to do with it?

Years later, Dunne said that Dawn Keegan was telling lies about this conversation. But why would she have chosen to concoct such evidence? Her story was investigated by Det.-Insp. Anders, who found it to be reliable, in so far as it could be checked. By contrast, Dunne's denials, under caution, to McCarrick and Camon appeared self-serving. The McCarrick report did not deal at all with this issue of the timing of Dawn Keegan's encounter with Dunne.

Brendan Leeson's notes of his conversation in the Royal Dublin Hotel in October 1986 show him asking the self-proclaimed driver of Eamon Gavin's car why he did not come forward and save Meleady and Grogan from jail. Part of the answer, as recorded by the researcher, was as follows: 'Since he was approached by Mrs. Grogan + boyfriend in such a hostile manner he wasn't now inclined to own up.' In other words, Dunne here maintained the precise opposite of what years later he told Det.-Supt McCarrick and Supt Camon. He said that bad-mouthing from Joan Grogan and Jimmy Brady had the effect of getting his back up and determining him *not* to come forward rather than persuading him to own up. It might also be noted that if Dunne really was as frightened by the abuse he got as he claimed, he still never actually did own up in a meaningful way at any time in the ten years since the crime.

Dunne's explanation for why he apologised to Joan Grogan in front of several witnesses, including the journalist Frank Connolly, for something he told the Gardaí he never did was also recorded by the investigators. He confirmed to the Garda inquiry the essence of Connolly's account, including admitting that he did indeed apologise to Joan Grogan. But why? Why apologise if he was not in the car?

'Because he thought it was the right thing to do at that particular point in time,' said the Garda report.

Other incriminating comments attributed to Dunne by Frank Connolly, bearing out the truth of Paul McDonnell's testimony and implicating Dunne as the driver of Eamon Gavin's car, Dunne simply denied making. One such was Connolly's report that Dunne had confirmed to him how he had gone on television in 1986 and admitted his involvement. If Dunne had given this television interview under duress, as he was claiming to Det.-Supt McCarrick, why did he endorse its authenticity in this later interview in 1988? Dunne's explanation was that Connolly had invented the quotations on this matter. (Connolly's notes of the interview showed later that Dunne *had* made the remarks he later denied making.) When he learnt years later, in 1995, that the McCarrick report had written up this claim by Dunne as if it were factual, Frank Connolly confronted Det.-Supt McCarrick personally, asking him why he had not contacted him before doing so. The officer, who undoubtedly had his own good reasons for proceeding as he did, did not reply.

McCarrick dealt briefly with the fact that Dunne had told Det.-Insp. Anders when he met him in Tallaght station in February 1987 that he was the driver of Eamon Gavin's car and that everything he had said on television was the truth. This exchange had not been commented on by Supt William McMunn of Rathfarnham station four years earlier in the course of a report that dismissed the conclusions of the Anders report, saying that not enough credence could be put in Anders's conclusions to warrant any action. How did Det.-Supt McCarrick deal with the exchange between Dunne and Anders? 'Gordon Dunne now states that he was just anxious to get out of the Garda station. He states that all the pressure that Mrs. Grogan, James Brady and others were putting on him were building up, and he went to Jersey a few days later.'

While Anders had gone on to conclude, on the basis of his research, that it appeared that Meleady and Grogan were not in the car, Det.-Supt McCarrick, like McMunn before them, dismissed that proposition. 'The present investigating officers are of the view that, on the available evidence, even at that time, this opinion is very difficult to support.'

Nor were the investigating officers impressed by another

incriminating statement they gathered from Dunne, this one made to
Supt Camon and Det.-Garda Patrick Bane on 10 November 1990,
when the Gardaí first began to question Dunne after the 'Wednesday
Report' programme. It was also before Dunne had begun his denials of
guilt. He told Camon and Bane: 'If I tell the truth about this, I will be
done in.'

There was one other tantalising detail hidden in the myriad of
statements and interviews accompanying the inquiry report. It was the
memo from Det.-Garda Felix McKenna indicating for the first time
that Dunne was, in March 1984, questioned in connection with the
crime against Eamon Gavin. No hint that Dunne had been suspected
of knowing anything had ever emerged in public; but the state files
released in early 1994 contained the statement made by McKenna in
December 1986, to a superior officer, noting that McKenna himself
had questioned Dunne, inconclusively, in relation to the Gavin crime
just one week after Meleady and Grogan were charged. The Garda
report included this memo in an appendix. It made no comment.

McCarrick and the girl in the car

In the McCarrick report a surprising amount of time and attention was
devoted to the question of the young woman supposedly sighted in the
car chased up the mountains by Gardaí after Eamon Gavin's car had
been abandoned. The story had arisen from the unsolicited phone call
from Finbarr Martin and his brother-in-law, Maurice Walsh. For
reasons of time and other editorial considerations, their story had to be
omitted from the television broadcast of October 1990. But the
producer submitted ST's name privately, with her consent, to the
DPP's office as being a person who could offer new evidence.

The story of a girl sighted in the back of the stolen car had
originated, indirectly, from the Gardaí, and appeared subsequently to
be corroborated by Paul McDonnell, Brendan Walsh, and ST herself.
ST was clear that Gus Dunne and Brendan Walsh were with her and a
second girl in the car, and that Joseph Meleady and Joseph Grogan
were not.

Martin and Walsh had been interviewed for the programme. In this
interview, which was not transmitted, and in a detailed briefing with
the producer in advance, they recounted how Gardaí had told them of
an identified girl having been seen in the back of Finbarr Martin's car.

They were told in the course of several conversations how the girl was spotted; they recalled being told of this on the night the car was taken and also early next morning at Tallaght station.

The inquiry team led by Det.-Supt McCarrick made extensive inquiries into this matter. The two men were interviewed; they confirmed to the investigating Gardaí what they had already told RTE and Sister Veronica. Each of them had retained a clear memory from the several Gardaí they spoke to that the girl in question was known and identifiable and could be picked up without difficulty.

When the inquiry team questioned the motorcyclist, Garda James Broe, he denied ever seeing any girl or making any reference to a girl in the car he was chasing that night. McCarrick and Camon's team spoke to him and to other Gardaí on duty in Tallaght station on the days in question; none of them could recall any dealings with Martin or Walsh, or having heard the story of a girl in the car. While the two men remembered speaking to several Gardaí, both on the night of the theft and when they went to recover their car next morning, no-one remembered talking to them. It was a blank wall.

At this stage, of course, it was seven years since the events in question, and memories naturally would have faded. The report stated that there was 'no doubt but that some Garda told Mr. Martin and Mr. Walsh something about a girl ... who allegedly went up the mountains with youths in stolen cars.' But, they concluded, 'it is possible that Mr. Martin and Mr. Walsh got the impression that the Garda who they say spoke to them was being specific when in fact he was generalising.'

As for ST, the inquiry was clearly heavily influenced by evidence it gathered that she had been a friend of Joseph Meleady and therefore could not be classed as a disinterested party. They were unimpressed with her powers of recall. She indicated that her memory of the events in question had been jogged by a conversation with the author at her house in Tallaght in 1990. The inquiry stated: 'The extent of the amount of information imparted to her by Michael Heney is unknown and difficult to quantify.' No clarification of this was sought from the author. In fact very little information was imparted by him. ST remembered very little of events that night. When it was briefly put to her that she had been a passenger in the car with Dunne and Walsh later that evening, she remembered being in the car with them and one other girl, and she remembered the youths talking about the man who had been on the bonnet earlier. She thought it had been earlier in the evening than 7:30 p.m.

Det.-Supt McCarrick stated that it 'seems to be unrealistic' to think that those who stole Eamon Gavin's car would then, with the Gardaí in hot pursuit, go and pick up two girls in the car they had stolen. He noted that both Gus Dunne and the other girl named denied that ST's account was the truth. Brendan Walsh refused to co-operate with the inquiry in either confirming or denying the story: Walsh would have no dealing with the inquiry at all. None of the Gardaí in Tallaght station were able to help.

The report concluded that the references heard by Martin and Walsh 'would seem to have been of a general nature, made in a reassuring sense rather than imparting specific information.' Martin and Walsh, in their statements to the inquiry, had depicted the references made to them by Gardaí as quite detailed and specific. The two men's view of what was being said to them had seemed to represent a shared understanding of a number of different conversations over a twelve-hour period. However, no Gardaí in Tallaght station could recall talking to Martin and Walsh; all the Gardaí there denied all knowledge of a girl in the car. The lead given by Finbarr Martin and his brother-in-law in the end went nowhere. The Garda report, seeking to reconcile the conflicting evidence, in the end took the view that the two men, separately and together, had misunderstood what was said to them. ST's corroboration was felt to be unreliable and could be disregarded.

Paul McDonnell and the petrol can

As we have seen, Paul McDonnell's account of how he threatened Eamon Gavin with a petrol can and with being burned off the car contained a vital clue to McDonnell's credibility as a witness. The clue lay in the colour of the can. McDonnell's sworn affidavit, made in May 1985, had described the can, quite incidentally, as being red. It was a detail no-one else in the saga ever referred to—neither Brendan Walsh, Gus Dunne, Eamon or Paul Gavin, nor indeed Joseph Meleady or Joseph Grogan. None of the Garda witnesses, in any of the court proceedings, ever referred to the can's colour.

In the state's case, Brendan Walsh was the supposed back-seat passenger. Could Walsh have told McDonnell? But Walsh was in jail when Meleady and Grogan were first convicted, and was still there when Paul McDonnell decided to come forward some weeks later. In these circumstances it was unlikely that he could have furnished McDonnell with such an incidental detail for his lengthy statement.

For years the author was intrigued by the question of the can's colour but was unable to acquire from the state witnesses verification or repudiation of McDonnell's claim that it was red. None of the many trials, not even those in which Paul McDonnell was in the dock, brought clarification. When Det.-Supt McCarrick investigated the whole matter, it seemed to the author that he and his team would assess the significance of this one way or the other but especially if it turned out that the can was red, as McDonnell claimed. The report, however, contained no comment on the matter. It was only quite incidentally, in the statements accompanying Det.-Supt McCarrick's report, that it was finally confirmed, by Eamon Gavin himself.

The two superintendents had interviewed Paul McDonnell, finding him angry and arrogant and very difficult to handle. But he said in his interview with them (though this was never part of his sworn evidence) that while threatening Gavin with the petrol can he had actually spilled petrol on the roof of the car. The investigators were anxious to clarify this point. In their report they pointed out that technical studies they had conducted showed that no petrol was spilled. But in asking Eamon Gavin to comment on this aspect they also secured written confirmation of the can's colour, something they showed no interest in, before or after receiving Gavin's statement. He said to them: 'You have asked me if the fellow in the rear seat of my car … did in fact unscrew the cap of the red petrol can as he had same on the roof of my car …'

If McDonnell had been wrong on the colour, it should have tripped him up years earlier. Only the person handling the can was remotely likely to remember such a detail: that meant either himself or Brendan Walsh, depending on whether one believed the state version or Meleady and Grogan's. Walsh, as we have seen, was locked up, and never spoke in public about the can or its colour. That left McDonnell as the only one ever to refer to it. He said it was red, and he was right.

10

The Fingerprint Issue:
The State's Defence, Part 1

The heart of the case made in the 1990 television programme was that
the state had mishandled and misrepresented the scientific evidence in
the Meleady and Grogan trials. It was this claim more than anything
else that forced the state into its three-year-long inquiry under the
instigation of the Attorney-General. It was hardly surprising, therefore,
that the authorities were found to have spent a great deal of time and
effort trying to establish precisely what had happened in regard to the
fingerprint of Brendan Walsh. The result of all this deliberation, as it
was presented to Meleady and Grogan's lawyers, was an exceptionally
complicated, almost byzantine defence of the state's conduct. There
was no explicit acknowledgment that the non-disclosure had been a
mistake.

Piecing the official response together from the various files,
statements, and reports, we can see that the state's argument—part
explanation, part defence—amounted to the following:

1. The failure to present the proper fingerprint evidence was not
   deliberate: it was unwitting and accidental.
2. There had been several unfortunate but innocent administrative
   errors at local Garda level that had prevented the evidence being
   included in the original Circuit Court file that went to the Chief
   State Solicitor's office. As a result, neither solicitors nor barristers
   on the state side were aware of the existence of this evidence.

3. The investigating officer, Garda Patrick Thornton, unfortunately but again quite innocently told the state's counsel at the first trial that the fingerprint was in the back of the car—because that was where he mistakenly thought it was—and not in the front.

4. The description in the Walsh book of evidence of the fingerprint's location—'inside of the passenger door window'—was, it was argued, ambiguous and could be taken as referring to either the front or the back. Those reading this description, it was claimed, could not be expected to realise that it referred in fact to the front.

5. The fingerprint evidence itself was not regarded as conclusive. It did not prove anything, and was in fact 'neutral' on the issue of where Walsh was in the car.

6. In any event, this evidence had been revealed in full at the McDonnell perjury trials in 1987, and the conviction there of McDonnell showed that it was of little evidential value to the defence.

This, then, was the essence of the state case, as distilled by the author from the various detailed files, including the report from the Director of Public Prosecutions to the Attorney-General. It seemed to add up to saying, 'Much ado about nothing.' There was, in the end, nothing to persuade the state to change its mind over the safety of the convictions; there was nothing to persuade them of errors requiring correction, nothing to apologise for. The files were thick, showing the number of staff hours required to investigate the whole affair; but in their conclusions there was little solace for Meleady and Grogan. There was, in particular, no acknowledgment that the rights of the accused to due process of law might have been infringed. There was no acceptance of the simple proposition that the fingerprint evidence should have been disclosed to the defence either before the first trial or, failing that, the retrial.

Overall, the files were of such a nature that they raised a completely different question: if the matters being investigated were judged finally to be of such little consequence, why had it taken such an inordinate amount of time and effort to investigate them?

No deliberate suppression

An unexpected concern of the state agencies and in particular of the DPP himself was to rebut a perceived charge in the television programme that there had been deliberate suppression of the fingerprint evidence. This supposed aspect of the broadcast, as seen in the report, came as a surprise to the programme-makers themselves, as they had consciously tried to exclude any such explicit or implicit message from the broadcast. The transcript of the 1990 programme, which was in the state's possession, recorded Barry White SC as stating very clearly: 'I am not suggesting that there was anything in this other than an innocent misleading of the jury.' Eamon Barnes stated in his report to the Attorney-General that the television programme 'implied' a 'deliberate suppression' and that it attributed 'base, indeed criminal motives to prosecutors.' One of the main concerns of his report, he said, was 'with the suggestion that there was a deliberate suppression of evidence regarding Mr. Walsh's fingermark.'

It was not stated how this suggestion was made in the programme, or how it squared with the broadcast view of the man whose findings governed the whole report that the mistake was an innocent one. The main focus of the documentary had not in fact been on the causes of the mishandled evidence but, firstly, on recording that it had occurred and, secondly, on the consequences of this for due process and the rights of the accused. The fact is that no suggestion of deliberate suppression was either made or intended to be made, just as no such suggestion is made by the author today.

Administrative errors blamed for failure to disclose

The Garda inquiry led by Det.-Supt McCarrick found that the reason the wrong position of the fingerprint was given to the first trial was simply that no-one on the state side knew the truth. How did this happen?

The explanation given in the report was as follows. In the first place, Brendan Walsh had not been tried with Meleady and Grogan but was tried separately, in advance. Walsh had been accused, with another person, of offences additional to and quite separate from the Gavin incident. The Garda file on Walsh and this other person was prepared in Tallaght Garda station by Det.-Garda Felix McKenna and Det.-Sgt John McLoughlin. The Meleady and Grogan file, on the other hand, because the offence was committed in the Rathfarnham district, was prepared in Rathfarnham station by Garda Patrick Thornton and his supervising officer, Sgt W. Egan.

Two actions were taken by the Rathfarnham Gardaí that would prove costly. Thornton and Egan were aware that Walsh had been charged with being in Eamon Gavin's car and that his fingerprint had been found in that car. They were also aware that this evidence was being included by Det.-Garda McKenna in the Walsh file, to be handled in separate court proceedings. They decided not to include the fingerprint evidence in the Meleady and Grogan file, the file that went on to the State Solicitor and to the DPP.

Having made this unfortunate decision, Sgt Egan then made what he later described to McCarrick and Camon as a typing error when making out a covering note for the file. The effect was that the note was seriously inaccurate. It contained a brief summary of the offences against Eamon Gavin, the last sentence of which read: 'A stolen car was left outside Mr. Gavin's house in Cremourne Estate and Brendan Walsh was charged in connexion with this by Det. Garda McKenna, Tallaght.'

This statement was incorrect. Brendan Walsh was not charged in connection with this other car but with Eamon Gavin's car. Sgt Egan told the inquiry that when he wrote the memo he intended to convey that Brendan Walsh was also charged in connection with Gavin's car.

McCarrick and Camon stated: 'Perusal of this report will show that with the use of a full stop after the word "Cremourne Estate," and the deletion of the word "and," the final sentence of this paragraph would then read: "Brendan Walsh was charged in connexion with this [i.e. Gavin's car] by D/Garda McKenna, Tallaght." Although grammatically incorrect this sequence of sentences could then be interpreted as conveying to the reader the fact that Walsh was also charged in connexion with Gavin's car.'

The combined effect of this error on the covering note of the Garda file and the decision not to include the Walsh fingerprint evidence meant that the Garda file on Meleady and Grogan showed no connection whatever between Brendan Walsh and evidence found in Eamon Gavin's car.

The DPP, Eamon Barnes, said of these errors: 'It may now be considered that there was insufficient contact regarding these cases between the Rathfarnham and Tallaght investigations and investigators. This may in retrospect be unfortunate, but there is no reason to believe that the Rathfarnham Gardaí consciously and deliberately chose to exclude from their file such knowledge as they may have got from their Tallaght colleagues regarding Mr. Walsh's involvement in the Gavin crime.'

The separate file from Det.-Garda McKenna and Det.-Sgt McLoughlin in Tallaght made no reference to the other file being prepared by Garda Thornton and Sgt Egan in Rathfarnham. However, the Tallaght file did connect the cases in one way, as it contained the evidence that Walsh's fingerprint had been found in Gavin's car, and specifically 'on the passenger door window.'

Both files were assigned to the same solicitor, Richard Walker, but there is no evidence that he made any connection between them. If he had, presumably they would not have been subsequently assigned, as they were, to different officials within the office of the DPP. The Walsh file was sent to the DPP's office on 1 May, the Meleady and Grogan file two weeks earlier, on 13 April. Different prosecutors thereafter handled each.

The net effect was that the file on Meleady and Grogan reached the courtroom floor and state's counsel without any reference in it to Brendan Walsh's involvement. In particular, it did not contain the statement of evidence from Det.-Garda Edward Donohue placing Brendan Walsh's print on the inside of the passenger door window of Eamon Gavin's car. As a further factor explaining what was to follow, the state side had no advance knowledge, any more than the defence, that Brendan Walsh would give evidence that he was sitting in the front seat, allegedly occupied by Joseph Grogan.

In all these circumstances the state argued that in not providing the defence with details of the Walsh fingerprint evidence in advance, it could not be held to be culpable. It did not argue that the evidence should not have been disclosed. In fact this question was not directly addressed. Instead, a totally separate argument was made that the non-disclosure was not deliberate but simply the result of a chapter of accidents. The DPP himself said later that it appeared that his own counsel was not aware that such evidence even existed before the first trial, 'nor was there any reason why he should have known.' Clearly the DPP felt that in the circumstances, one of the principal state witnesses, Garda Thornton, who was aware of the existence of the fingerprint, could not have been expected, at some preliminary stage, to inform counsel about it. Nor did he feel that the state solicitor who had handled both files, given all the circumstances, should reasonably be expected to have informed counsel of the fingerprint's existence.

At any rate, as a result of a series of unfortunate errors, mishaps, and misapprehensions, counsel for the DPP, through no fault of his own and despite having the whole apparatus of the state's prosecution system behind him, arrived in court on the morning of the Tallaght Two's first trial completely unaware that a third party had been convicted in connection with the same crime after his fingerprint was found in Eamon Gavin's car. Truly, the truth seems stranger than fiction.

Although counsel for the DPP, Eamon Leahy, became aware of the existence of the fingerprint evidence during the first trial, and sought to use it to discredit a central defence witness (mistakenly, as we now know), the DPP himself was able to write in 1991: 'Nobody in the D.P.P.'s Office who dealt with the prosecution of Messrs. Meleady and Grogan was aware … that there was any fingerprint evidence which could be relevant to the Meleady and Grogan prosecution until long after those proceedings had finished.' Eamon Barnes's statement appeared to mean that no official in the DPP's office attended the first trial; no official in the DPP's office read the transcript prepared for the appeal; no official in the DPP's office discussed the cross-examination of Brendan Walsh in any detail subsequently with their own counsel in advance of the retrial. None of this, it seems, is unusual in itself, but the consequence here was that the DPP and his staff were completely in the dark, not only about Eamon Leahy's error but also, it seems, about the very existence of a fingerprint that could affect the case.

What remained unclear was what the DPP and his office did when they finally became aware of these aspects of the case, including Eamon Leahy's misstatement.

An explanation for Garda Thornton's error

If there was an explanation for the failure to disclose the evidence *in advance of* the first trial, this left still to be explained, among other things, the further evidence given when the case reached the Circuit Criminal Court. Here, in the first Meleady and Grogan trial, Garda Thornton was a witness. In that evidence Thornton made no reference whatever to the Walsh fingerprint found in Eamon Gavin's car.

Garda Thornton was asked by defence counsel, Bernard Madden, about the scientific examination of Gavin's car; he was asked if

Meleady's or Grogan's fingerprints were found in it. He was not asked specifically about Brendan Walsh's fingerprint, and, accordingly, made no reference to it. The inquiry team questioned whether the defence team should have had their own knowledge of the evidence that had convicted Brendan Walsh. This had been made available to Walsh and his legal advisers at the time. These, of course, had been quite separate proceedings, with separate lawyers; nonetheless, the Garda report felt that the lawyers for Meleady and Grogan could have been kept informed as a result of them. Of course they were not so informed, and could hardly be faulted for this.

The inquiry considered in detail what had happened in the Circuit Criminal Court when Brendan Walsh took the stand as a witness for Meleady and Grogan. In an attempt to discredit Walsh's claim that Meleady and Grogan were not with him, Eamon Leahy put it to him that he was in the back of the car, 'where your fingerprint was found.' Walsh replied that he was in the front of the car.

Eamon Leahy later offered an explanation for his mistake to Det.-Supt McCarrick. 'In the course of my cross-examination of Brendan Walsh, I spoke with the Garda in charge of the prosecution, and he informed me that Walsh's fingerprint had been found in the back of the car.' Garda Thornton, questioned later by the Garda inquiry team, could not recall saying this to Leahy. However, he agreed he was sitting behind him in the courtroom and that he did have a number of conversations with him during the trial. If he did tell Leahy that the fingerprint was in the back of the car, it was in the genuine belief that this information was correct. 'How I came to be of this belief I am not now aware.'

The Garda report concluded—as indeed the evidence suggests— that if Thornton did mislead Leahy he did it unwittingly and without malice aforethought. They noted that his diligence, integrity and competence had been commented on favourably throughout the case by several judges and officials.

But how had Garda Thornton, one of the few people, it seems, who really should have been on top of the evidence on the state side, become misinformed on such a matter? The Garda report had no clear answer. The fingerprint evidence had been processed by Det.-Garda McKenna from Tallaght station, who stated that he had visited

Rathfarnham Garda station and spoken to Sgt Egan and Garda Thornton on the subject.

It might reasonably have been expected that Det.-Garda McKenna would have been aware of the position of the print; it was evidence, after all, that had won him a conviction against Brendan Walsh. But it is not clear that McKenna was aware that the print was in the front. He said in his statement to the McCarrick inquiry that when he processed the evidence, 'the precise location of the fingermark on the inside of the car was not of particular relevance at this time.' It was true that, in so far as the prosecution of Brendan Walsh was concerned, the relevant fact was that the fingerprint was found inside the car—where inside did not matter. So did Det.-Garda McKenna himself come to believe that the fingerprint was in the back, and if so, how? The origin of the view that it was in the back could not be traced.

As we saw earlier (chapter 3), the fingerprint evidence always held the potential to challenge Eamon Gavin's identification of Joseph Grogan as the front-seat passenger. Det.-Garda McKenna, at the time, did not appear to see this; nor did it seem a point of substance to the Garda inquiry.

Garda Thornton for his part told the investigators that it 'may' have been Det.-Garda McKenna who told him of the fingerprint being found in Gavin's car, but he just did not know. He said he would have had casual conversations with McKenna, but he never went into 'any specific detail in relation to the location of Brendan Walsh's fingerprint' with McKenna or with any other Garda. Once again it did not occur to him that Walsh's position in the car, and anything touching on it, was an essential component of the prosecution case against Meleady and Grogan. Whether in the front or the back, its location was relevant to the case.

The McCarrick investigation established that while Garda Thornton had never been formally sent the fingerprint evidence by the Forensic Science Section—it had gone to Det.-Garda McKenna— nonetheless he had been in direct touch with the Fingerprint Section, where someone had given him the information about various smudges being found in the car. He had referred to these in his evidence at the first trial. But how did he come to think the fingerprint was in the back of the car? The matter remained a mystery and was not clarified in the inquiry report—nor, indeed, in the final hearing of the Court of Criminal Appeal on the case in January and February 1995.

Det.-Garda McKenna was present at the first trial of Meleady and Grogan, but not as a witness. He stated years later to the *Sunday Business Post* that he was not present in the courtroom at the moment when Eamon Leahy made his misstatement. So, in all these circumstances, he could do nothing either to prevent or later to correct the false impression given by the state's counsel on the whereabouts of the fingerprint. There is no suggestion that either he or his Garda colleagues behaved improperly in any of this.

Eamon Leahy himself was asked by Det.-Supt McCarrick specifically if he felt that his misinformed question altered the result of the trial. There was no report of this question being put to any other lawyer. Leahy's response, in the final report, was given extra emphasis by being underlined by the authors: *'I can say that I believe that it did not.'* But Leahy had no way of calculating the deliberations of the jury, or indeed of the defence lawyers, had they had open to them a possible line of argument based on the whereabouts of Walsh's fingerprint. There was no evidence that he was asked a related question: did the non-disclosure of the proper evidence, as opposed to its misstatement by himself, alter the result of the trial?

What was clear from the McCarrick report was that Garda procedures had failed in the run-up to the case. Compounding errors were made when the case came to trial. McCarrick concluded that none of this arose from a deliberate intention to mislead but rather from innocent and quite inadvertent human error. He assigned no blame to anyone involved.

'Passenger door window' regarded as ambiguous

As a further and significant part of its explanation for the mishandling of the scientific evidence, the state argued, retrospectively, that the actual statement of evidence from the Garda concerned had been too vague to place the fingerprint precisely. The location was 'inside of the passenger door window'; this was felt to be an ambiguous term, which did not indicate whether the fingerprint was in the front or the back. This proposition was advanced most forcibly in the report of the DPP and by Barry Donoghue of the Chief State Solicitor's office. It was a vital proposition from the point of view of the state, which had to explain why neither solicitors nor barristers on the state side acted to correct their error after they came into possession of the statement of evidence.

McCarrick concluded that 'a more detailed location for the identified fingerprint … would have been beneficial.' Such a statement came eventually in 1987, when Det.-Insp. Anders's inquiries uncovered part of the truth. A second statement of evidence was then taken from the detective who found the fingerprint, Det.-Garda Donohue. In this he very specifically described the print as having been found 'on the inside of the front passenger window.'

In an accompanying statement to McCarrick on this matter, Det.-Garda Donohue said he regarded the locations in a four-door car as being driver's door, passenger door, and rear passenger doors, and that when he used the term 'the passenger door' he felt this placed the print on the front passenger door. But Barry Donoghue in the Chief State Solicitor's office took a different view when reporting later, in 1991. He felt the initial forensic science report was 'silent' on the fingerprint's exact position in the car. Even had the state solicitor had the statement of evidence, he felt, it would not have rung alarm bells regarding Leahy's statement. 'The original statement of Det. Garda Donohue would not have raised in the mind of the solicitor preparing the Book of Evidence in the Meleady and Grogan case any anxiety that the statement was inconsistent with the prosecution evidence in that case. Even if that statement had been served on the solicitor for the accused (and I do not accept that in the circumstances of the case there was any duty on the prosecution to serve the statement) it would not have assisted him in ascertaining the exact location of the print; nor would it have assisted him in correcting the unwitting error made by State Counsel during the trial.'

This then was the position taken by the senior solicitor in the Chief State Solicitor's office. The term 'the passenger door window' he regarded as 'silent' on the issue of exact location within the car.

Barry Donoghue's clear position in this regard seemed to refer only to the first trial, and only to the issue of inclusion in the book of evidence. It did not refer to the fact that there was a retrial, or to the fact that obligations of disclosure could and should be met outside of actual inclusion in the book of evidence. The defence could simply be informed by word of mouth.

By the time of the retrial, those handling the Meleady and Grogan case in the office of the Chief State Solicitor were in possession of Det.-Garda Donohue's statement of evidence. They were also aware—or should have been—of Brendan Walsh's claim to have been in the front of the car. With the retrial, therefore, there was a fresh opportunity to make a disclosure to the defence of evidence that had hitherto been overlooked. This should now, in normal circumstances, have been known to the state to be both material and relevant. Because of the apparent misunderstanding of Det.-Garda Donohue's original statement of evidence, it seems that once again it was not.

The innocence of the error, of course, was entirely immaterial to the defence. They would have been no less and no more disadvantaged had the failure been deliberate. And it was a moot point whether Det.-Garda Donohue's statement of evidence was 'silent' on the issue of whether it was found in the front or the back of the car.

Further complications in the way of these explanations arose from the entry on the state files by John Rohan of the Chief State Solicitor's office. It had clearly occurred to him, before the retrial, that the fingerprint might be in the front of Gavin's car. Both he and counsel for the DPP, Eamon Leahy, had now in their possession the actual evidence of Det.-Garda Donohue.

The Director of Public Prosecutions, Eamon Barnes, commented: 'Mr. Donoghue states that a copy of the Walsh Book of Evidence was furnished to Mr. Leahy shortly before the retrial. This was presumably because of the evidence Mr. Walsh gave at the first trial, and in anticipation of his testifying again. However, only the first version of Det. Garda Donohue's statement, which did not specify the front passenger window as the location of the fingermark, was then in existence. It would, in my view, be unreasonable to suggest that Mr. Leahy had to have been alerted by that Book of Evidence to the possibility that any mistake or mis-statement had taken place at the first trial regarding the location of the fingermark.'

The DPP also said in his report: 'While in retrospect it is unfortunate that D. Garda Donohue was not a little more specific in his original statement as to the location of Walsh's fingermark, his explanation for this ... seems entirely reasonable.' (Det.-Garda Donohue's explanation was to the effect that in saying 'passenger door' he felt he was identifying the front passenger door.) If this was an 'entirely reasonable' view in the DPP's opinion, did this imply that Eamon Leahy might have realised that he had made a mistake?

One further point arises concerning this issue of the term 'passenger door window'. A survey was conducted among a thousand adults in Dublin in the spring of 1994 under the auspices of the Psychology Department of Trinity College. Each of the thousand adults was handed an image of a four-door car and asked to identify where they thought 'the passenger door' could be found. Eighty per cent pointed to the *front* passenger door.

Eamon Leahy's own reports to the DPP on this and other matters did not indicate what his awareness was when he came into possession of Det.-Garda Donohue's statement of evidence before the retrial. He did not explain why he did not then notice a potential discrepancy between what he had told the court and the actual evidence. He gave no indication of his own view on whether this could or should have been set straight during the McDonnell perjury trials. He had, of course, no responsibility for the prosecution in the case; but did he feel some responsibility in relation to the misstatement of the fingerprint evidence, given his own role in that regard? No reference was made to this.

Eamon Leahy told the investigators that he had no recollection of a fingerprint issue arising at the consultation with John Rohan in November 1985, the week before the retrial, despite the solicitor's note to that effect. Unquestionably, however, something at that conference put into Rohan's mind the idea that the fingerprint was in the front of the car. One possibility not raised in the state files on the case was that Rohan had in front of him the Walsh book of evidence, including particularly the statement of evidence placing the fingerprint on the passenger door window. Did Rohan simply read the evidence and the reference there to 'the passenger door window' and draw the (intended) conclusion that the fingerprint was on the *front* passenger door?

11

The Fingerprint Issue:
The State's Defence, Part 2

In his report to the Attorney-General, the Director of Public Prosecutions, Eamon Barnes, dealt with the central question of the 'evidential significance' of the location and orientation of Brendan Walsh's fingerprint. His conclusion, in essence, was that it had no significance.

It is worth recording the DPP's comments on this matter in full, as they raised further important issues. 'The mark was in fact made by Mr. Walsh's right thumb. It was inverted, and was left close to the top of the front passenger side window, on the inside and nearer to the front pillar. Such a mark could have been made by a person sitting in the front passenger seat. It would however involve a somewhat unusual, even uncomfortable posture or movement by such a person.

'The way that springs to mind would be if he turned leftward towards the back of the car and steadied himself by holding the roof over the door with his right hand, letting his inverted thumb rest on the closed window.

'Mr. Gavin in his statement of 6.3.84 refers to two of the hi-jackers rooting in the boot of his car prior to the production of the petrol container. One of the two must have gone from the front to the back and it would, I would think, have been possible for the mark to have been left in the course of that operation. However, the initial entry to Mr. Gavin's car appears to have been gained by breaking a rear quarter light. The location and orientation of the fingermark is at least as consistent with the explanation that it was made by a person in the rear of the car leaning forward to unlock the front passenger door, as with having been made by a person in the front passenger seat.

'I am of opinion that the location of Mr. Walsh's fingermark is neutral relative to the issue of whether he was a front or rear passenger in the car, and that insofar as it may have any significance at all on that issue, the fact that it was inverted would tend somewhat towards the explanation that he left the mark when he was in the back leaning forward and resting his hand over the front passenger door near the front pillar, while he unlocked the door with his left hand.

'In short, I consider that the location of Mr. Walsh's fingermark has no clear or compelling significance in the context of the question of where Mr. Walsh was in the car when he deposited his thumb mark on the left window, that it does not call for any action by my Office now … and that had my Office been aware of it in 1984 it would not have affected or altered the decision to prosecute Messrs. Meleady and Grogan.'

Thus went the DPP's considered view of the matter. In the claim that the fingerprint was neutral on the issue of location, Eamon Barnes appeared in effect to contradict his own counsel in the McDonnell perjury actions, Erwan Mill-Arden. Also, Eamon Leahy, his counsel in the Meleady and Grogan trials, had made a direct assumption, in his misguided question seeking to discredit Brendan Walsh, that the position of the fingerprint indicated where Walsh was seated in the car. Furthermore, Garda Patrick Thornton, in initiating the perjury action against Paul McDonnell in 1985, had stated to his superiors: 'Fingerprint evidence found in the rear of the car would suggest that Brendan Walsh was in the back seat of the car at the time in question.' To none of these Garda officers and lawyers on the state side had the fingerprint appeared neutral on the issue of location.

The McCarrick report offered an opinion similar to that of the DPP on this issue. It stated: 'The present investigating officers would suggest that the presence of the fingerprint on the inside window on the left front passenger side, simply suggests he handled the window on the inside, and not necessarily while occupying the front seat passenger position.'

The DPP's report left a number of particular questions unanswered, notably in relation to the McDonnell case. The DPP's office and the Chief State Solicitor's office were aware of the fingerprint evidence at least by June 1987; yet again this evidence was not disclosed to the defence in advance of the perjury trials, which began in July 1987. Nor was the irregularity in the previous handling of this evidence brought to the attention of the courts hearing McDonnell's case. Had the prosecution authorities a reason for this? Had they assessed the situation and decided that the irregularities were incidental to the prosecution of Paul McDonnell? Were they simply leaving it to the defence lawyers to bring the matter up if they so wished? Did anyone actually realise that a serious mistake had been made?

The DPP went on to consider the question whether an accurate account of the location and orientation of the fingerprint might have influenced the verdict of either of the two Meleady and Grogan juries. This, the DPP felt, was 'quite impossible to answer. It is totally in the realm of speculation.' A more relevant and answerable question, he felt, might be: 'If either jury had heard all the evidence relating to the location and orientation of the fingermark, and had been properly instructed in relation to it, should such jury have been influenced by it on the issue of where Mr. Walsh was in the car when he deposited the mark?' Eamon Barnes, with delicious but obviously unconscious irony, answered thus: 'I consider the evidence to be inconclusive and without significance on that issue, and that a jury would have been most appropriately advised that they could not safely draw any conclusion from it one way or the other.' The irony was that advice very similar to this had in fact been given to the juries in the Meleady and Grogan case—in regard to the DPP's own evidence. Jurors in both Tallaght Two trials were told it would be positively dangerous to convict on the visual identification alone.

Eamon Barnes did not refer to the nature of the prosecution evidence against Meleady and Grogan. Uncorroborated visual identification, made in extremely stressful circumstances and in relation to people never before seen by the witness, amounted to far from cast-iron evidence. The weight of the scientific evidence could only be measured by comparison with the evidence on the other side. In the circumstances of the case, while the fingerprint evidence was certainly less than conclusive, was it really, as Eamon Barnes suggested, 'without significance'? The issue here was the seriousness of the error made by Garda Thornton, transmitted to the court by the DPP's own counsel, Eamon Leahy, in 1985.

There were a number of other issues raised by the DPP's analysis of how Walsh's fingerprint might have been deposited where it was. Firstly, he did not refer to evidence of how the passenger door window was wound down at some point in the course of the action. The person in the front seat had hauled himself out into a seated position on the window edge, holding a golf umbrella in his left hand while gaining balance and leverage with his right hand. This was all explicit in Eamon Gavin's evidence. Clearly the right hand was being used to grip the inside of the car as that person climbed out on the window and when he climbed back in. Such activity could explain the 'unusual, even uncomfortable posture' the DPP felt was required to place the fingerprint where it was: the top of the window would have been much more accessible when wound down. (See illustrations preceding page 83.)

The evidence in court was that the front-seat passenger eventually climbed back into his seat, probably clutching the window and door as he did so. Would all this explain the fingerprint's unusual location and orientation? If the DPP considered this possibility, he did not refer to it in his report to the Attorney-General. Of course it followed that, if this was how the print was deposited, then it was likely that Brendan Walsh was the front-seat passenger, not Joseph Grogan.

The propositions Eamon Barnes did advance to explain how the mark could have got where it was raised certain difficulties. A person in the front seat turning to face the back of the car, as contemplated by the DPP, would naturally turn to his right, not his left—especially in a car with large head-rests, as there were in the car in question. No explanation was given of how a person moving from the front seat to the back could leave such a mark. In fact there was no evidence in any of the hearings that anyone did move from the front seat during the course of the action. Eamon Gavin did refer at one point to two of the raiders rooting in the boot but never at any time to anyone moving out of the front seat.

The proposition that Eamon Barnes appeared, eventually, to favour involved someone leaning forward to open the front door from the back—but only in what would have been a clumsy and far from urgent manoeuvre. The person involved would in all probability have had to be left-handed. The idea that a person would reach beyond and above the handle with his right hand before hurriedly opening it with his left hand, while certainly possible, does not seem persuasive. It is reasonable to assume that the opening of the door would have been a hurried and urgent task: a reaching hand would most likely have gone direct to the handle area, not to the top of the glass.

It seemed implicit throughout Eamon Barness's report to the Attorney-General that his view on these matters was, at least in part, being formulated years after the events in question. There was, at any rate, no reference to any such analysis, or explanation, or justification, having been arrived at, for example, before the McDonnell perjury hearings. There was no reference to any review by the DPP or the Chief State Solicitor of the consequences of Eamon Leahy's error throughout 1987, 1988, 1989, or 1990—up to 10 October. It may have occurred, but no mention was made of it. This time delay was simply not dealt with in his report to the Attorney-General. Eamon Leahy referred in one of his reports to a report being prepared by a solicitor in the Chief State Solicitor's office; but no document by the solicitor in question was released to Meleady and Grogan.

Neither the DPP nor the Chief State Solicitor were of course in any sense directly responsible for the original error made in 1985. This error had been on foot of mistaken information provided by the investigating Garda. But when the irregularity became manifest, as it must have done during 1987, who on the prosecution side had responsibility for seeing that it was acknowledged and addressed? There was very little in the related files or in the various reports submitted to the Attorney-General to confirm that this had happened between 1987 and October 1990.

Claim that verdict of third jury confirms Tallaght Two's guilt

The final argument on the state side regarding the Walsh fingerprint was that it had been fully disclosed at the McDonnell perjury hearings and that still the verdict there went against Meleady and Grogan. Eamon Leahy stated in his report to the DPP that the outcome of the second perjury trial 'appears to confirm' his view that the fingerprint evidence would not have altered the verdicts against Meleady and Grogan. But was this really so?

In the same report to the DPP, Eamon Leahy made this statement in relation to the perjury hearings: 'I understand that the trial judge charged the jury to the effect that they would have to be satisfied beyond all reasonable doubt that both Mr. Meleady and Mr. Grogan were in the car before they could convict.' In fact it is not clear that either trial judge did this. Eamon Leahy, in fairness, added that he was not present in court at the time, nor had he the transcripts to confirm this point. Yet he made the claim to the DPP, and his assertion was not contradicted in any of the reports. A close study of the transcript of both judges' charges in the McDonnell case shows that at no point in either of them was such a statement made.

In fact in the first McDonnell trial, where the jury disagreed and had to be discharged, Judge Buchanan placed a very different reality before the jury. He said: 'You must be very clear in your mind that you are in no way retrying the prosecution brought against Meleady and Grogan. You have heard that Meleady and Grogan were convicted in two separate criminal trials. There is nothing that you do that will affect the conviction of Meleady and Grogan. It is part of the evidence against the accused [McDonnell] that these things happened ...' So the judge in fact told the jury *not* that they must first be convinced that Meleady and Grogan were in the car but simply that Meleady and Grogan were already convicted of being in the car. That had already been decided by a court. The question to the jury was whether, in the light of that unalterable fact and the rest of the evidence, they thought McDonnell was lying when he said they were not there. The prior conviction of Meleady and Grogan loaded the dice heavily against McDonnell from the start.

Det.-Supt McCarrick shared Eamon Leahy's view of the perjury case finding. He recorded at some length how the evidence that the fingerprint of Walsh was in the front of the car was made available to both McDonnell trials and yet McDonnell was convicted of perjury. The implied argument was that the McDonnell case was, if not a retrial of Meleady and Grogan, then the nearest imaginable thing to it, only with the fingerprint evidence on display. The McCarrick report stated that the three jury findings were 'a fair judgement on the facts of this case, especially as the third convicting jury had all available evidence and all correct information placed before them.' This position, as we have seen (see also chapter 6), was open to challenge as an assessment of the nature of the issue and the verdict in the McDonnell perjury prosecution.

The charge to the jury in McDonnell's second trial, by Judge Michael Moriarty, also made it explicit that it was not Meleady and Grogan who were on trial in the perjury proceedings but Paul McDonnell. The judge stated that the McDonnell trial was no retrial of Meleady and Grogan. As Judge Buchanan had done in the previous trial, Judge Moriarty reminded the jury how Meleady and Grogan had already been convicted twice, unanimously, 'on essentially that evidence' (of Eamon Gavin and his son). He went on also to point out that a third person, Brendan Walsh, had been proved to be in the car; that it was agreed by all that there were only three people involved in the crime; that Meleady and Grogan had exhausted all means of appeal; and finally that as a result of all this it was difficult to see how Paul McDonnell, who claimed to be present, could ever be charged with being in the car.

The judge had pointed out that McDonnell's alleged perjury had consisted of a dual reference—that he was in the car, and that Meleady and Grogan were not—and that these two aspects were intertwined in McDonnell's evidence and had to be treated as one. The jury was not to be affected in its deliberations in any way, he charged, by the previous trials.

Had Meleady and Grogan not already been convicted, and had the juries not been aware of their conviction, the McDonnell case might have had the significance apparently placed on it by McCarrick and by Eamon Leahy. As it was, while the fingerprint evidence was—partially—adduced in evidence, also before the jury was the unalterable guilt of Meleady and Grogan. The McCarrick report did not advert to the fact that these previous convictions were used—and, it seems, used successfully—by the state in the McDonnell proceedings to persuade the jurors to draw the logical conclusion: that Paul McDonnell had to be guilty of perjury. Eamon Leahy, in fairness to him, did not have access to the transcripts when he made the incorrect observation quoted above to the DPP.

The Garda inquiry and, separately, Eamon Leahy appeared to have constructed a circular argument. In this it was maintained that because McDonnell was found guilty of perjury, this confirmed that Meleady and Grogan were guilty; but McDonnell was only found guilty after trials in which the predetermined and unalterable guilt of Meleady and Grogan was a significant factor. The records showed that the guilty verdict against the Tallaght Two (which legally appeared final) was used to help secure the conviction of McDonnell. Was it open to the state, therefore, to argue that the verdict against McDonnell, which might not have been obtained without the prior conviction of Meleady and Grogan, was a confirmation of the justice of that conviction?

Mill-Arden's astonishment over television programme

Det.-Supt McCarrick, in the course of his investigation, received a report from the state prosecuting counsel in the McDonnell perjury trials, Erwan Mill-Arden. The report was included among the appendixes to the full McCarrick report. In this, Mill-Arden revealed that he himself was unaware of the full history of the scientific evidence at the time he was prosecuting McDonnell. He stated: 'My consideration of this matter proceeded on the basis, as I understood then to be the truth, that the correct evidence concerning the placing of the fingerprint had already been adduced, and that all of these matters were cleared up with the approval of the Court of Criminal Appeal.' He stated that Eamon Gavin's evidence, 'as I understood my instructions, had already been challenged by the fingerprint evidence.' Of course, it had not.

In the full Garda report, sections of Erwan Mill-Arden's account were included, but in the course of doing so Det.-Supt McCarrick also included what appeared to be a misprint. The section in question was dealing with the fingerprint evidence, and in its original form Mill-Arden stated as follows: 'My understanding was there had been a contest over this issue, which of course would mean that there had been a dispute as to where the print was placed and which would have resulted in it being sorted out as to where it really was. This I understood had occurred.

'I recently watched a television programme on RTE ['Wednesday Report', October 1990] about the Meleady and Grogan case, and was genuinely astonished by what the programme had said took place on the second trial, as I was expecting it to say that the problem was cleared up then. I particularly remembered Garda Thornton stating that the State Counsel had got something wrong about the place of the fingerprint in the first trial.'

The Garda report omitted the second paragraph completely, and so included no reference to the astonishment of the state's own counsel at what he had learnt from the television programme about the fingerprint evidence years after the fact. In addition, in relation to the first of the two paragraphs quoted, the short sentence 'This I understood had occurred' became 'This I *understand* had occurred', with, in brackets immediately afterwards, '[incorrect]' added. The reference to the television programme, which explained the use of the past tense, was not included. The effect of this was to leave the reader unaware (*a*) that Mill-Arden had since realised that his understanding may have been mistaken and (*b*) that he had only gleaned the correcting information from a television programme in 1990.

Erwan Mill-Arden stated that he had at least two consultations with Garda Thornton and at least one with Det.-Insp. Anders. Also present at consultations, he recalled, was a legal executive from the Chief State Solicitor's office. Garda Thornton had raised the issue of the fingerprint evidence; at one of the consultations Thornton had explained to him that 'State Counsel had got something wrong about the place of the fingerprint in the first trial.' He said that as a result of these consultations 'my understanding was that between the first trial, the appeal from that, the second trial and the appeal from that, all of this had been cleared up.' In this, of course, he was mistaken.

A statement from Garda Thornton taken by Det.-Supt McCarrick in November 1990 insisted that he had brought to the notice of Erwan Mill-Arden and the state solicitor that in both Meleady and Grogan trials the fingerprint had been referred to as being in the back. Mill-Arden, regardless, and by his own account, laboured under a significant misapprehension during the McDonnell trials. As a result of his misunderstanding over what had happened previously he explained how, very deliberately, he had not passed on the elusive fingerprint evidence to the McDonnell defence lawyers. First of all he thought (wrongly) that they knew of it; secondly, because he thought it had already been adduced in court to challenge Eamon Gavin's evidence (which it had not) he felt it was not open to the defence to use it again in court. He also noted that he had summoned witnesses to deal with the matter if it arose—which it did—and that he had observed all legal proprieties on the basis of his instructions.

Erwan Mill-Arden's statement, among other things, tended to undermine the basis of the argument that the state would seek to use to defeat the Meleady and Grogan appeal in 1995: that in the McDonnell case the fingerprint evidence was fully available to challenge Eamon Gavin's identification. Clearly, on the basis of his account, it was not. The prosecution held the view that any such tactic in the McDonnell trial would have been inadmissible. Mill-Arden also appeared to differ in 1987 from the later claims of his own client, the Director of Public Prosecutions, in accepting that the accurate fingerprint evidence *could* be used to challenge Eamon Gavin's identification. As we have seen, Eamon Barnes argued in his report to the Attorney-General in 1991 that the location of the print was 'neutral' in regard to whether Walsh was in the front or the back of the car. Erwan Mill-Arden seemed to have been of the same view as Meleady and Grogan's lawyers, namely that this evidence could have been used to suggest that Eamon Gavin was wrong about the occupant of the front passenger seat.

Mill-Arden went on: 'The prosecution case was not that there were two comparable stories, one which might be right and one which might not be—i.e. Mr. Gavin's or Mr. McDonnell's. The prosecution situation was that Mr. Gavin's evidence, with all the challenges having been made to it, had been accepted and affirmed, and was embodied in the conviction of the two car thieves. To my mind to use evidence which had already been adduced (as I understood to be the case) to re-challenge Mr. Gavin's evidence, was in fact to use the perjury trial as a re-opening of the hearing before the previous jury in the car theft case and before the Court of Criminal Appeal, and was therefore not an acceptable procedure.

'It was my understanding in all these considerations that the proper fingerprint evidence about the correct placing of the print had already been adduced and would in fact of course be public knowledge, certainly within the legal advisers concerned.' In all of this, of course, he was misinformed about the prior use of the fingerprint evidence.

But Erwan Mill-Arden's remarks to this effect were not included in Det.-Supt McCarrick's detailed analysis of the case, sent to the DPP. The report noted how Mill-Arden said he had approached the first perjury trial on the basis that it emanated from a procedure that was in itself proper, acceptable, and adequate, and not one that itself would be open to challenge. It did not note his surprise at hearing that the evidence had never been adduced, nor the matter cleared up previously. It noted how he said that Garda Thornton had raised with him the issue of confusion or mix-up over the fingerprint evidence; it did not note that his recollection was that Thornton had only told him of a problem at the first trial, which he had then presumed, wrongly, to have been subsequently cleared up.

As an experienced officer at the top of his profession, Det.-Supt McCarrick will have had his own good reasons for writing his report as he did. Inevitably, only a very abbreviated series of extracts from Erwan Mill-Arden's full statement could be included in the McCarrick report. In addition, the full statement would have been passed to the DPP as an appendix. So, clearly, there was no deliberate attempt to misinform, nor is any such suggestion being made here.

But if Mill-Arden was correct, then once again a barrister representing the DPP in proceedings relating to the Tallaght Two had gone to court inadvertently misinformed about aspects of the evidence. Garda Thornton may have thought he told him how the fingerprint evidence had never been adduced and how the error of the first trial had never been corrected; but Mill-Arden, by his own account, was under the impression that all these matters had been raised, and resolved. Eamon Leahy, a witness in the perjury trials for Mill-Arden, had no opportunity to clarify the history of the matter for his colleague, despite his own intimate role in that history. Mill-Arden, for the best of professional reasons, ruled out consultations with Leahy as inappropriate in the circumstances of the case. And, whatever instructions came from the Chief State Solicitor's office, it seems that the best efforts of the staff there could not avoid a recurrence of the chronic difficulties that had dogged this fingerprint evidence since 1984. (Finally, it should be noted that Mill-Arden told the Court of Criminal Appeal in 1995 that he himself had no access to the transcripts of the Meleady and Grogan trials while preparing for the McDonnell case.)

Officials on the state side languished for years in a state of ignorance regarding, first, the existence, then the location, of Walsh's fingerprint. Now, in 1987, they were in possession of the facts—but once again, it seems, when their counsel went into court, he went in under some very considerable misapprehensions. The implications of this for the conviction of Paul McDonnell for perjury were not addressed in their respective reports by either the investigating Garda officers or by Eamon Barnes himself. Their focus was on the case of Joseph Meleady and Joseph Grogan.

Judge Moriarty refuses Séamus Sorahan's request

There was a further, related omission in the McCarrick report regarding the retrial of Paul McDonnell. In seeking to show that the fingerprint evidence had been fully aired in those proceedings, it recorded how defence counsel, Séamus Sorahan SC, asked the judge to amend his charge to the jury to make specific mention of the fingerprint having been found in the front of the car. This location of the print, Sorahan claimed, corroborated Walsh's claim to have been in the front. The Garda report then recorded how Judge Moriarty politely refused to do this. The judge told Sorahan that he had already made the reference Sorahan was referring to. Sorahan then conceded the point, apologising, and saying he was absent during part of the charge.

All this McCarrick recorded in his report. What he did not record, and what the transcript clearly showed, was that Judge Moriarty had *not* in fact made the reference in question. Contrary to what he said in reply to Sorahan, he had not, anywhere in his charge to the jury, stated where Walsh's prints were found inside Eamon Gavin's car. He referred the jury, in general terms, to the location of the print, but described it only as being inside the car, not specifically in the front. Nor did he at any time explain to the jury how this location could, arguably, be seen as corroboration of Walsh's claim to have been in the front.

Det.-Supt McCarrick had at his team's disposal the full transcript of the judge's charge, and a close reading of this shows that Judge Moriarty had assigned no importance to this aspect of the case when briefing the jury earlier. When he assessed the evidence of Brendan Walsh he had not informed the jury that the fingerprint's location was potentially corroborative of Walsh's claim to have been in the front of the car. Nor did he say that the fingerprint was in the front.

12

The Quashing of the Convictions

The convictions of Joseph Meleady and Joseph Grogan were quashed by the Court of Criminal Appeal on 22 March 1995, just under ten years after they were first imposed. The court found that the convictions were unsafe and unsatisfactory. As a consequence of the quashing, it stated that a presumption of innocence now applied to the two young men.

The judgment was the result of an eight-day hearing before Mr Justice Séamus Egan, Mr Justice Ronan Keane, and Mr Justice Richard Johnson, during which a large number of witnesses were called. The court's decision amounted to a rejection of arguments the state hid behind for years.

However, the court refused to certify, under the terms of the Criminal Procedure Act, 1993, that a miscarriage of justice had occurred. This appeared to conflict with the court's finding that the two had been jailed for five years without due process and were now to be presumed by law to be innocent citizens, just as if they had been acquitted in a full jury trial. The practical effect was to deny the two appellants automatic compensation; the more significant effect, however, was to create confusion in the public mind about what the court had actually decided.

The hearing was a tense and dramatic occasion, dominated to a large degree by the evidence of Richard Walker, a solicitor from the Chief State Solicitor's office. He displayed determination in the witness box, standing over the accuracy of his 1984 memo regarding the purported showing of photographs to Eamon Gavin. He refused to be shifted from this position, despite emphatic sworn denials from Garda Thornton and Eamon Gavin that there was any truth in the contents of the memo.

The state solicitor also found himself in what appeared to be an irreconcilable conflict of evidence with Det.-Supt Gerard McCarrick. The conflict concerned a purported telephone conversation between them in February 1991. Walker surprised the court by producing, to support his version of this incident, a memorandum in his own handwriting that he said he had made during the purported conversation; Det.-Supt McCarrick denied that the conversation had ever taken place or that he ever said what Walker had noted him as saying.

The appeal court hearing, although a climactic act, was far from being a comprehensive review of the long and twisting saga of the case. Much was excluded from the start. For example, the role of Gordon (Gus) Dunne and Paul McDonnell, the two young men who had publicly, in different ways, owned up to the crime, never featured. The case was confined to the consideration of specific new facts that had arisen since the second trial in November 1985.

There were in effect three grounds on which the appeal was brought. These were the non-disclosure, and mishandling in court by counsel for the DPP, of the fingerprint evidence of Brendan Walsh; the non-disclosure of the 1984 Walker memorandum, which had been present on the Chief State Solicitor's files and appeared to contradict prosecution evidence on the identification of Meleady and Grogan; and the failure of the Gardaí to set up a formal identification parade for Paul Gavin after his father's identification thirty minutes earlier had made Joseph Meleady a genuine suspect.

The last of these arguments was dismissed with little ceremony by the court, on the grounds that it could not accept that the applicants' legal advisers were not fully aware of such an argument at the time of their trial.

Significance of fingerprint evidence upheld

The court found that the fingerprint evidence of Brendan Walsh should have been disclosed to the defence. It found that Eamon Leahy's misinformed question in the first trial, asserting that the print was in the back of the car, must have created the possibility that

Walsh's own evidence—that he was in the front of the car—had been discredited in the eyes of the jury. The court agreed that this error of Eamon Leahy's 'contaminated' the second trial, where defence counsel still believed the print to have been found in the back. It said that it was not prepared to assume that the supposed location of the fingerprint did not weigh with defence counsel in this retrial, particularly over the question of deciding whether Brendan Walsh should or should not be a witness.

In reaching this conclusion, the court implicitly rejected the arguments of the Director of Public Prosecutions, and indeed those contained in the McCarrick report, that the Walsh fingerprint had no significance for the issue of who was seated where in Mr Gavin's car. It stated that Mr Leahy's question wrongly referring to the print being in the back had the effect of discrediting Walsh's claim to be in the front. This was a long-awaited acknowledgment of something the state for years had refused to concede: that if the defence had known that the fingerprint was in the front they could have used it to challenge Eamon Gavin's evidence.

The judgment also represented the end of the road for another argument the state had used to protect itself against the implications on the fingerprint issue, an argument developed at great length in the McCarrick report, endorsed by Eamon Leahy, and presented to the court in documentary form on behalf of the DPP as grounds for refusing the appeal. This was that, as the fingerprint evidence had been adduced at the perjury trials of Paul McDonnell, and the outcome of these proceedings allegedly confirmed the guilt of Meleady and Grogan, this proved the unimportance of Walsh's fingerprint having been found in the front. This proposition was passed over in silence in the judgment.

The court's views in relation to the fingerprint evidence differed sharply from those expressed by the senior investigating officer, Det.-Supt McCarrick, by counsel for the DPP, Eamon Leahy, and by the DPP, Eamon Barnes. None of these had accepted or acknowledged that damage had been done to Meleady and Grogan's right to a fair trial by the state's mishandling of material evidence. The court's finding could be held to have implicitly backed the view of Det.-Insp. Paschal Anders in 1987 that the fingerprint evidence relating to Brendan Walsh could not be ignored.

The judgment also raised questions over the failure of the authorities, including several Ministers for Justice, to take action on this matter, particularly between mid-1987 and October 1990. This was the period when they could not have failed to be aware of the irregularity in the 1985 court proceedings. It was on this latter date of 1990 that it fell to an RTE television programme to report the information already in the state's possession, thereby provoking the Attorney-General's inquiry, which led in turn to the successful appeal.

Walker memo should have been disclosed

The Court of Criminal Appeal found that the Walker memo on the purported showing of photographs to Eamon Gavin should have been disclosed to the Meleady and Grogan defence team in 1985. It was, the court said, 'unquestionably relevant' to the identification and could have been used in cross-examination to weaken the reliability of Gavin's evidence. Its non-disclosure also rendered the convictions of Joseph Meleady and Joseph Grogan unsafe and unsatisfactory. 'It was imperative', said Mr Justice Keane, 'that in a case which depended exclusively and critically on that [identification] evidence, all the relevant material relating to the identification should have been before the juries.'

Some of the most dramatic moments in the appeal centred around Richard Walker himself and his evidence. This evidence was contested vigorously, in separate respects, by both Garda Thornton and Det.-Supt McCarrick, leaving the judges with irreconcilable differences in testimony that, in the end, they felt they did not have to resolve.

The case had begun—typically enough, given its history—with the acknowledgment of another state error, this time regarding Walker's 1984 memo. The DPP, acting through the Chief State Solicitor, initially pleaded complete ignorance of this memo, prior to its discovery in 1991, on behalf of himself, of officials in his office, of prosecuting counsel, and of any of the staff of the Chief State Solicitor's office who dealt with the Meleady and Grogan prosecution on indictment. This virtually blanket claim was made in court documents, presented in the months before the hearing, in which the DPP opposed the grounds for the appeal. But on the day the appeal opened it emerged that one of these claims was inaccurate.

It appears from the evidence in the Court of Criminal Appeal to have been Walker himself who first noticed the error. The law clerk who had seen the memo in the Circuit Court section, Tadhg O'Neill, *had* in fact been the official there who dealt with the indictment and who sent the Meleady and Grogan file to counsel to advise on proofs and witnesses. The problem arose because O'Neill's own, quite brief report of just several paragraphs had not included this fact, nor had any of the other state papers, reports or statements that went to Meleady and Grogan's lawyers. The documents did not pinpoint O'Neill's specific role as *the* law clerk who dealt with the file on indictment. It was a matter that accordingly escaped everyone's attention, until Richard Walker, just two days before the appeal began, noticed the inaccurate claim in the grounds given for opposing the appeal. He brought it to the attention of his superiors; the inaccuracy was thereafter withdrawn by counsel for the DPP at the first opportunity on the first day of the hearing.

It was, of course, a matter of some embarrassment to the Chief State Solicitor that Tadhg O'Neill should have read the Walker memo in the course of his normal duties, as, clearly, no action had ensued to investigate the matter of a purported photographic identification. O'Neill, it emerged in court, had not only read the memo but, extraordinarily, said he had also understood that the matters referred to were unusual. In the witness box he said that when he read the memo he had recalled that on the only other occasion on which he had encountered the question of a photographic identification preceding an identification parade, the judge had thrown out the prosecution case. He had realised when he read the memo on the file that it was unusual, that it could be significant. He said he was just a law clerk at the time. He imagined that he would have brought the memo to the attention of one of the two solicitors in the office; however, he had no specific memory of having done so, and could not say that he had. His own role was purely administrative.

The evidence from Tadhg O'Neill indicated that Richard Walker's note, addressed specifically to the Circuit Court section, had in fact been read and noted in the Circuit Court section, by the only official there who read the file in the normal way. No solicitor read the note, nor had they any involvement, it appeared from the evidence, in the Meleady and Grogan file as it reached the section. The evidence was that neither Richard Walker nor Tadhg O'Neill nor anyone else in the

Chief State Solicitor's office had investigated the contents of the note, that neither of the two solicitors in the office at the time had seen it, or had it referred to them. This was where Patrick MacEntee's quip about the office being on 'autopilot' had arisen. The upshot was that no-one disclosed it to the defence.

Nor, critically, did the Walker memo ever reach counsel for the DPP. Form 8, the form on which it was inscribed, did not, in the normal course of events, go to counsel: it was not at the time regarded as a necessary part of the papers that had to be furnished to counsel in order for him or her to advise on proofs. This practice had changed by 1995, but in 1984 and 1985 counsel did not get the form containing this memo; it was counsel who in effect was going to direct and control the state's case in court.

Richard Walker's superiors, in particular the Assistant Chief State Solicitor, John Corcoran, argued in court that the fault for the failure of the office to take action lay with Walker himself. Form 8 was not the right vehicle for a message of such importance, he said in evidence. Walker was junior at the time, he said; his correct response should have been to communicate directly with the DPP when he received what he believed to be a vital piece of information from Garda Thornton; form 8 was a totally wrong means of communication chosen by Walker.

This argument was vigorously resisted by Walker himself, despite his subordinate role to John Corcoran within the office. He insisted that he had used the correct form, and pointed out in support of this that his memo *was* in fact read in the Circuit Court section, by Tadhg O'Neill, who dealt with the file on indictment.

This public row between solicitors in the Chief State Solicitor's office arose from a highly unusual breakdown in systems. The court, in its judgment, said it did not find it necessary to resolve the disagreement between Walker and Corcoran; but it did comment on the situation where a memo with vital significance for a prosecution could apparently go uninvestigated, and ultimately ignored, in such a fashion. This drew a stinging comment from Mr Justice Keane, who read the judgment: he said that if adequate procedures were in existence in the Chief State Solicitor's office in 1984 to deal with the communication of such 'unarguably significant material', then 'they signally failed to operate effectively.'

On the underlying issue of the contents of Richard Walker's memo about the showing of photographs to Eamon Gavin, Garda Patrick Thornton said in evidence that the memo had no basis in fact. He had never shown any photographs to Mr Gavin, nor had Mr Gavin ever asked to be shown photographs. He had not had any such conversation with Mr Walker, as alleged, either on the telephone or in person, on 16 May or on any other day. Eamon Gavin also emphatically denied that he had ever been shown any photographs.

Richard Walker's evidence was that he had no doubt that Garda Thornton had said to him, on 16 May 1984, what the memo recorded him as saying. He could not recall the conversation, he said, after eleven years, but from the rest of the contents of form 8 on which he wrote it down, he was happy that on that particular day he would have been in touch with Garda Thornton over additional evidence required for the court. That day he was preparing the book of evidence for the Meleady and Grogan trial, he said, and the notes showed he had a specific reason for contacting Garda Thornton, as the investigating Garda, in relation to additional evidence that was being sought. He felt he would have telephoned him in Rathfarnham Garda station and that the conversation as recorded then took place. He was sure his note was an accurate account of what Garda Thornton had told him on 16 May.

Garda Thornton's surprise evidence

In his evidence, Garda Thornton surprised the court, and in particular counsel for the DPP—whose witness he was—by stating that he had been shown the Walker memo in the Circuit Criminal Court in November 1987 by a solicitor from the Chief State Solicitor's office who was attending counsel in that case. The occasion, he stated, was the second perjury trial of Paul McDonnell; the case had just ended, the jury had been discharged, and the court was clearing, he asserted, when the incident occurred. A female solicitor had shown him the memo, asking him what it meant, and he had said it was completely untrue.

Garda Thornton was unable to recall the name of the solicitor who showed him the memo. In the Court of Criminal Appeal various officers from the Chief State Solicitor's office who had any dealings with the case, and some others who had none, were asked to stand up and identify themselves to the witness. Thornton was unable to identify the person who had spoken to him.

Several difficulties were raised by this evidence of Garda Thornton's. Firstly, no female official attended counsel for the DPP at the case in question; the court was told that that official had been male. Secondly, Garda Thornton said that counsel for the DPP, Erwan Mill-Arden, had become involved in this conversation; yet when called to give evidence on this, Mill-Arden could not recall any such conversation. He told the court that if he had seen the Walker memo at that time he presumed he would have brought it to the attention of the authorities; he felt that had he become aware of the memo as recounted by Thornton, he would definitely have acted on it. He agreed that it appeared to contradict sworn evidence that Thornton had given in the case then just concluded.

A third problem was that Garda Thornton had stated that, having been shown this memo, he had then gone into the corridor outside the courtroom and brought the matter to Mr Gavin's attention. Eamon Gavin did not corroborate this evidence: he did not recall having any such conversation with Thornton in 1987. On the contrary, the evidence before the court was that he had first heard of the allegations in the Walker memo in February 1991, over three years later.

The final problem was that Garda Thornton had given no hint of this 1987 incident to Det.-Supt McCarrick and Supt Camon when they questioned him on this general matter in early 1991. Under questioning about the Walker memo, Thornton had made no reference to having seen or heard of it before. He was asked why he had not mentioned the alleged incident with the solicitor to Det.-Supt McCarrick; he said simply that he was not asked. He said that he had answered every question put to him honestly and fairly.

Det.-Supt McCarrick in his evidence described Eamon Gavin as showing 'surprise and bewilderment' when asked in 1991 about the showing of photographs. Mr Gavin was, he said, 'in total amazement' at his line of questioning; he had no doubt that Mr Gavin reacted like a man hearing of the allegation for the first time.

Drama of second Walker memo

The main drama in the Court of Criminal Appeal came with the unexpected emergence of a second controversial memo, also made by

Richard Walker, this time in 1991. This was a contemporaneous note of a purported telephone conversation between Walker and Det.-Supt McCarrick on 7 February 1991. The subject of the conversation was the Garda investigation into Walker's 1984 memo; this had come to McCarrick's attention just three days previously.

The authenticity of Walker's 1991 note, which was scribbled and almost indecipherable, was not challenged in the court. Also produced in evidence by Walker was a printed version of the contemporaneous note, which he said he made some forty minutes later, when he deciphered his notes into a legible account of what he believed McCarrick had said.

Det.-Supt McCarrick challenged the note's contents and said that the conversation as described had never taken place; he could not possibly have said the things that Mr Walker recorded him as saying. He said the only conversations he and Walker had had were in the company of the Chief State Solicitor, Louis Dockery.

Walker's evidence was that he was disturbed and uneasy at the conversation he had had with Det.-Supt McCarrick. He said that McCarrick had told him that he had been told by Garda Thornton the previous day (6 February) that no photographs were ever shown to Eamon Gavin, and that the matter had been resolved. He was told definitely that no photographs were shown. They were not, he was told, talking about mistakes: McCarrick (in Walker's account) made a reference to 'confusion' on Walker's part.

Det.-Supt McCarrick in his sworn evidence said that his report showed that he did not talk to Garda Thornton until 27 February, three weeks after the date of this alleged conversation. If Garda Thornton had called in to him on 6 February the file would show a statement taken from him at that time. The account was therefore impossible.

Richard Walker, with reference to his notes, said that Det.-Supt McCarrick told him on 7 February that Eamon Gavin had left his office just ten minutes before their conversation. Gavin had told him he had not been shown any photographs. McCarrick denied this account by Walker; he said he did not see Gavin until 26 February. He could not have made such a statement about Gavin on 7 February.

Richard Walker gave evidence of how he had protested on the phone to Det.-Supt McCarrick that although questions had been asked and denials had been made by Garda Thornton, no statement had been taken from the Garda. He also pointed out, he said, that questions should have been addressed simultaneously to Thornton and Gavin: a 36-hour gap should not have been left between their interviews. This, he said, drew a comment from McCarrick: 'If anyone could be so twisted as to suggest that Thornton would do such a thing …' The superintendent then remarked, according to Walker, that the Gardaí did a lot of work for the Chief State Solicitor's office. 'We don't want to make problems for you.' 'Questions will be asked as to why the note was not followed up.' In Walker's account, McCarrick said that there was loads of evidence against Meleady and Grogan, and there would definitely be no tribunal.

Det.-Supt McCarrick said he had no such conversation with Mr Walker. He had not concluded his investigations at this time, and could not have said what Mr Walker alleged. He said that when he undertook the investigation he intended to carry it out as a neutral person, irrespective of who he pleased or did not please, and that was how he went through the investigation.

Richard Walker said that immediately after the phone call ended he spoke to the Chief State Solicitor, Louis Dockery, about his unease over the call. Dockery, in his presence, had phoned Barry Donoghue (the senior solicitor who had first uncovered the Walker memo) in relation to this. Called to give evidence, Barry Donoghue confirmed that there had been a phone call to him in Cork; he said that Mr Walker had been concerned about something but he could not recall at this distance in time what was troubling him. Louis Dockery was not called to give evidence.

Det.-Supt McCarrick said in his evidence that if such a detailed conversation with Mr Walker had occurred at this time he would certainly have remembered it. He assured the court that it had not. He totally rejected Walker's recollection and the contents of his note.

For state witnesses to find themselves in such unbridgeable conflict was unusual in the extreme. On one side was Richard Walker himself, described by counsel for the DPP as a witness of honesty and integrity, while on the other side, Det.-Supt Gerard McCarrick and Garda Patrick Thornton were, equally, witnesses of the highest calibre. The court declared in the end that it was 'unnecessary' for it to resolve these conflicts of evidence.

Issues over the conclusion of Det.-Supt McCarrick

Det.-Supt McCarrick and his deputy, Supt Seán Camon, confirmed separately in their evidence that when they interviewed Garda Thornton in 1991 they did not ask him if he had ever seen the Walker memo before or if anyone had ever questioned him about it. They said they had been surprised in the Court of Criminal Appeal to hear Garda Thornton state that he had been shown the memo by a state solicitor as far back as late 1987. If this remark by Thornton was true, why had he not said this before?

Thornton, as noted above, said he was not asked. Det.-Supt McCarrick, asked by Patrick MacEntee SC why Garda Thornton was not asked by him when he first saw the Walker memo, said that he took it for granted at the time he spoke to him that this was the first knowledge Thornton had of the document. His colleague, Supt Camon, gave evidence that Garda Thornton, when questioned, had not given the slightest sign, either by his demeanour or by any word, that he had any prior knowledge of the Walker memo. He said the impression he got from Garda Thornton was that if anyone had asked him about the showing of photographs to Mr Gavin he would have said as much. The impression was that he knew nothing about it, that it did not feature in his memory in any way. Det.-Supt McCarrick agreed with this account.

This evidence in 1991 from two senior Garda officers raised some new problems. At issue was not just the decision not to ask Garda Thornton the simple question but, more so, the treatment of this matter in McCarrick's report to the DPP, completed in the spring of 1991. In this report the following conclusion was drawn, at paragraph 86.33: 'Mr. John Corcoran suggests the possibility that the relevant note [Walker's memo] was adverted to and acted upon and that it was found upon enquiry that the contents were incorrect and necessitated no further action. Bearing in mind the integrity of the staff of the Chief State Solicitor's Office and of the members of the Garda Síochána involved, and of their dedication to their chosen professions, the possibility of this course of action having been taken is most likely.'

The proposition of John Corcoran's referred to here was outlined in a report by him to Det.-Supt McCarrick on 1 March 1991: 'The second possibility is that the note was adverted to and acted upon, in that the Garda was asked about it orally and indicated that no photographs were shown to Mr Gavin ...' How could the McCarrick report have reached the conclusion it did in view of the evidence presented by its author and his deputy to the Court of Criminal Appeal? If the 'most likely' possibility was that either Thornton or Gavin, or both, were asked by some unknown official at some point about the Walker memo and denied its contents, then one or the other, or both, would have known about it before 1991. The two senior officers said in evidence in the appeal court that they believed at the time that neither Thornton nor Gavin knew about it. The reason given in the court for not asking Thornton the simple question—had he seen the Walker memo before—was the stated belief that it was quite evident that it was the first Thornton knew of it. Equally it was the officers' view in evidence that Gavin had definitely heard nothing of the Walker memo before February 1991. How could the McCarrick report state, in apparent contradiction, that it was most likely that they had been questioned about it earlier? Clearly there must have been a good reason for such a conclusion; but it was not elaborated in the report.

The conclusion in the McCarrick report referred to above followed an exhaustive inquiry in the Chief State Solicitor's office, during which no official was found who had investigated the Walker memo. Having failed to ask Garda Thornton the simple question, what then was the basis for Det.-Supt McCarrick's statement that it was most likely that someone—unnamed and unknown—had investigated the memo and found it to be incorrect?

The court's refusal to certify miscarriage of justice

Towards the end of its judgment, having already quashed the convictions of Joseph Meleady and Joseph Grogan on the several grounds described above, the Court of Criminal Appeal said: 'The evidence of Mr Gavin, which was accepted by the juries in the two trials of the Appellants and was given again on oath to this Court, has never been considered by a jury in a trial not flawed by the irregularities identified as a result of the present application. In these circumstances, the Court is not in a position to certify that the newly discovered facts show that, in the case of either applicant, there has been a miscarriage of justice.'

This was a reference to the provision of the Criminal Procedure Act,

1993, that the court could certify a miscarriage of justice on foot of quashing a conviction. Its decision in this respect came as a disappointment to the two men's legal advisers, who immediately prepared to seek a review of the ruling in the Supreme Court. The Court of Criminal Appeal had declared that because the men had already served their sentences, it would not be appropriate to order a retrial.

In submissions to the court before the judgment was delivered, Patrick MacEntee SC, for Meleady and Grogan, argued strongly against the court adopting the posture it eventually took: quashing the convictions but failing to certify a miscarriage of justice. He insisted that to do so would leave his clients in a form of limbo, where they would not be completely innocent, not completely guilty, but somewhere in between. 'The wholly absurd position would arise in which a person not having been tried in due course of law and having been declared innocent by the quashing of the conviction is nonetheless held not to have been the subject of a miscarriage—in other words, to be in a sort of limbo situation, where this court takes the view that there was a miscarriage but there wasn't a miscarriage.' A decision not to certify a miscarriage of justice, he said, 'would be a decision that trenched on the revived presumption of innocence; in other words, it would be saying that the accused is guilty, or slightly guilty, but one way or the other is not entitled to the benefit of the revived presumption of innocence.'

The court rejected this argument. Mr Justice Keane stated its view: 'The court rejects the submission advanced on behalf of the applicants that a decision not to certify [that] the facts show that there has been a miscarriage of justice in some sense abridges or qualifies the presumption of innocence to which the applicants will be entitled as a result of the quashing of their convictions.

'That presumption … runs like a golden thread through the web of the Anglo-American system of criminal justice. It applies to every person who is acquitted on a criminal charge, whether the acquittal be the result of a verdict by the jury on the merits of the case, a mere failure of technical proof in a case where there is overwhelming evidence against the accused, or, as here, the quashing of a jury verdict because of material irregularities which render a trial unsafe and unsatisfactory.'

13

Conclusions

The heart of the Tallaght Two case was the insistence of Eamon Gavin that he was correct in identifying Joseph Meleady and Joseph Grogan as the culprits. His passionate, unbridled commitment to this view was such as to persuade many disinterested observers over the years that he had to be correct. The tragedy, for the man himself and for everyone else concerned, was that he was not. The two people in the front of his car on the night of 26 February 1984 were not Joseph Meleady and Joseph Grogan: they were Gordon (Gus) Dunne and Brendan Walsh, with Paul McDonnell in the rear. Mr Gavin was wrong.

The evidence for the claim that Meleady and Grogan were innocent has been outlined in the pages of this book. First of all, McDonnell and Dunne—though never charged with the crime—separately have said they were in the car; they also said that Meleady and Grogan were not. Secondly, Brendan Walsh, who was in the car, supported the view that Meleady and Grogan were innocent. Objective analysis of the circumstances in which Walsh and McDonnell gave their sworn evidence in the 1987 perjury trials leads to only one conclusion: they were telling the truth.

In all the eleven years of the case, from 1984 to 1995, no credible conspiracy theory was ever advanced to explain the diverse, quite separate admissions of guilt that marked this case. No credible explanation was produced to explain the common ground between the accounts of McDonnell, Dunne, and Walsh, or to explain the persistence of McDonnell's and Walsh's attachment to the proposition that Meleady and Grogan were innocent.

The location and orientation of Brendan Walsh's fingerprint in Eamon Gavin's car strongly corroborated his claim to have been sitting in the front passenger seat, the seat supposedly occupied by Joseph Grogan. This print was of Walsh's right thumb, upside down, near the top of the glass near the front pillar on the passenger door window. It was probably deposited by him in the course of his climbing out onto the window ledge, holding the umbrella in his left hand to beat Eamon Gavin, holding on with his right hand while exiting and re-entering the window.

In Paul McDonnell's 1985 sworn affidavit he made correct reference to the colour of the petrol can in the car, a detail that came from no-one else before or since. The reference, only publicly confirmed as accurate many years later, should immediately have signalled the bona fide nature of his confession. Similarly, Gus Dunne's correct description, in his 1986 television interview, of the make and model of the car stolen before Eamon Gavin's was taken at Cremorne pointed up the truth of his admission of involvement.

Overall, Dunne's various recorded admissions of guilt during 1985, 1986, 1987 and 1988 left no room for reasonable doubt about his involvement in the crime. In particular there was his admission of guilt to Dawn Keegan in June 1985 in Shanganagh Detention Centre; his detailed, spontaneous television interview in November 1986; his statement endorsing the contents of this interview to Det.-Insp. Paschal Anders in February 1987; his interview with Frank Connolly for *Magill* in 1988; and his witnessed apology to the mothers of the two wrongly convicted young men, also in 1988.

Det.-Insp. Anders, since retired, told the author in 1995 that he believed that Meleady and Grogan were not in Gavin's car; he believed that Gordon Dunne and Brendan Walsh were the people sitting in the front seats.

It was a tragedy for Eamon Gavin that he made a mistaken identification. Even more was it a tragedy for the Meleady and Grogan families. They found themselves as a result subject to a decade of suffering; Joseph Meleady and Joseph Grogan served five years' penal servitude, all for a crime in which they had no involvement. In fairness to Eamon Gavin it must be said that it was obviously the furthest thing from his mind to punish two innocent young men and their families in an unfair way. The truth was that he was so certain of his own identification that the idea of a mistake did not arise; consequently he could not but be blind to the damage his mistaken identification caused in two families' lives. For him it was simply justice in action. But it had a price, and Eamon Gavin himself and his family also suffered as a result of his obsession with the case.

The problem was that he had placed himself in a false position, where the presentation of any evidence suggesting that Meleady and Grogan might not be guilty appeared indistinguishable to him from a direct attack on his own good name and reputation. As the years passed and the convictions appeared more and more suspect, culminating eventually in their being quashed in 1995, the case became a personal crisis for the innocent victim of a nasty and brutal crime committed years before.

What was also tragically clear was that the authorities had never fully come to grips with a case that went seriously wrong very early on. By mishandling important evidence, they failed in one of their most important obligations to an accused: to provide due process of law. Subsequently, they failed to correct their own errors. They compounded the problems they had themselves created with a misconceived and misguided prosecution of Paul McDonnell for perjury. Not one but several Garda inquiries, years after the fact, misread the situation, missed important clues, and went on to arrive at mistaken conclusions. The office of the Director of Public Prosecutions and the office of the Chief State Solicitor each contributed to the tragedy of the case, by errors both of procedure and of judgment, culminating in a period of inaction between November 1987 and October 1990, for which, by the spring of 1995, no proper explanation had been offered.

In the end, the hearing of the Court of Criminal Appeal in January and February 1995 proved a debacle for the prosecution authorities. Witnesses contradicted each other. Failures in internal procedures were graphically exposed. Judgments made in relation to evidence affecting the rights of the two accused were rejected by the court. Meanwhile, three separate Ministers for Justice—Alan Dukes of Fine Gael and Gerry Collins and Ray Burke of Fianna Fáil—before the transmission of the television documentary in October 1990 were seen to have sat on their hands; this was at a time when the prison sentences of Meleady and Grogan had only been partly served.

There was no evidence that any of these unfortunate official failings were deliberate, or that any individual or agency connived at a deliberate obstruction of the course of justice. The problem was simpler than that: the authorities thought that Meleady and Grogan were guilty, and they could, for two years, cite two jury verdicts as proof of that. That these verdicts might be unsafe and unsatisfactory did not, it seems, occur to them, though it occurred to many others. The result was the creation of a particular mental attitude that did not grasp the significance of the mounting evidence that Meleady and Grogan had been wrongly convicted.

If this failure of vision was, in all the circumstances, a forgivable one, it would be easier to accept had the authorities been seen eventually to act promptly—or indeed act at all—to correct their own mistakes, when these became apparent, and to take steps to vindicate the rights of the accused to a fair trial.

Few cases in recent years made as many appearances in court. Yet even when the Court of Criminal Appeal had heard the matter for the third time, the outcome was not fully satisfactory. Two questions in particular were unresolved. Had there or had there not been a miscarriage of justice? The court appeared to have given two contradictory answers: yes and no. But which was it? One way or the other, the outcome, while restoring Meleady and Grogan's presumed innocence, left matters still to be clarified.

The second issue concerns the conduct of the state itself, conduct that was never specifically addressed as an issue in any of the various court hearings over the years from 1984 to 1995. These had been narrowly focused criminal proceedings, centred on the guilt or innocence of the two accused, or, as in the appeals, on some other defined points of law. None included in their terms of reference the specific task of assessing the conduct of the prosecution authorities. The only partial attempt to review the facts comprehensively had been the McCarrick Garda report. Apart from being non-judicial, this had also failed to identify the problems and, generally, could not be regarded as a satisfactory overview.

So, in the spring of 1995, important questions still remained to be addressed, including the question of who in the state's criminal justice system was responsible for setting right a material irregularity in a prosecution case once it had been identified. Also, while there had been no deliberate attempt to obstruct the course of justice, if, as suggested above, there was a particular view of this case in the office of the Director of Public Prosecutions, the office of the Chief State Solicitor, the Department of Justice, and some sections of the Garda Síochána, only an inquiry could establish what this view was, and how it might have affected the case.

There remained also the conviction of Paul McDonnell for perjury, another unfortunate legacy that had not been cleared up. The quashing of the convictions against Meleady and Grogan implied that the McDonnell perjury conviction could also be unsafe and unsatisfactory. A legal snarl had been created and had to be disentangled.

For all these reasons, a strong argument existed for a more widely mandated inquiry into the whole Tallaght Two saga. Possible terms and conditions for such an inquiry could be found in section 8 of the Criminal Procedure Act, 1993, which empowers the Minister for Justice to set up a tribunal or committee of inquiry into presumed miscarriages of justice. Such a tribunal could hear whatever evidence it thought fit, including evidence not normally admissible in a court of law, and make recommendations accordingly.

Fourteen questions for a tribunal

Fourteen specific questions need to be answered by such an inquiry.

1. Why did Det.-Insp. Anders's report on the case, completed in mid-1987, not lead to a rethink, at a time when both young men still had to serve the bulk of their sentences?

2. Why did the McMunn Garda report in 1987, and the more extensive McCarrick report in 1991, both miss the significance of the mishandling of the fingerprint evidence in 1985?

3. Why was there a delay of almost four years before a statement was sought from Gordon Dunne after his televised admission of guilt in December 1986, and in particular after his subsequent indication to the Gardaí, in February 1987, that the contents of this interview were authentic and truthful?

4. Why was Dunne's fanciful disavowal (under caution, and many years later, in early 1991) of his several admissions of guilt made

in 1985, 1986, 1987 and 1988, to various parties, including journalists, accepted by the authorities as significant new evidence, without any attempt being made to confirm it with the journalists involved?

5. On what basis was it thought that Gordon Dunne could help the Gardaí with their inquiries when he was questioned by Det.-Garda Felix McKenna in March 1984 in connection with the crimes against Eamon Gavin?

6. Why was a vital clue to Paul McDonnell's bona fides in confessing to the crime in May 1985 never picked up? This was when he made a sworn admission of guilt in which, among other things, he revealed knowledge unlikely to be known to anyone not previously in Eamon Gavin's car—i.e. the colour of the petrol can.

7. Why did the Director of Public Prosecutions and the Chief State Solicitor not acknowledge publicly at any time from 1987 to 1990 that, as a result of prosecution errors, a material irregularity had occurred whose effect had been to deprive two convicted men of due process of law?

8. What responsibility for redressing the damage done by the state's mishandling of the scientific evidence in this case lay with (a) counsel for the DPP, (b) the DPP himself, and (c) the Chief State Solicitor?

9. Why did the authorities persist with the prosecution of Paul McDonnell for perjury in 1987, at a time when a material irregularity in the previous proceedings, relevant to that prosecution, should have been known to them?

10. Why did the state subsequently not advert in court during the McDonnell hearings to this irregularity, given that the prosecution in that case sought to use the (flawed) convictions to assist in gaining a conviction against Paul McDonnell?

11. Why did successive Ministers for Justice, from 1987 to 1990, fail to acknowledge the significance of the fingerprint evidence and its mishandling in court, even in the face of advice from such influential figures as Gareth Peirce, solicitor for the Birmingham Six?

12. What attempts should be made to resolve fundamental conflicts of evidence that arose in the Court of Criminal Appeal in March 1995?

13. Are new procedures required in the office of the Chief State Solicitor to ensure that the failures identified by the Court of Criminal Appeal in relation to communicating important material, such as the Walker memorandum, do not recur?

14. Are new procedures required in the Garda Síochána to ensure that the failures that occurred in 1984 and 1985 in the processing of the fingerprint evidence cannot be repeated?

Appendix 1

Visual Identification and Case Law

Experience has shown that one of the most fraught, most problematical and most dangerous areas of the criminal law system is that concerning uncorroborated visual identification.

Almost ten years before Eamon Gavin made his disputed identification at Rathfarnham courthouse, Lord Justice Scarman in the English Court of Appeal said: 'We all know there is no branch of human perception more fallible than identifying a person.' A former Director of Public Prosecutions in Britain, Sir Norman Skelhorne, once described visual identification as 'the Achilles heel of British justice.'

Psychologists' studies of the processes of memory and recall have emphasised over the years the need for juries to approach eye-witness identification with great caution. These studies show a complex interaction in the process of recall between a person's observation of an incident and other sensory awareness, including the observer's prejudices, attitudes, and expectations. Together these combine to create a tendency to distort the ability to recall precisely. Added to this difficulty is a general inadequacy in the average person's powers of memory.

Because of all these factors, an extensive body of case law has built up, in Ireland as elsewhere, much of it concerned with creating conditions where serious errors can be avoided by juries. But there is a question mark over the effectiveness of the various stipulations, including those involving statutory warnings. The reason for this scepticism is that a large number of mistakes have been made over the years, in the Irish and British courts as well as in other jurisdictions.

One of the most celebrated failures of identification evidence was in the case of Adolf Beck. He was twice convicted (in 1896 and 1904) in English courts of various frauds perpetrated on a number of women. He was identified as the culprit by eleven of these women on the first occasion and by four on the second. Despite this weight of numbers, Beck was innocent, and was eventually proved to be so. The true culprit was discovered some time after Beck's second trial. Beck was granted a free pardon.

Legal experience has shown that when the witness has had no previous acquaintance with the suspect being identified, his or her visual identification is particularly questionable. The Devlin Interdepartmental Committee on Identification Evidence (1976) quoted the British psychologist D. E. Broadbent to the effect that certainty in the field of identification was actually *unattainable*, since, he said, the acts of perception and recall have to deal with what he called disconnected rationalisation by the perceiving subject.

One of the great problems for judges and jurors faced with this form of evidence is the difficulty of assessing it. Typically, the witness asserts his or her confidence in their own identification—and has little more with which to assist the jury. There is no story to probe, no dubious motives to question. The task is just to judge the accuracy of the single assertion by a witness who, typically, is acting in complete good faith. The assertion is either correct or it is incorrect. The difficulty is that there is no ready test for its technical validity. And whereas juries are normally directed specifically by the trial judge to assess the demeanour and credibility and attitude of a witness, when presented with this type of eye-witness assertion they may need almost to ignore such factors.

The Devlin Report said of this: 'Demeanour in general is quite useless. The capacity to memorise a face differs enormously from one man to another, but there is no way of finding out in the witness box how much of it the witness has got; no-one keeps a record of his successes and failures to submit to scrutiny.

'If a man thinks he is a good memoriser and in fact is not, that fact will not show itself in his demeanour. Witnesses who are themselves convinced of the truth of their identification and who are able to impart to a jury their own sense of conviction, have not infrequently been found to be mistaken.'

The further point is made by lawyers that while psychologists and others involved in the criminal law are in general well aware of the risks and dangers involved in identification evidence, the average juror is not. This raises questions, central to the Tallaght Two case, about a juror's capacity to respond to a warning delivered by a judge.

The People v. Casey

The law on visual identification evidence is governed by a landmark case, *The People v. Casey*, heard in the Supreme Court in 1962. The judgment in the matter was handed down by the Chief Justice, Mr Justice Kingsmill Moore, in 1963, when he ordered a complete retrial.

A man had been convicted of sexual assault on the sole basis of visual identification by two people, neither of whom had been known to him before the offence. The court said that it was concerned by the increasing evidence of 'the potentialities of error in visual identification, however honest, however convinced.' Mr Justice Kingsmill Moore went on: 'We are of opinion that juries as a whole may not be fully aware of the dangers involved in visual identification, nor of the considerable number of cases in which such identification has been proved to be erroneous …

'In our opinion it is desirable that in all cases where the verdict depends substantially on the correctness of an identification, their attention should be called in general terms to the fact that, in a number of instances, such identification has proved erroneous, to the possibilities of mistake in the case before them, and to the necessity of caution.

'Nor do we think that such warning should be confined to such cases where the identification is that of only one witness. Experience has shown that mistakes can occur when two or more witnesses have made positive identifications …

'They [juries] should bear in mind that there have been a number of instances where responsible witnesses, whose honesty was not in question and whose opportunities for observation had been adequate, made positive identifications in a parade or otherwise, which identifications were subsequently proved to be erroneous.'

As a result of *Casey*, judges ever since have been required to charge juries that are faced with this kind of evidence with such a warning. It is a recognition of an exceptional situation, with exceptional dangers, born of experience; the warning from *Casey* is also a recognition of the basic fallibility of human memory in such matters.

But despite this precaution, serious doubts exist in legal circles whether any such warning can be effective. Legal opinion is divided on the matter. Judges in English courts, although equally aware of the dangers in this kind of evidence, as indicated above, are required to issue no such mandatory warning. The argument against a mandatory warning is not that it is unnecessary but that it may simply be ineffective.

Part of this argument is that the message to a jury is quite subtle and may not easily be understood by a lay person. In the first instance, jurors are warned, as mentioned, that it will be dangerous to convict. But then, probably in the next breath, they are told they *can* convict, just that they must be sure before they do so. But juries always have to be sure before convicting anyone: this is their overriding instruction in all cases. So what then is the message? What is the point of the warning? The form of words used, according to many lawyers, could well be valueless to a jury in making them understand the difficulties and dangers involved; the result often may just be confusion.

Those holding this view argue, as eventually the Devlin Committee did in its report, that in fact something stronger than a warning is required. In Devlin's view, juries should be directed *not* to convict on the basis of uncorroborated visual identification unless 'there were other exceptional circumstances which warranted it …'

In the Tallaght Two case, the judge in the retrial followed the general direction given by the Supreme Court in *Casey* and warned the jury of the risks in convicting. But Judge Gleeson, after delivering this brief warning as required, immediately continued: 'Having given you that warning, I must then say to you that there's no rule of law, it is not the law that you can't convict on evidence of visual identification alone. That is not the law. These various cases—there have been some where convictions were set aside because of unsatisfactory evidence of visual identification, but there's no rule of law that you can't convict on the uncorroborated visual identification. There's no legal requirement of corroboration.

'Once I warn you of the dangers of mistakes, grave mistakes, that have happened occasionally in the past, you, having heard that warning, should bear it in mind when considering the facts of this case, and if you're satisfied beyond reasonable doubt that Mr Gavin is surely right in his evidence of identification, then not only can you convict but *it's your duty on oath to convict.'* (Emphasis added.)

This was a very different emphasis from that given by Mr Justice Kingsmill Moore in *The People v. Casey*. This was how the law had been stated on that occasion: 'If, after careful examination of such evidence, in the light of all the circumstances, and with due regard to all the other evidence in the case, they [the jury] feel satisfied beyond reasonable doubt of the correctness of the identification, they *are at liberty* to act upon it.' (Emphasis added.)

There was a further difference. The warning under *Casey* was not intended to be taken as a stereotyped formula, the Chief Justice had said. In fact, he said, it might have to be amplified. 'It may be too condensed to be fully appreciated by a jury without some further explanation, and the facts of an individual case may require it to be couched in stronger or more ample terms, as when the witness or witnesses had no previous acquaintance with the appearance of the accused, or had only an indifferent opportunity for observation.' Referring then to any other relevant evidence, he stated: 'It is for the judge to deal with the lesser or greater probative value of any item of corroborative evidence.'

There is no doubt that Judge Gleeson, acting with the discretion that was open to him as the trial judge, put his own emphasis and his own gloss on the obligation before the jury. It was nonetheless unusual that he made no concession to Mr Justice Kingsmill Moore's specific concern about an identification where the witness had no previous acquaintance with the accused—though these were exactly the circumstances in the Tallaght Two case.

The People v. Fagan

The case of *The People v. Fagan* strongly illustrated a paradox at the heart of the issue of identification evidence. While *certainty* about the accuracy of such an identification is virtually unattainable, a witness who wavers from a position of certainty—to even a slight degree—virtually guarantees that their evidence will be disregarded and that the case against the accused will fail. In the courtroom, an enormous, almost inhuman onus rests on the witness to express certainty if a conviction is to result.

The People v. Fagan was heard in the Court of Criminal Appeal in 1976, with judgment delivered by Mr Justice Séamus Henchy. This case centred on a robbery at a petrol filling station in Dublin. In pursuit of a suspect, the investigating Garda decided to bring one of the witnesses down to a sitting of the Dublin Circuit Court, in the hope that there he might identify the culprit. And in fact the witness, when he got there, did identify a man as being one of those who robbed him. The man was duly convicted on this evidence.

The conviction, however, was later overturned, on the basis of two issues that also arose prominently in the Tallaght Two trials. The first of these was what the Garda said to the witness in asking him to come down to the Circuit Court. Did he 'mark his card,' to the extent that he knew he was expected to identify someone? Such an attitude would have devalued the worth of his subsequent identification.

The second critical issue in *Fagan* was the level of certainty or doubt in the mind of the witness over his visual identification. The witness gave evidence that the Garda told him the man who robbed him *would* be at the Circuit Court that day. If this evidence was accurate, commented Mr Justice Henchy, 'the subsequent identification would be virtually valueless, as he might have felt bound to identify somebody.' The Garda, however, maintained in evidence that he told the witness he *might* see someone he could identify at the court.

Mr Justice Henchy found that the judge's charge had failed to identify and to underline this critical clash of evidence on the prosecution side and its implications for the jury's findings. The judge also criticised the failure of the Garda in question to hold a proper identification parade. The Garda had given as his excuse for this omission the fact that the suspect did not live at home and was as a result 'not that readily available.' This the judge found 'less than satisfactory' as an explanation.

But the main factor leading to the overturning of the conviction in *Fagan* was that at the last moment in the court proceedings the witness acknowledged the possibility that he could be wrong in his identification. Asked by the trial judge if he was satisfied beyond all doubt that this was the same man or if there was room for a doubt, the witness had replied, 'Well, I'd say there is room for a doubt.' His evidence otherwise was that he was satisfied that he had made a correct identification. Mr Justice Henchy found that the fact that the witness had been unable to empty his mind of uncertainty was crucial. It was 'an inescapable fact' that at the time of the trial 'his identification had lost certainty in his own mind,' said the judge.

In the Meleady and Grogan trials, equally, the state witnesses had to show certainty. Unattainable though such certainty might be in the opinion of some experts, it remained a *sine qua non* of a successful prosecution. The Tallaght Two prosecution depended totally on eye-witness identification.

Not surprisingly, the case of *The People v. Fagan* was cited at some length in the retrial of the Tallaght Two in the Circuit Criminal Court. Michael Feehan SC, counsel for Meleady and Grogan, used it when strongly urging Judge Gleeson not to allow the case against the accused to go to the jury at all.

But it was a double-edged sword. The Tallaght case had some significant differences from the case involving Fagan. Firstly, there was no evidence that the Gardaí told Eamon Gavin that the culprits *would* be present in Rathfarnham courthouse that morning; secondly, Gavin never said that he had lost certainty in the accuracy of his identification. These points distinguished the Fagan case from that of Meleady and Grogan and served to blunt the force of Michael Feehan's argument.

Among the arguments he did make, and tellingly, was that in neither case had the witness seen the accused before the crime was committed. Also, while in *Fagan* there was a four-day interval between the criminal act and the identification, in the Gavin case the interval was eight days, increasing the likelihood of error. In each case there had been a failure to hold an identification parade. In *Fagan* the Gardaí's reason was that the suspect did not live at home and was not always that readily available; this excuse Mr Justice Henchy had found 'less than satisfactory.' Feehan argued that even that unsatisfactory excuse could not be made in this case, because the people were available.

Michael Feehan reminded the court of what Mr Justice Henchy had said in the Fagan case about the identification being virtually valueless, and said: 'That is practically the case here, my lord. Your lordship will have to assess the actual evidence given by both the guard and Mr

Gavin in relation to that. Mr Gavin knew very well he was being brought in to identify somebody in the court, and that, in the words of Mr Henchy, renders this identification as virtually valueless ... It is a useless identification, in my submission to your lordship.' Feehan specifically reminded the judge that under the terms of the *Casey* ruling it might not be sufficient merely to recite the warning to the jury, that it could be necessary to have it 'couched in stronger or more ample terms.' The judge chose not to act on this advice.

With hindsight, and with the aid of the court transcripts, one can detect a critical moment in the discussion between the judge and Michael Feehan. It came when Judge Gleeson interrupted Feehan, suggesting to him that the appeal court judgment overturning *Fagan* had not faulted the trial judge on 'the adequacy of the direction on the *Casey* lines.' To this Feehan assented, saying, 'They weren't faulting the adequacy of the direction as such.'

However, the record appears today to show that the trial judge may not have appreciated that *Casey* had indicated that certain cases required stronger and more ample warnings to the jury. The *Fagan* judgment by Mr Justice Henchy did in fact fault the trial judge's direction. It faulted him specifically for failing to observe that the case in question was one of those referred to in *Casey* 'where the facts of an individual case may require it [the warning] to be couched in stronger or more ample terms.'

Michael Feehan had earlier pointed out this aspect of the *Fagan* appeal court ruling to Judge Gleeson, in the course of an impressive and comprehensive argument on the basis of the then case law. But, for some reason, when the judge revealed his belief that there was no faulting of the direction given by the *Fagan* trial judge, Feehan, critically, did not argue the point, despite the factual record he had earlier adverted to. In the end, in the judge's charge to the jury, rather than the statutory warning being couched in stronger and more ample terms, Judge Gleeson added an emphasis that tended if anything to weaken and reduce the force of the mandatory stricture.

Michael Feehan in his submission acknowledged that Eamon Gavin had not lost certainty in his identification; whereupon Judge Gleeson interjected: 'A jury could take the view that he seemed very sure.' But Feehan countered: 'Your lordship is correct in saying that. In my submission to your lordship as judge in this matter, you should not allow it to go to the jury, for fear, my lord, they might accept his certainty … They might think that the mere identification and the mere positiveness of Mr Gavin was sufficient to convict. It is, in my submission, not sufficient.'

But Judge Gleeson did not take the point. He in turn pointed out that the only time he had refused to let a case like this go to the jury was, as in the Fagan case, when a witness wavered in his certainty. He felt the case was dissimilar to that of Fagan. He said there was no rule saying there had to be an identification parade, nor any absolute rule that an explanation had to be given when a parade did not take place. 'The evidence indicating what happened here is that the identifiers, that is, Mr Gavin and his son, were, according to the evidence, told to go along to the courthouse. Their card wasn't marked for them like the identifying witness in Fagan's case … I believe there was no leading, no prompting, no influencing, and I believe it's completely distinguishable from Fagan's case, where the weight of evidence suggests that the witness was told: your man will be there.'

The People v. O'Reilly

Two important rulings by the Court of Criminal Appeal further refined the law on visual identification in the years since Judge Gleeson charged the jury in 1985. The first of these was *The People v. O'Reilly*, handed down in January 1990. The conviction and sentence of Patrick O'Reilly for a larceny offence in Mullingar were quashed by Mr Justice Hugh O'Flaherty, Mr Justice Robert Barr, and Mr Justice Vivian Lavan.

The facts of the case were as follows. A woman aged eighty-one was in her front garden when a man appeared and offered to do a painting job for her, which she declined. He asked for a drink of water, and while she was providing this another man appeared with a bedspread around him and offered to sell it to her for fifty pounds. The injured party—later the prosecution chief witness—described him as 'a stout butt of a fair-haired man' and said that he had 'a most notorious face, an awful face,' and she thought he was insane or an idiot. Some time after this encounter she discovered that missing from her house was £850 or thereabouts.

The matter was reported to the Gardaí. Suspicion centred on one Patrick O'Reilly, because of the fact that a car similar to his was seen outside the woman's house at the relevant time. About two months after the crime, the woman was brought by the Gardaí to the main street in Edgeworthstown, at or near the courthouse. Here she was able to observe people in the street; the purpose was to see if she could identify anyone as having been in her house on the day of the crime.

After she had seen twenty or thirty people, a group of five people approached, two women and one man in front and two people behind. She said of the man in front, 'I think that's him there,' and 'I didn't get a good look at him.' The people went into the courthouse and emerged about an hour later, and she said of the same man, 'That's him, that's him, the fellow with the ugly face,' and she pointed out Patrick O'Reilly.

Mr Justice O'Flaherty in his judgment pointed out that the single issue in the trial was whether the identification was adequate. He felt it was a mistake on the part of the Garda in question not to have held a formal identification parade. He pointed out that a formal parade, rather than the informal one that was held, was fairer to the accused. It meant that the accused could, for example, see the composition of the parade, and that he or his solicitor could object if they felt it was unfair. Also, a detailed account of the parade and those participating in it would be available to any subsequent trial. By contrast, the accused had no input into an informal parade, and was unlikely even to have knowledge of its happening. As a result, Mr Justice O'Flaherty said, the accused might be seriously inhibited in challenging the identification's fairness at the trial.

Mr Justice O'Flaherty also made substantial criticism of the manner in which the trial judge discharged his obligation, under the *Casey* ruling, to warn the jury of the risks inherent in visual identification. He emphasised that there were two parts to the *Casey* stipulation; one part had been observed in the judge's charge, the other had not.

The judge, he felt, had correctly warned the jury that there were great risks in convicting in such cases. However, what he had not done was to pay heed to Mr Justice Kingsmill Moore's ruling that in such cases a simple warning might not be sufficient. The law was that the warning might require 'further explanation', and 'the facts of an individual case may require it to be couched in stronger or more ample terms.' The O'Reilly case was a case in point, according to Mr Justice O'Flaherty, and the trial judge should have given firmer guidance to the jury on the weaknesses in the identification, in particular the fact that the witness was elderly, that she was in a state of shock, that she suffered a good deal of pain from an arthritic condition, and that she had only a short time in which to observe the men in her house.

This ruling in *The People v. O'Reilly* held a clear retrospective relevance to the Tallaght Two case. Far from emphasising the infirmities in the state case against Meleady and Grogan, Judge Gleeson in his charge in 1985 passed swiftly over them.

The People v. McDermott

The ruling in *The People v. McDermott* also came in 1990. It arose from a case where uncorroborated visual identification had led to a criminal conviction. The Court of Criminal Appeal quashed the conviction and discharged the accused. The ruling in the case was delivered by the Chief Justice, Mr Justice Thomas Finlay, supported by Mr Justice Séamus Egan and Mr Justice Richard Johnson.

The *McDermott* ruling included the following firm statement of the law: 'The Court is satisfied that there must, in a case where no identification parade is held, be added, as it were, to the very special warnings that must be given to a jury, a warning as to the difference in opportunity, control and credibility between an informal identification … and an ordinary controlled identification parade.'

Such a warning had not been given to the jury in the McDermott case—nor, indeed, had it been given by Judge Gleeson in the Tallaght Two case five years earlier. Judge Gleeson, addressing counsel, had stated that the procedure followed by the Gardaí 'bore all the hallmarks of the structure of a formal identification parade.' This remark was vigorously disputed by the defence, to no avail.

In the McDermott case, Mr Justice Finlay found that the trial judge had failed to point out to the jury 'an adequate, particularised relationship of the problems of identification in this case to the particular facts as proved.' The judge had failed to identify particular factors that could have impeded an accurate identification. Among the grounds for quashing the conviction Mr Justice Finlay stated: 'There was no attempt to point out to the jury the differences that would exist between this form of informal identification and a formal identification parade, and the potential superior strength as proof of the latter.' In these circumstances, the court felt the conviction should be quashed.

A reading of the judge's charge to the Tallaght Two jury in 1985 suggests that, had it been subjected to the test the Chief Justice applied in 1990, it too might well have been found to be unsatisfactory.

Appendix 2

The Case of Lazlo Virag, 1969

A case heard in the English courts in 1969 involving a Hungarian immigrant called Lazlo Virag bears an uncanny resemblance to the Tallaght Two case. While one cannot say that judgments made in one case can be applied directly to another with different facts, individuals, and backgrounds, some of the parallels between the two cases are interesting. Virag was convicted in 1969 on various charges, including theft and wounding a police officer with intent to cause grievous bodily harm. He was convicted solely on the basis of visual identification. In court, the alibi evidence presented on Virag's behalf was shown by prosecuting counsel to be contradictory and implausible. Yet five years later, in 1974, Virag was shown conclusively to have been innocent of the charges against him, and he was granted a free pardon.

Part of Virag's case for pardon was that scientific evidence, involving a fingerprint of another person found at the scene of the crime, was not revealed to the defence at or before the trial. But the primary case was that initially he had been falsely identified.

Virag's supposed offences included threatening policemen in Liverpool with a revolver. The actual crime happened early one Sunday morning in January 1969. Two policemen were within ten feet of the man whom they suspected of robbing parking meters, under street lighting described as good enough to read by. The man's face was uncovered, though he wore a trilby hat. About two months later, in a properly conducted identification parade, the two policemen,

Constable Callon and Constable Roberts, identified Virag as the culprit.

In the meantime another offence, also involving theft of parking meters, had taken place in Bristol in February 1969. This led to a car chase, during which the police were fired on by the driver of the car they were chasing. After a time the car being pursued pulled up. The gunman started to walk, with two policemen following him on foot at a distance. One of these, Constable Smith, got to within fifteen feet of the man in broad daylight, when he was shot by him in the arm. The gunman shouted at him to give up the chase. Smith, however, continued. Shortly afterwards two colleagues, Constable Davies and Constable Bragg, were confronted at a distance of about fifteen yards by the man, now holding a gun in each hand. He spoke to them in a Hungarian accent before they backed away.

These three policemen—Smith, Davies, and Bragg—all later identified Virag at an identification parade as the man they had seen with the guns. Virag had already been implicated in the Liverpool incident by the identification made by the other two policemen, Callon and Roberts. In addition, a further three witnesses identified Virag as a man involved in other incidents closely related to the various crimes.

While a total of nine other witnesses failed to identify him as the criminal, the prosecution case appeared very convincing, and indeed was successful. Virag was convicted.

The Devlin Report on Issues of Visual Identification looked in some detail in 1976 into how the Virag case had happened. Devlin noted that of all the prosecution witnesses, Constable Smith in particular had proved very influential and had greatly impressed the jury. He was later awarded a medal for bravery in the case. The report commented on his evidence as follows: 'P.C. Smith in particular was a most impressive witness. His gallantry and devotion to duty would naturally dispose any jury to listen to him with the utmost attention … He was clearly himself convinced beyond a shadow of a doubt that the accused was the man who had shot him; he said when he was interviewed by Det. Supt. Allen—"His face is imprinted on my brain."'

The Devlin Report noted that at the time of the trial it seemed almost absurd to suppose that the many identifications of Virag as the criminal could be misplaced. 'Among the classic cases of wrong identification, there are few in which the evidence was as strong as in Virag's case. This was not a case of fleeting glimpses, or of a single witness on a single occasion. Eight witnesses, on six separate occasions, identified Mr Virag as the man ... Five of the witnesses were police officers, trained to identify, and all were looking at the man with the knowledge that they might well be asked to identify him later.'

The Devlin Committee took the view that the mistaken visual identification had been the main cause of the miscarriage of justice on Virag, as otherwise he would not have been convicted. It also listed three important contributory factors.

1. The fingerprint issue

The police investigating the case recovered, early on, a number of stolen containers for the coins inserted in parking meters. On six of these, fingerprints were found. Five of these fingerprints could not be identified; they did not tally with fingerprints taken from current or past employees of Bristol City Council. They belonged, most probably, to someone involved in the theft.

But no evidence relating to these unidentified fingerprints was included by the police in the trial documents. A summary of the case prepared by a police inspector did refer to the existence of finger impressions that did not match those of Virag, and noted that the true owner of these had not been identified; but the inspector did not elaborate. Devlin observed that the police appeared at the time to have discounted the importance of these fingerprints. They did not pass them on to the defence, nor inform the defence of the facts regarding them.

Yet later these fingerprints proved crucial. They were found to belong to another Hungarian immigrant, Thomas Payen, who, it turned out, also owned the firearm used in the shooting of Constable Smith and who also had in his possession documents from the car stolen in the Bristol car chase. But Virag had been convicted and jailed on impressive visual evidence.

The non-disclosure of the fingerprint evidence had been a grave error and contributed to the miscarriage of justice, the Devlin Report concluded. At the same time the report ruled out, unequivocally, any idea that there had been deliberate suppression by the police of this evidence. It was, said Devlin, a case of its significance being misunderstood. Had it been introduced in evidence it would have altered the prosecution argument considerably: it would have required them, at the least, to argue that Virag had an associate in his crime, that there had been a change of driver of the car at some stage, or other unargued propositions, all of which the police would have had some difficulty in proving. It would have changed the case completely.

Devlin concluded: 'If there was a duty on the prosecution to disclose the fingerprint evidence, it was not in our opinion fulfilled ... The defence was not to blame for overlooking the potentiality of the fingerprint evidence ... If it is something that ought to have been considered by the Court—we think it is—the prosecution should either have brought it out and adapted their case to it, or given it to the defence in good time for them to study.'

The report concluded that the failure to make the fingerprint evidence in this case available to the defence was a major factor contributing to the miscarriage of justice that occurred.

2. *The alibi factor*

A second major contributing factor to the wrongful conviction, in Devlin's view, was the unconvincing presentation of the alibi evidence on Virag's behalf, which only added strength to the prosecution's case.

While Devlin felt there was no reason in hindsight to presume that Virag's alibi was anything other than the essential truth, the report concluded that it was improbable that the alibi could have been made to appear convincing, however well the defence prepared its presentation.

But Devlin was critical of the defence counsel and solicitor in this case. 'If the alibi had appeared simply as insufficient, its effect would merely have been neutral. Inadequate preparation made it appear as false. That is the appearance it shows on the written record, and the impression which the trial judge received. In his view it harmed rather than helped Mr Virag's case. The inadequacy in preparation was made up of the failure to obtain proper statements from the witnesses, and the failure to study the Club Book' (the attendance book of the club where Virag was supposed to have been).

And Devlin noted: 'There are two ways in which an ill-prepared alibi can cause or contribute to a miscarriage of justice. The first is when it would—if properly presented—have proved innocence. The second is when a true, but insufficient, case is, through lack of preparation, made to appear false.

'An explanation of some sort, even if it is only a failure of memory, is virtually a compulsory answer to identification evidence of any substance. When thereafter a conviction results, it is impossible to say whether it was the strength of the identification evidence, or the weakness of the alibi evidence, that was the deciding factor.'

3. The factor of official resistance to new evidence

Devlin felt that a third factor contributing to the miscarriage of justice was an error of judgment in the Home Office in failing to notice that something was fundamentally unsafe about the conviction. A decision had been made at higher and senior executive officer level that there was no need for further inquiry into the case. This decision was, says Devlin, 'astounding'.

At the stage, in 1971, when officials decided to pigeon-hole the concerns over the case and in effect take no action, police investigations had already established that the fingerprints on the coin containers at Bristol belonged to Payen, not to Virag. It had been proved that he was the one who had stolen from the meters and the one who stole the car the police had chased, an occupant of which had shot Constable Smith.

A report that contained all this information had gone to the Director of Public Prosecutions from a police inspector. From the DPP's office it had been sent to the Home Office. While containing the dramatic new information on the newly found culprit, the inspector's report also gave the opinion that it was still 'difficult to believe' that all the identification witnesses were mistaken in accusing Virag, and that it did not necessarily follow from the new evidence that Payen, and not Virag, had shot Constable Smith.

So, in the Home Office, the matter was pigeon-holed. It was almost two years before a senior principal officer took the file out and decided that further inquiries were necessary. This was to lead within a year, by April 1974, to Virag's pardon and acquittal.

Devlin says, in trenchant language: 'What we cannot understand is how the officer [in the Home Office] could have reached the conclusion that there was no need for any further inquiry.' The official had the same information available then, in 1971, as was available to the Devlin Committee, reporting in 1976. 'It is not our business to look for a culprit, and we are therefore quite content to accept the view of his superiors that there was no incompetence or neglect. On the other hand, we cannot accept the view that the explanation lies simply in an individual error of judgement.'